MW00764758

America's Music

JAZZ IN NEWARK

America's Music ♪

JAZZ IN NEWARK

BARBARA J. KUKLA

*To my friend Donna
— a jazz aficiando!
Best wishes.
Barbara Kukla
February 28, 2014*

Swing City Press

Swing City Press
336 Northfield Avenue
West Orange, New Jersey 07052

Copyright © 2014 by Barbara J. Kukla
All rights reserved
Published 2014
Printed in the United States of America

Type: Dante
Composed and designed by P. M. Gordon Associates

ISBN 978-0-9768130-3-3
Library of Congress Control Number: 2013954940

Viola Wells, "Miss Rhapsody," 1944. *(Author's collection.)*

For Miss Rhapsody (1902–1984),
who made jazz in Newark
a vital part of my life

CONTENTS

America's Music

JAZZ IN NEWARK

INTRODUCTION

America's Music: Jazz in Newark examines the vibrant jazz history in New Jersey's largest city during the second half of the 20th century and the early years of the 21st century, picking up where my first book, *Swing City: Newark Nightlife, 1925–50*, left off. As with *Swing City*, this book details the careers of hundreds of singers and musicians who played locally through the years as well as jazz icons like Sarah Vaughan, Wayne Shorter and Woody Shaw.

Although more than twenty years have passed since Temple University Press published *Swing City* in 1991, it continues to serve as a source of pride for the musicians and singers whose careers are documented in it and their families. It also is an invaluable reference work for jazz historians and aficionados worldwide. Both the hardcover edition of *Swing City* produced by Temple and the subsequent soft-cover volume published by Rutgers University Press a decade later were dedicated to Viola Wells (Miss Rhapsody), whose six-decade career as a blues and jazz singer dates to the roots of America's classical music.

My interest in jazz goes back nearly fifty years, when I began hanging out in Newark at the Bridge Club and Key Club as a general assignment reporter for the *Star-Ledger*. When I met Rhap on an assignment, I never imagined myself running around to jazz events all over the world with an old black woman more than forty years my senior. But that's what happened. At her invitation, I became

1

a regular at jazz parties at the Larchmont, New York, home of Al and Dot Vollmer, where scores of roots-of-jazz musicians gathered. It's where I made many musical friends, including Al Casey, Fats Waller's guitarist; Johnny Williams, who recorded with Billie Holiday, and Eddie Durham, who played with Count Basie. Before long, Rhap introduced me to just about every old-time musician in Newark, including Clem Moorman, Hal Mitchell, Leon Eason and Duke Anderson. Those experiences became the genesis for *Swing City*. By then, I also began hosting annual birthday parties for Rhap at my home, where my guests included pianist June Cole and his brother, Cozy Cole, the famous drummer, and Maxine Harvard, who organized Newark's first Jazz Week.

In its heyday, Newark's once-rich jazz scene allowed enthusiasts like myself to go from club to club each night nearly until sunrise. One by one, these venues shut down until only the Priory on West Market Street remained. The scene is different now, but jazz in Newark still flourishes at the recently renovated Priory Jazz Club and at the New Jersey Performing Arts Center, the Newark Museum, and new spots like the Ideal Bar and the Dinosaur Bar-B-Que.

In creating *America's Music: Jazz in Newark* I conducted nearly two hundred interviews with those who know the lay of the land best—musicians, singers, club owners, bartenders, historians, family members and anyone else who had a story to tell or information to share. I cannot thank them enough for their trust in me and faith in my ability to convey, as accurately as possible, what they had to say. Other information came from books, liner notes and a variety of Internet sources.

It should be said that I am not, nor do I profess to be, a jazz critic. When it comes to evaluating jazz artists and their performances, I look to the experts, especially my friend Amiri Baraka, whose writings on jazz and blues are unparalleled. Old-timers Tiny Prince, Robert Banks, Stan Myers and Charlie Cann, who were on the scene long before I arrived in Newark, also have been invaluable resources.

Nor am I an expert on the complexities of drug and alcohol abuse that claimed so many of our most talented jazz artists in their prime, especially the bebop generation. Except for the compelling words of Gene Phipps Sr., I leave that subject to the experts and refer my readers to professionals in that field. A panel discussion on *Dope Addiction and the Jazz Musician* in the November 1960 issue of *Playboy* is another interesting source of information. In short, I am simply a jazz fan-turned-storyteller who believes that Newark's jazz history should not be lost to time, lest the contributions of so many talented musicians and singers be forgotten.

I understand, too, that whatever I write will be subject to controversy, for there's always someone who believes that their friends or loved ones did not get their due or simply likes wagging his or her tongue. In putting my blood, guts, time and money into this project, all I can say in response is that I've been blessed to do what I've done, criticism and all. My only regret is that I did not get to interview Wayne Shorter or Andy Bey. Nevertheless, this has been a magnificent journey. So let me thank those who have taken it with me, the singers, musicians and fans who allowed me to interview them and/or provided photographs, flyers and other vital information.

I particularly want to thank Bruce Lundvall, chairman emeritus of Blue Note Records, and Michael Cuscuna, founder and president of Mosaic Records, for granting me permission to use otherwise inaccessible materials. Thank you, too, Michael, for sharing your insights about so many musicians from Newark and allowing access to so many extraordinary photographs taken by world-famous photographer Francis Wolff. Neither Wolff's photographs, which are copyrighted by Mosaic Images, nor any others in this book, I might add, may be reproduced or used for any purpose without the express consent of the owners. All clubs are located in Newark unless otherwise noted.

Special thanks go to Maxine Harvard for supporting this project every step of the way; Jimmy Scott and his biographer, David Ritz; Woody Shaw III and Larry Young III for providing insights into their fathers' legacies; John Hamilton for providing historic jazz photos from the 1950s and 1960s, and Celeste Bateman for sharing the Newark Jazz Festival archives. Thanks, too, to Alice Camp-isi O'Keefe, my sounding board; Joan Vidal, my former editor, for her advice; Robin Taylor for assisting with publicity; and my former *Star-Ledger* colleagues Janice Carter Brown and Reginald Roberts for their editing and technical assistance. As always I am indebted to P. M. Gordon Associates of Philadelphia, my production team, especially Peggy and Doug Gordon.

As with all my projects, I also have benefited tremendously from the assistance of my friends at the Charles F. Cummings Information Center at the Newark Public Library, especially Tom Anker, who answered many questions for me. George Hawley, the center's supervisor, and staff members James Lewis and Dale Colston also assisted me. I also want to thank my friend Wilma Grey, director of the Newark Public Library.

This is my fifth book about the people of Newark. In addition to *Swing City*, the others are: *Defying the Odds: Triumphant Black Women of Newark*; *Sounds of Music: The Dolores Collins Benjamin Story*; and *Newark Inside My Soul: A 50-Year Memoir*. My body of work also includes three calendars: *Remembering Connie: A Life Well-Lived; Newark Songbirds: Jazz Through the Years*; and *Rejoice! Newark Gospel Greats*. As editor of the *Newark This Week* section of the *Star-Ledger* from its inception in 1979 until my retirement in 2004, I also wrote thousands of articles that appeared in that section of the newspaper.

With the gentrification of downtown Newark in full swing, new jazz spots are gradually emerging. For me, the days when my friends and I loved hanging out at the Key Club and Sparky J's can never be replicated. Glory be to the memories those of us who were there hold dear.

1 ♪

Old Roots, New Branches

*The memory of things gone is important to a
jazz musician. Things like old folks singing in
the moonlight in the backyard on a hot night or
something said long ago.* —Louis Armstrong

Newark's rich jazz history dates to the early 1920s, around the
time twenty-one-year-old Louis "Satchmo" Armstrong came
north from New Orleans to Chicago to join Joe "King" Oliver's Cre-
ole Jazz Band. In those days the new music often had a tinny sound
that southern folks called potty-tot, as evidenced in Satchmo's early
recordings. Other southern influences, including the blues, were apparent, too. Armstrong's *Royal Garden Blues*, a tribute to a popular
Chicago nightclub, is a key example.

Some of the earliest jazz in Newark could be heard at the Kinney
Club on Arlington Street, the Palace Lucille on Plane Street (now
University Avenue) and the Radio Inn on Halsey Street. The Kinney Club, old-timers say, was home to the hustlers, a magnet for
high-class prostitutes, pimps, gamblers and numbers bankers as well
as curious, law-abiding patrons, black and white. Everything taboo
was available.

"Elmer Chambers, who usta play with (big-band leader) Fletcher
Henderson, was one of the old-timers at the Kinney Club," according to trombonist Clyde Bernhardt. "He couldn't improvise, but he
was a helluva musician. If you put it down proper, he'd play it."
Bernhardt, who was born in Gold Hill, North Carolina, in 1905,

joined King Oliver in 1931. By then, Armstrong, who became one of jazz's brightest lights, no longer was with the band.

After the Kinney Club was renovated and the music moved to an upstairs room, the Arlington Street watering hole became a gold mine for owners Benny Gilsider and Herman Pontischoff. "We had two shows a night, often produced by Billie Byrd, the emcee," waitress Lucille Morton recalled. "I'd say the Kinney Club was the center of all entertainment in Newark."

Many of the Kinney Club shows were built around blues singers like Mamie Smith, whose 1920 recording of *Crazy Blues* set off an avalanche of sales for Columbia Records, and Mamie Miller, who coordinated the entertainment and was known as "The Boss." Jazz musicians like trumpeter Leon Eason, bassist Wes Clark and alto saxophonist Al "Rex" Williams remained in the background unless invited to solo. But the Kinney Club was not for everyone. "I played there once, but that was it," said Miss Rhapsody, a beloved jazz and blues singer born in Newark in 1902. "It was too risqué."

The Palace Lucille near West Market Street opened for business in 1918. Other than a small advertisement billing blues singer Hattie Dukes as a headliner in the early 1920s, little else is known about it. The Radio Inn on Halsey, between Hill and Pearl streets, was a different story. Its owner, Alfred C. Gibson, was the father of Swing Era drummer Danny Gibson and uncle of promoter Tiny Prince, a seminal figure in Newark jazz history.

Big-band jazz did not take off in Newark until the mid-1930s, when civic and social clubs began hiring jazz musicians to play for dances and other events at the Terrace Ballroom and Krueger's and Graham's auditoriums. Graham's, run by promoter Henry Graham, eventually became the national headquarters of the Prince Hall Masons. During the Swing Era, orchestras led by Johnny Jackson, Brady Hodge, Duke Richardson, Frank Gibbs and Pancho Diggs provided the music.

The Barons of Rhythm, a group of young musicians out of South Side and Arts high schools, was another hot little act, opening for nationally known big bands at the Shady Rest Country Club in

Scotch Plains, where upwardly mobile blacks gathered to play tennis and golf and socialize. Because Newark was so close to New York, well-known Swing Era bands led by Duke Ellington, Count Basie and Lionel Hampton often played Shady Rest as well as the Adams and Mosque theaters in downtown Newark.

In the late 1930s and early 1940s, the debate among fans in Newark's black community was always the same: which city-based band was the best—the tightest, most musical and most talented. With rare exception, opinions came down to two: the Savoy Dictators, led by trumpeter Hal Mitchell, and the Savoy Sultans, led by bassist Grachan "Brother" Moncur's half-brother, Al Cooper. As the intermission band at the Savoy Ballroom in Harlem, the Sultans were far better known than the Dictators, yet in head-to-head competition, the two groups seemed equally matched.

At the height of the Swing Era, Newark had a tavern on every corner, where hundreds of local musicians, including rising stars like trumpeters Hal Mitchell and Leon Eason and saxophonists Ike Quebec and James Moody honed their skills. The scene was so hot newly minted beboppers Charlie Parker and John Coltrane came from New York City to hang out at clubs in the old Third Ward. Newark also was what writer/poet Amiri Baraka calls a "ticklers' town," a haven for stride pianists like Fats Waller and James P. Johnson, as well as home to two of the best in the business, Willie "The Lion" Smith and Donald Lambert.

Prohibition or not, Newark was a beer town, home to a half-dozen or so major breweries, so it had its fair share of speakeasies. For jazz musicians, that meant plenty of work. Spacious venues like the Kinney Club put on full-scale revues, replete with singers, comedians, dancers and musicians. At the Nest Club on Warren Street, patrons came to see more family-oriented shows. The owner, Euralee Reeves, was one of the city's few black businesswomen.

Singers like Miss Rhapsody, Grace Smith and Geneva Turman often starred in the shows or were the attraction at smaller spots like Fisher's Tavern, Dodger's Bar & Grill and the Alcazar. Miss Rhapsody was a mother figure to younger musicians and singers as well as one of the city's most popular jazz and blues vocalists. In the late 1930s and early '40s, she and her friend Smith took turns reigning as Newark's top female vocalist when the *New Jersey African-American* conducted readers' polls. Smith, who had a reputation as a torch singer, started out as a chorus girl at the Nest Club. Billed as the "Queen of the Blues," she was best-known for her renditions of *Easy Living, I Cried for You* and *Them There Eyes*. Geneva Turman, also quite popular, came from a musical family. Her sister Helena was a dancer; another sister, Gertrude, sang and danced and their brother Buddy was a comedian and emcee.

Through the war years, nightlife in Newark remained brisk in the Third Ward, where most of the musical action took place. Although many musicians left to serve in the military, workers, especially in the black community, couldn't wait to let loose at night after toiling by day in the city's wartime factories. The club scene, where small combos took over the role once played by large orchestras, became their escape. "I used to go to all the clubs," says Charlie Cann, now in his nineties. "Even though I wasn't much of a drinker, the entertainment was great and there were lots of places to go to have fun."

At the Mosque (now Newark Symphony Hall), everything from dance recitals to pop performances by artists such as Judy Garland and Jackie Gleason took place on its grand stage. When Ella Fitzgerald and other stars came to town, jazz was also part of the mix. Downstairs in the Terrace Ballroom, bands led by Duke and Billy Anderson, Nat Phipps, Johnny Jackson and Mandy Ross played for dances sponsored by black middle-class social and professional groups. The hot spot for jazz, however, was the Adams Theater on Branford Place, where bands led by Basie and Ellington performed on their way in or out of New York.

In 1945, with many musicians back from the war, the scene began changing. An age of rampant acquisition and materialism was evolving, and television was the new kid in town. Everyone wanted to watch it. Cashing in on the novelty, club owners who acquired a television set for a few hundred dollars found it a far more profitable investment than having to pay musicians on a regular basis.

No longer did they have to worry about musicians showing up on time or arriving drunk or high. All they had to do was plug in the set and rake in the cash.

Eddie Mosby, manager of the Picadilly, was one of the converts. Instead of hiring a band, he bought a TV set and put a sign in the window: "Jackie Robinson vs the Giants." Robinson, the Brooklyn Dodgers' dynamic young second baseman, had just broken Major League baseball's color barrier. Live music was out. The boob tube was the new attraction.

The music was changing, too. For the next decade or so, rhythm and blues drove younger fans out of the clubs and into record stores. Then, in the late 1940s, a generation of young musicians, tired of traditional jazz, burst on the scene, devoting themselves to a more modern style called bebop. Many of them, like Hank Mobley, Charli Persip, James Moody and Wayne Shorter, got their start at the Picadilly on Peshine Avenue or at Lloyd's Manor on Beacon Street.

When the Key Club first opened on West Street in 1956, Chuck Nolley, who taught art in Newark by day, was behind the bar at night. Nolley also appeared on Broadway in *Carmen Jones*, presented Thursday-night talent shows at the Key Club, and booked acts there and at the Mosque. After World War II, he brought entertainers from Newark to a resort in the Catskills owned by one-legged novelty dancer Peg Leg Bates. Drummer Herbert "Geronimo" Johnson, for one, broke into show business there. Singer Betty "Bebop" Carter was another one of Nolley's clients. "I wound up booking her at the Mosque," he says, "but then she went off with someone else."

Traditional jazz in Newark was still going strong in the late 1950s at places like Sugar Hill opposite City Hall on Broad Street, where Billie Holiday performed for a week in 1957, and at Teddy Powell's Lounge a few doors away, where Abbey Lincoln was a key attraction the following year. Other popular spots included Broadway Open House and the Front Room, both on Broadway, and the Playbill Lounge on Central Avenue.

In 1958, Holiday made four appearances on Art Ford's *Jazz Party*, telecast live on Thursday nights from the Mosque. The series of ninety-minute unrehearsed jam sessions lasted only from May until December of that year, but attracted jazz greats such as Coleman Hawkins, Billie Holiday, Roy Eldridge, Buck Clayton and Buster Bailey. Gradually, rhythm and blues shows, like those staged by promoter Teddy Powell, took over.

Among white teenagers, rock and roll was the new thing. According to historian Nat Bodian, it was concocted as a marketing tool to make rhythm and blues more acceptable to whites. Rock and roll made its debut in Newark when Cleveland disc jockey Alan Freed, who coined the term, brought the first East Coast rock and roll concert to the Newark Armory on Sussex Avenue on May 1, 1948. Advertised as the "Mayday Moondog Coronation Ball," the show featured the Clovers, Harptones, Muddy Waters and Charles Brown. More than 10,000 people, mostly teenagers, showed up. According to one report, "thousands were unable to gain entrance." About a fifth of the audience were white, an indication, Bodian believed, that foretold the future of rock and roll.

Even after Newark's middle class fled the city following the civil rebellions of 1967, the city's reputation as a jazz center continued. Other businesses suffered, but the club scene refused to go softly into the night. Bebop proponents and jazz organ fans still supported places like the Key Club and Sparky J's, where jazz and blues continued to thrive. In the ensuing decades, spots such as Mr. Wes's, Midas Gold, El C's and the Four Leaf Deli came and went.

With the club scene in decline, today's jazz fans generally get their kicks at the Priory, one of Newark's only remaining jazz venues, or at larger places like the Newark Museum, Newark Public Library, Newark Symphony Hall and the New Jersey Performing Arts Center. Or, they tune in to WBGO-FM/Jazz 88, the only station nationwide with an around-the-clock jazz format. No one knows how the future of jazz in Newark will unfold but, as Bob Queen, longtime editor of the *New Jersey Afro-American*, once wrote, "It keeps popping up in the strangest places."

2 ♪

The Hipsters

Bop Comes to Town

Hipness isn't a state of mind, it's a fact of life. —Cannonball Adderly

Newark radio host and jazz historian Stan Myers was a die-hard Swing Era fan, expert on the music of Louis Armstrong, Duke Ellington and Count Basie, when he entered the Army during World War II. By the time he got out in 1947, bebop was the rage and Newark was at the center of it all. Just a hop across the Hudson from Manhattan, the city had become a second home to Charlie Parker, John Coltrane and Dizzy Gillespie as well as a musical playland for those who emulated them.

Unlike the music that came before it, bop was spontaneous, fast-paced and free-wheeling. Instead of charts, improvisation got the musicians' creative juices flowing. "Guys like Bird (Parker) and Dizzy were tired of playing the same old thing," Myers explains. "So they turned to bebop."

In those days, bebop could be heard all over Newark—at upstairs jam sessions at Lloyd's Manor on Beacon Street, at Len & Len's on Warren Street, at the Picadilly in the Third Ward and at the Front Room on Broadway, where Coltrane performed when he first came to town.

Neal Patterson, a retired Newark police lieutenant, was just a kid living upstairs over the old Picadilly Club at Waverly and Peshine avenues when he met Parker in the early 1950s. By then, Parker, or Bird, as his friends called him, was gaining traction as a jazz legend after making his famous Ko-Ko sessions on the small, but thriving, Savoy record label. By then, too, Newark had become a haunt for Bird and his cronies, including Dexter Gordon, Fats Navarro, Miles Davis and Eddie "Lockjaw" Davis.

"Most of them were just starting out," Patterson says. "They weren't all that well-known." But the owners of the Picadilly, one of the city's most popular hangouts for middle-class blacks into the early 1950s, had an eye for top talent. Billie Holiday played there. Erroll Garner, too. "If You Clic at the Pic, You'll Clic with the World" was the club's catchy motto.

On the night Patterson met Parker, Bird had come to town to play at a Monday night jam session run by Hank Mobley, a tenor saxophonist who went on to play with Gillespie. "I can't remember what he (Parker) said to me," Patterson says, "but he took the time to talk to me. He was a real nice guy." A few years later Bird was dead, vanquished by drugs, the scourge that also claimed many of his contemporaries. He was thirty-four.

Except for the blue and white awning that beckoned patrons from the outside, the Picadilly, like many neighborhood clubs in the old Third Ward, was nondescript. An oval bar with a piano in the middle and a few tables on risers surrounding it dominated the interior. As tiny as it was and inconsequential as it seemed, the Pic was a magnet for young musicians who idolized Parker, Coltrane and Gillespie. When Mobley hosted his Monday jams, Larry Young Jr., Charli Persip, Grachan Moncur III and Walter Davis Jr. were among the regulars.

"It was raw bebop at its best," said Ozzie Cadena, who taped several live sessions at the Picadilly, including the recent Uptown release *Hank Mobley: Newark 1953*. Except for trombonist Benny Green, the musicians on the LP—Mobley on tenor, Davis on piano, Jimmy Schenck, bass, and Persip, drums—were jazz newcomers. Cadena, a 1950s Savoy Records producer, also created a two-hour daily jazz program on WNJR, the *Newark Evening News* station. The disc jockeys, Carl Ide and Chris Cunningham, promoted everything from Jazz at the Philharmonic to local music events.

If bebop had an unofficial home in Newark, it was Lloyd's Manor which operated out of a factory-like building on Beacon Street just off Springfield Avenue. The front room catered to house rock fans. Bebop was played in the back. "I used to call it the Bebop Room," Myers says. "A lot of the guys from New York, like Miles Davis, used to hang out there. That's where I first heard Fats Navarro." One of the guys Myers liked best was saxophonist Joe Holliday, one of the few white musicians who came to jam. "He was good and he stood out, just like Vinnie Burke (a bassist from Newark who later played with Bobby Hackett and Marian McPartland)."

Parker and his bebop friends also played at the Blue Mirror on Clinton Avenue, one of a growing number of clubs offering more avant-garde music. They included Teddy Powell's Holiday Inn at the edge of Weequahic Park, Sugar Hill on Broad Street and, later on, Mr. Wes's on Hill Street. "The owner of Sugar Hill had a direct connection to New York," Myers says. "When a lot of the musicians left Birdland, they'd come right over here (to Newark). So did Billie Holiday, Max Roach and Anita O'Day."

By the early 1960s, promising young musicians from Newark like Woody Shaw and Wayne Shorter were headed for the big time. So was saxophonist Tyrone Washington, who left the jazz scene after converting to Islam. Others who showed great promise but rarely left Newark included Herb Morgan, who played in bands led by Jackie Bland and Nat Phipps as a young man. Later in his career he was a fixture at Kimako's Blues People and the Lincoln Park Music Festival. Trombonist Moncur remembers Morgan hanging out with his Jazz Informers at Teddy Powell's Lounge and engaging in saxophone battles with Wayne Shorter. "Herbie was a great musician," Moncur says.

According to author Scott DeVeaux, bebop engenders two diverse schools of thought: Those (mostly writers and critics) who see it as an evolutionary continuation of the music that preceded it and those who see it as revolutionary, something totally unique in music history. Poet Amiri Baraka takes the latter stance, claiming that jazz in general, or bebop as its more innovative successor, is a racial misnomer. "There can be no inclusion as 'Americans' without full equality, and no legitimate disappearance of black music into the covering sobriquet 'American' without consistent recognition of the history, tradition and current needs of the black majority, its culture and it creations," Baraka believes.

Here's a look at some of the most gifted bebop musicians from Newark, starting with Babs Gonzalez, an offbeat character who achieved a semblance of international fame as a pianist, singer and bandleader.

Babs Gonzalez

No examination of the history of bebop would be complete without a look at the life and career of Babs Gonzalez, one of the hippest cats Newark ever knew. Born Lee Brown in New Jersey's largest city on October 27, 1919, Gonzalez was one of several names he went by. Although he performed all over the world, he always returned home to Newark.

As a teenager, Gonzalez spent Saturdays at the Savoy Ballroom in Harlem, where his friend Rudy Williams played saxophone with the Savoy Sultans, the house band. Ever the hustler, Gonzalez was still in school when he landed a job handing out leaflets at the Savoy to get in free. "I would take a few friends over with me so they could see me walk up to the door like the stars," he boasted. At the same time, he began ingratiating himself to icons like Duke Ellington, Count Basie, Lionel Hampton and Billie Holiday, who headlined shows at the Adams Theater. For a few bucks he would show the celebrities around town, which, as he put it, made him feel "sort of like a celebrity."

In his teens, Gonzalez also began crisscrossing the country with Jimmie Lunceford, a popular Swing Era bandleader. After playing Newark-area clubs with local leader Pancho Diggs and forming a club called Los Casanovas that sponsored big-name bands at Newark spots, he took off for California to find fame on his own. Instead, he became a wardrobe attendant at the West Side Country Club in Beverly Hills, where he mingled with the stars and was offered a job as actor Erroll Flynn's chauffeur. In keeping with his wacky ways, he began wearing a turban and calling himself Ram Singh. When the Army tried to draft him, Gonzalez headed back east to take his physical. To his delight and his mother's dismay, he was ruled 4F after dressing in her clothes and posing as a homosexual.

Oddly perhaps, Gonzalez chose not to play piano when he formed his first group, Three Bips and a Bop, in 1946. "I realized by then I'd have to become a singer if I wanted to make it," he concluded. And so, Tadd Dameron, a veteran of Count Basie's band, became his pianist with Peewee Tinney on guitar and Art Phipps on bass. "We rehearsed at Helen Humes' pad in the basement of the Douglas Hotel (in Newark) every day for a month," Gonzalez recounted in *I Paid My Dues*, his autobiography. One of their first gigs was at Minton's in Harlem, where Alfred Lion, who founded Blue Note Records, came to see them. "He said we gassed him, but we were too far out for the people," Gonzalez recalled. After regrouping, the band recorded on Blue Note in early 1947. *Oop-Pop-A-Da*, later a hit for Gillespie, was one of the tunes.

After Gonzalez and his musicians separated, he toured Europe, then spent the next two years traveling the United States with saxophonist James Moody and drummer Chink Wing, friends from Newark. "It was the most fun I ever had," he said. When the band broke up in 1956, he went back to Europe, recorded for a Swedish label, then moved to Paris, where he opened a nightclub called Le Maison du Idiots (the Insane Asylum). Three weeks later a labor strike shut it down. But the name stuck. In the early 1960s, he used it again for a new club on Sugar Hill in Harlem. In true Gonzalez fashion, the waiters dressed in strait-jackets. But that venture, too, was short-lived. After the owner of the building demanded a seventy-percent cut, Gonzalez wrecked the joint and headed south to work in Tampa and Atlanta.

Before long he was off to Europe again for a gig in Holland. Between jobs he worked a one-night stint as a doorman for a celebrity party in New York and had a one-line role in a movie that Sammy Davis Jr. got him called *A Man Named Adam*. Despite his spotty career, Gonzalez recorded frequently. He even made a comedy album, *Tales of the Famous*, stories about his celebrity friends.

In 1966 Gonzalez dropped out of the scene to write his book. "I haven't worked but ten weekends in seven months because I refuse to play bars in nothing places anymore," he said. "I just hope I run into the right connection." He never did. Instead, he spent his remaining days doing what he did best, hustling a gig here and there. Following a long illness, Gonzalez died January 23, 1980, in United Presbyterian Hospital in Newark.

Grachan Moncur III

Just as Duke Ellington wrote *A Train*, Grachan Moncur III—"Jazz" or "Mr. Jazz" to his followers—composed *G-Train*, a journey into the Land of Hip for one of the hippest musicians around. During a career that's spanned more than six decades, the tune is one of many compositions that's put Moncur, the architect of jazz trombone, in a singular category. "Jazz is everything in my life," he says. "There's a certain jazziness to the way I talk that I put into my music and the lyrics that go with it." Tunes like *G-Train* and *Hipnosis* are proof. That's also why Moncur has embarked on the American Jazz Vocal Project in conjunction with Don Sickler, who directs jazz ensembles at Columbia University. "The idea is to have some of the best jazz singers we can find record some of the hippest music ever written," he explains.

These days Moncur spends most of his time working on the project from the house in Newark's West Ward where he and his wife Tracy raised their children. With the exception of his latest project, life is docile compared to the days when he was on the road constantly, playing all over the United States and Europe. Moncur first performed in Europe in the mid-1960s in *Blues for Mr. Charlie*, a musical that debuted on Broadway. The next time he went abroad was with the Archie Shepp All-Stars, a group that first appeared at the Newport Jazz Festival. Miles Davis was the star. "It was the first time musicians featured at the festival played in Europe," he says. "But we were the ones who upset the place. We got a twenty-minute standing ovation. After that, Miles always said he hated us."

While Moncur's name is legendary among jazz musicians, he's achieved only a modicum of fame. His friend Ed Berger attests to that in a 2002 issue of *JazzTimes.* "For a time," Berger wrote, "it seemed like Grachan Moncur III was destined for jazz stardom. But for various reasons, some of his own doing and some beyond his own control, Moncur never enjoyed the sustained success of his peers, although his talent was never at issue."

Moncur, who won rave reviews for his work with Ray Charles, Art Farmer and Benny Golson and accolades for his daring bebop compositions, most notably *Evolution*, doesn't disagree with Berger's assessment. But his definition of success is far different than his critics. "It's not a matter of money," he says. "My royalties are good because my work has been re-issued. It's a matter of expressing my freedom through my horn." Nor was having big-band recognition the be-all and end-all for him. "The best performances usually come from having the right personnel for your music," he believes, "but I haven't always been fortunate to get the right people to work with me. I've kept going because of the love I have for my instrument."

Moncur was ten when his father, who played bass for the Savoy Sultans, an important Swing Era band, brought home the best gift he ever received—a shiny silver trombone. It cost only $5, but to young Grachan it was worth a mint. "From the moment I picked it up, I could play it," he recalls. Before long, he was taking lessons at Dorn & Kirschner's on Springfield Avenue, the biggest music store in Newark.

By then, his father's longtime gig with the Sultans was coming to an end. Moncur Sr., better known as "Brother," was about to take up residence at Club 83 on Warren Street, while his brother, saxophonist Al Cooper, the Sultans' leader, was building a reputation as a music promoter. Grachan III's mother, Ella Moncur, a well-known Newark hair stylist, was musical, too. She could sing and play piano.

Grachan Moncur III met Robert, his best friend, at Morton Street School. "He was the most hip dude in the school," he says. "His older brothers, who had a huge record collection, put me on to bebop. Until then, I was listening to Benny Green. Once I heard J.J. (Johnson), I was into a whole new movement. At lunchtime I think I put every cent I had into the jukebox at a greasy spoon on Court Street, listening to Lester Young play *Up and At 'Em.*"

After he graduated from Morton Street, Moncur's parents sent him to Laurinberg Institute in North Carolina, where his predecessors included Woody Shaw's father and trumpeter Dizzy Gillespie. "I think I was sent away to school because my mother wanted me off the streets," he reflects. "She didn't want me hanging out when the drug epidemic hit Newark, so I was spared." From the moment Frank McDuffie, the president, picked him up at the bus station in the fall of 1951, Moncur felt at home at Laurinberg. "I can't tell you how good I felt when I pulled my horn out and the guys in the marching band said excitedly, 'We got us a trombone player.' I didn't know nothing except one riff by Trummy Young that I played over and over. Just that one thing." But he learned quickly, especially from Philip Hilton, "the most advanced cat in the whole band," who taught him bassoon parts, and Frank McDuffie Jr., the president's son, who gave him a solo in his jazz orchestra.

By summer vacation of his junior year, Moncur had advanced to the point where the Club Varsity in Newark hired him to play on Sundays. "That's where I met Nat Phipps," he says. "Wayne Shorter, who was playing with Nat's orchestra, brought him to see me." Moncur was seventeen when he joined Phipps's band. "I was the youngest cat in it," he says. "We played at all the social dances at places like the Terrace Ballroom for groups like the Pacesetters. After the band disbanded, Wayne Shorter and Nat Phipps chose me to be the leader of the Jazz Informers and we began playing at Teddy Powell's Lounge. Teddy would bring in all the big acts like

Abbey Lincoln, Titus Turner and Redd Foxx." The group, which featured Ed Lightsey on bass and Bobby Thomas on drums, also played at Sugar Hill a few doors away from Powell's, another magnet for top-name attractions.

As Moncur delved deeper into jazz, he also learned one of the greatest lessons of his young life. "One night my friend Robert and I went to a party with his older brother Calvin. By then, Calvin, who had been the cleanest, hippest guy I knew, was a stone addict. We were told to stay in the living room while the other guys went in the back. I knew what they were doing, so I went back and told Calvin I wanted to try some (drugs), too. 'I don't ever want to hear about you doing drugs,' he screamed at me. Calvin was one of the most influential people in my life. First, he got me into bebop. Then, he saved my life. I don't think I would be living today, if it weren't for him. I did do drugs, but I never shot up. That made all the difference."

After returning home from Laurinberg, Moncur's father offered him a job with his band, but he turned it down to pursue his growing interest in avant-garde music. "I could have been playing six times a week for six or seven years with my father, but I had a sense of urgency about what I was playing. My head was in a different place," he says. Fortunately, his father was not disappointed. "My dad was the most supportive cat in the world," he explains. "As long as I was happy, he was, too."

Because he wanted to learn all there was to know about the trombone, Moncur eventually enrolled at the Juilliard School of Music and studied with trombone master John Clark at the Manhattan School of Music. "When I left Juilliard in 1958, I traveled with Ray Charles for three years, then was recruited by Art Farmer and Benny Golson to play with their Jazztet," he says. "I took them up on it because I wanted to be a contributing force on the music scene in New York. Art was the one who really started me writing. He sat me down and taught me notations. At the time, writing was the last thing on my mind, so I am forever grateful to him for inspiring me."

Moncur worked next with Sonny Rollins, Jackie McLean and Shepp before forming groups of his own. Both McLean and Shepp recorded many of his compositions. In addition to touring Europe as a composer and trombonist, his travels abroad include an appearance at the Pan-African Festival in Algiers in 1976. Among many honors, *DownBeat* voted him No. 1 Trombonist Deserving Wider Recognition in 1964. In 1970, the Paris publication *Jazz* named him Top Trombonist Among European Fans. In 1975, *Melody Maker*, the British magazine, selected his recording of *Echoes of Prayer: To Free All Political Prisoners* as Jazz Album of the Year.

Because he's marched to his own drummer—or perhaps that should be trombonist—Moncur believes he's been miscast at times. Like his friends Wayne Shorter and Miles Davis, he's refused to trade the truth and freedom of his music for commercial success, often a costly choice for a world-class musician.

Now he's returning to his roots, putting words to the first two tunes he ever wrote—*Sonny's Back* and *Space Station*—as part of the CD he's compiling with Sickler. To mark Moncur's seventy-fifth birthday in 2012, his family threw a party at Skipper's, where he released a new CD: *Homecoming: This One's for Jackie*, his first as a leader recording his own material. Dedicated to his friend McLean, it features four of his pieces that McLean recorded. At seventy-five-plus, Moncur's still doing things his way.

Wayne Shorter

Wayne Shorter's reputation for blowing the competition away at events all over Newark was legendary by the time bandleader Nat Phipps returned home from the Army in the mid-1950s and persuaded Shorter to join his orchestra. Like Phipps, Shorter had burst onto the Newark jazz scene as a teenager, playing with a group of progressive young jazz musicians led by Jackie Bland.

Trombonist Grachan Moncur III, bassist Chris White and saxophonist Ken Gibson, Newark's future mayor, also were in Bland's band. "Wayne was simply phenomenal," says Gibson. "We were friendly rivals with Nat's group. Our band alternated every Sunday, playing for canteens at Graham's auditorium at 188 Belmont Avenue (Irvine Turner Boulevard). Wayne was so dedicated to his music, so wrapped up in it, a lot of people thought he was weird."

But that didn't faze Shorter or his brother Alan, who also was in the band. In their quest to be hip they did everything possible to call attention to themselves, going so far as to paint "Mr. Weird" and "Doc Strange," respectively, on their horn cases and relishing the reactions they got.

Bland, who wore a goatee and horn-rimmed glasses, à la Dizzy Gillespie, was different, too. Although he didn't play an instrument, he got considerable feedback by waving a baton and distinguishing himself as the band's leader by wearing a leopard-skin coat. In keeping with their oddball antics, the Shorter brothers, according to Phipps, often wore dark suits "that made them look like undertakers."

But it was the music that mattered, the fact that Shorter, despite his late start at age fifteen and limited experience, was light years ahead of other musicians his age. "I could read (music), but I couldn't improvise, so I was always amazed when Wayne played," Gibson says. "He was out of sight."

"When our bands went head to head before I left for the Army, Jackie Bland's band was *it*," Phipps recounts. "They were into bebop and way ahead of us musically, mostly because of Wayne. By the time I got back we were into bebop, too, so you can imagine how glad we were to have Wayne join us."

Born in Newark on August 25, 1933, Shorter and his brother Alan were the children of Joseph Shorter, who worked in a nearby factory, and his wife Louise, a homemaker. Alan played trumpet after starting out on saxophone. Wayne's musical genius became apparent soon after he graduated from Oliver Street School in the Ironbound section of the city, where he grew up, and entered Arts High, Newark's training ground for the performing arts.

Like many young men his age, Wayne Shorter began skipping classes at Arts High to sneak into shows at the Adams Theater downtown. His interest in jazz took root there after hearing Lester Young, Stan Kenton, Count Basie and Woody Herman. Shorter also enjoyed practicing at the Oliver Street School playground with Joe Thomas, who was two years behind him in elementary school. "Wayne would play Leo Parker's *Leo Leaps In* on clarinet and I played Illinois Jacquet's *Flying Home* on saxophone," Thomas recalls.

By then, Shorter had made an art out of forging his parents' signatures on excuses from school to get into the Adams. Rather than punish him, the principal sent him to Miss Paparo, the vocal music teacher, for instruction. Until then, he had been a talented art major who produced a science fiction comic book of professional quality called *Other Worlds*—a perfect name coming from such an oddball kid. Once his musical talent became apparent, he changed his major to both art and music and began devoting himself to jazz.

Soon after, Shorter formed the Jazz Informers and began hanging out at Lloyd's Manor, where saxophone icons, including Charlie Parker and Fats Navarro, sat in at weekly jam sessions. Shorter was taking it all in, absorbing everything there was to know. Shortly after joining Bland's band, the word went out: No other young musician could touch him.

Shorter's interests in other worldliness extended to the music he played, not unusual perhaps for someone who grew up in a city that produced such individualists as Babs Gonzalez, Woody Shaw, Grachan Moncur III and Larry Young Jr. "Maybe there was something different in the water," a musician once joked. Whatever the reason, Shorter's interests, including his sense of spirituality as he grew older, were unconventional for a teenager, especially a young black man growing up in the inner city. Like Shaw, who followed him at Arts High a decade later, Shorter's zest for learning eventually led him to explore his spiritual leanings. Shaw wound up embracing the Baha'i faith. Shorter became a Buddhist.

After serving in the Army, Shorter worked his way through New York University, where Nat Phipps and trombonist Al Patterson also were enrolled. "At the rehearsals of the Nat Phipps Big Band, Wayne always practiced during the breaks," Patterson recalls. "It was the first time I had witnessed anything like that. What he was practicing was so complex everyone would wonder in amazement what he was playing."

While in college, Shorter cracked the New York music scene, which led him to sign with Horace Silver after graduation. By then he was playing all over New York with trumpeter Freddie Hubbard and saxophonist Sonny Rollins. He also was part of John Coltrane's inner circle. Keyboardist/composer Joe Zawinul, who came to the United States from Austria to study at the Berklee School of Music and was playing with Maynard Ferguson, was another new friend.

In those days, the old Birdland in New York was the place to be for any East Coast jazz musician. Shorter was no exception. Days after joining Ferguson's band at Zawinul's suggestion, he got his first write-up after performing there. The piece in the *Jazz Review* was written by Amiri Baraka, his friend from Newark. "Everything that comes out of the (Shorter's) horn seems not premeditated, but definite and assimilated . . . no matter how wild or unlikely it may seem at first," Baraka wrote.

In July 1959, Art Blakey recruited Shorter for his Jazz Messengers, one of the most successful bands in jazz history. Blakey needed a tenor, so he convinced Ferguson to let Shorter go, focusing his pitch on his contention that Shorter was not cut out for a career as a big-band musician. By then Shorter was a gifted composer and arranger, prompting Blakey, with whom he played for the next four years, to hand over complete control of the Messengers' music. Soon after joining Blakey, two of his tunes, including *Africaine*, were featured on Blakey's LP of the same name.

Shorter's association with Blakey greatly expanded his heretofore limited jazz experience. Before long, he began touring Europe and Japan and recording, first on Vee-Jay, then on Blue Note, where he made a string of LPs over a seven-year period in the 1960s. Hardly a day went by when he didn't write a new tune.

After he left Blakey, Shorter spent five years with Miles Davis at a time when Davis's band was getting into a more radical form of jazz. Playing with Davis gave him the opportunity to cement his reputation as a composer. Two tunes, *Miles Smiles* and *Footprints*, the name of Shorter's biography, did the trick. After leaving Davis in 1966, Shorter played club dates in and around New York, then came into his own as the founder, with his friend Zawinul, of Weather Report, the jazz world's quintessential quintet. During the latter 1970s he traveled constantly, to the point where he spent forty-two weeks of 1977 touring with Weather Report and another group led by Herbie Hancock.

Shorter was a lone wolf on the road, remaining in his room to read, watch old movies or, most often, compose music while the other guys were socializing or out drinking. Despite changes in personnel and style, Weather Report kept going for fourteen years. Since the group broke up, Shorter has led the Wayne Shorter Quartet with Danilo Perez on piano; John Patitucci, bass; and Brian Blade, drums.

Over time, however, Shorter got away from playing and composing music as his devotion to Buddhism gained strength. His religious beliefs intensified as his daughter Iska, brain-damaged in infancy, grew older. Iska, who was fourteen when she died, was the center of his world, one he seemed to better understand and feel more comfortable in through Buddhism more than music. The depth of his faith also compelled him to put aside a life of hard drinking that sometimes impaired his performances. Although he's won nine Grammys, worldly achievements appear of little interest to him.

One of Shorter's most recent appearances was at Town Hall in New York in mid-2013, where he kicked off a five-city tour marking his eightieth birthday. The year before he appeared at NJPAC in Newark as a board member of the Thelonious Monk Institute, a training ground for young musicians.

In August 2013, Shorter appeared on the cover of *DownBeat* after capturing top honors in four categories of the Annual Critics Poll: Jazz Artist, Jazz Album, Jazz Group and Soprano Saxophone. "Wayne Wins," the headline read. Shorter's reaction to these accolades was typical, humble and grateful, yet cryptic. "Metaphorically," he told *DownBeat*, the LP is "a chronicle of how segments of life have been perceived and how the perception changes, and what visionary means. You break out of the chains of safety zones and boxes and pyramids and circles, and get into this unknown."

While Shorter was on his birthday tour, friend Baraka paid tribute to him at the annual Lincoln Park Music Festival in Newark, where the NewArkestra spent an August afternoon playing his music. Al Patterson, the band's co-director with Steve Colson, described the tribute as very special "because it gave me the opportunity to arrange six of the eight Shorter compositions played by the eight-piece ensemble—five horns plus the rhythm section. It gave me insight into the music that I had heard many times in Wayne's performances with Blakey and Miles." Colson arranged the other tunes on the program, while Baraka read a poem about the murder of Florida teenager Trayvon Martin.

3 ♪

Newark's Most Musical Families

Jazz in Their Genes

When families adorn the pages of jazz
history, it's possible that the most numerous
are pairs of brothers. —Jazz Mostly

The unparalleled legacy of the Phipps family in New Jersey jazz history is the story of two diverse branches of Newark's most musical family. On one end of the spectrum are Nat and Billy Phipps, college-educated twin brothers who became prominent music educators; at the other end, their older cousin, Gene Phipps Sr., and his son, Gene Jr., whose genius was plagued by drug abuse.

Before his death in November 2013, Gene Phipps Sr. was a resident of the White House Nursing home in Orange, New Jersey, where he had more than enough time to mull over the costly mistakes he had made early in life and paid for dearly. His gift for music, he said, proved his downfall because he became hooked on drugs so young and took fifty years to finally clean up. Unfortunately, his son, Gene Jr., continues to struggle with his addiction. Conversely, cousins Nat and Billy Phipps became highly respected music educators and musicians who enjoyed fruitful careers.

Born December 17, 1927, in Newark, Eugene Phipps Sr. started playing alto saxophone at Webster Street School in the city's North Ward, where his gift for music was immediately apparent. At graduation, he played two solos: *Nola* and *Flight of the Bumble Bee*, quite a feat for a young musician. By then he had played his first gig at the Court Street Y in his older brother Ernie's band, the Marlarks of Rhythm. "I think I got $6 for the night," he said. With their mother's permission, he began hanging out on 52nd Street in New York with Ernie, taking in the burgeoning jazz scene on "The Street That Never Slept." "I was a young teenager when I got to hear all the greats—Don Byas, Coleman Hawkins, Charlie Parker and Dizzy Gillespie," he recalled. "Don Byas was my idol."

When his brother left for the Army, Phipps, then a student at Barringer High School, took over the Marlarks. When he dropped out of school at seventeen to tour with Billie Holiday's orchestra, he was the only black member of the Barringer Blue Jackets, the school jazz band. "Hal Mitchell (a big-band trumpeter from Newark) took me to New York to audition for Billie, and I made it," he said. After five months on the road with Holiday, he joined a band led by Oran "Hot Lips" Page, one of the hottest trumpeters of the era. "We did one-nighters up and down the East Coast," he noted. "I was making $75 a night. That was big time. We also played places like the Apollo Theater and Tavern on the Green in New York."

Subsequently, he toured with a band led by pianist Sonny Thompson, whose recording of *Long Gone* became a hit. Along the way Phipps got married and returned home for a breather. When a call he was waiting for to rejoin the band came, his wife answered and told the manager he had quit. "By the time I found out, it was too late," he said, "so I stayed in Newark and began playing at the Washington Bar, which had music seven nights a week. That's when I began drinking and using dope. It was a mistake, and it ruined me."

At the age of forty Phipps had a chance to join Lionel Hampton's band, but wasn't ready. "It would have taken me two weeks to clean up," he said, "so I missed out." From then on, finding work became more difficult Dope was readily available and taking its toll. The once-premier player was losing his edge. "I was seventy when I quit," Phipps said, "only because I got sick. Don't be a wise guy," he advised young musicians who think drugs will enhance their play-ing. "Don't be stupid."

Phipps's cousins, Nat and Billy Phipps, fraternal twins who en-tered the world minutes apart in December 1931, were master musi-cians too. Oddly enough, they were born on different days. Billy arrived shortly before midnight on Christmas Day, Nat just minutes into December 26. During their childhood they learned the rudi-ments of music from their mother's brother, William O'Laughlin. "My uncle didn't only teach us," Nat says. "He taught our cousins—Gene Phipps Sr., Joe O'Laughlin and Stanley (Stash) O'Laughlin—as well as all the other kids in the neighborhood. Everyone wanted to be in the marching band he led at Queen of Angels Roman Cath-olic Church."

Billy and Nat were in knee pants when they began studying with their uncle. Nat started out on trumpet before switching to piano, while Billy stayed with the saxophone. After practicing arduously, the brothers joined their uncle's band, which played during inter-mission at Ruppert Stadium in Newark's Ironbound area when the Newark Eagles of the National Negro League were at home. By then, the O'Laughlin brothers were playing professionally—Joe O'Laughlin as a saxophonist with Buddy Johnson's and Brady Hodge's orchestras and Stash as a pianist with the Millard Trio and Brother Kelly's band.

The Phipps brothers made their mark on Newark's musical land-scape as teenagers at Barringer High School, where Nat held sway over the Nat Phipps Orchestra. With Nat on piano and Billy on tenor sax, the band was immensely popular at dances at the Terrace Ballroom and battles of the bands at teenage canteens that pitted them against their contemporaries.

"Another guy was leading the orchestra when we started out," Nat notes. "But my friends wanted me to take over." Despite their youth, their group was one of the most musically precocious among Newark's up-and-coming bands. So was a band led by Jackie Bland. "We were rivals," Nat explains. "That's why we were invited to compete against each other at the Court Street Y," a hangout for black teenagers and young adults.

Bland didn't just have a good band, he had a secret weapon: tenor saxophonist Wayne Shorter, whose legendary career in jazz includes nine Grammys and thirteen Grammy nominations. Although they grew up in different areas of the city—Shorter Down Neck (in the Ironbound) and the Phipps twins in the predominantly Italian First Ward—music was their bond. While Billy and Nat were at Barringer, Wayne and his brother Alan, who played saxophone before turning to trumpet and flugelhorn, were at Arts High. "Both of them were playing with Jackie Bland when we first went head to head," Nat recounts. "We had Bobby Thomas on drums; Eddie Lightsey, bass; Owen Francis, trumpet; Louis Miles, trombone; Clarence Walker, alto; and two tenors, Julius Hickson and my brother. Neither Wayne nor his brother read (music) then. They played lines off records, note for note, which I thought was fabulous."

By the time the rivals met at the Y, "Jackie's band was playing hard-driving bebop, while we were still playing conventional Swing Era standards," Nat says. "All the kids were into bebop, so they blew us away."

"They ran us out of there, playing pieces Miles Davis had recorded, while we were still playing *Blue Moon*," Billy said years later. Things evened up the next time around when the rivals met at the Masonic Temple at 188 Belmont Avenue. "By then we were playing bebop, too," Nat explains. "So we outdid them."

After Nat came home from the Army and enrolled at New York University, Shorter wound up playing with Nat's new orchestra as well as a scaled-down version of it. "Our tenor player left and Wayne agreed to fill in. By that time, we were heavily into bebop, too," Nat says. The tight little unit also included avant-garde trombonist Grachan Moncur III and bassist Chris White, along with Billy Phipps on tenor; Bobby Thomas, drums; Charlie Mason, trumpet, and cousin Harold Phipps, congas. White, who went on to play with Cecil Taylor and Dizzy Gillespie, was in the band from 1956–58. "I heard about it from Ed Lightsey when we both were at the Manhattan School of Music," Nat says.

"While I was in the Army I was always drawn to older guys in the band who were in college," he says. "I learned that you'll always have teaching as a means of earning a living, even if you don't make it big. After I got back home I was thinking of going to Juilliard, but Wayne convinced me to go to NYU because so many other jazz musicians were there." Billy followed suit a year later.

Both brothers enjoyed stellar careers as music educators. After transferring to the Manhattan School of Music for his undergraduate degree, Billy taught in Newark public schools for more than thirty years. Along the way he earned a master's degree in music from Jersey City State College. Following his graduation from NYU in 1959, Nat taught music in New York City for nearly twenty years. During that time he received his master's degree in music education from NYU and certificate in administration and supervision from Hunter College. In 1976, he was named Teacher of the Year for his work with emotionally disturbed children at Sterling High School in Manhattan, where he created the Sterling Average Teenage Band, a student rock group that wound up playing at the Kennedy Center in Washington, D.C., for President John F. Kennedy and his family. "My work with these talented young people was extremely rewarding because it reflected the importance of music as a way of stimulating and motivating them to go to class and behave," he says.

In the latter part of 1979, Nat Phipps moved to upstate New York, where he joined the New York State Education Department as an associate in music education, overseeing choral studies at Skidmore College. For many years he also taught a course called *Jazz: America's Music* at the State College of New York. He retired in 1995 as chief of the Bureau of Arts and Music Education.

Reflecting on his long career in music, he remembers the thrill of opening for Nat King Cole at the Newark Opera House in 1951. "As part of a trio, I got to play *Tea For Two* for Bunny Briggs, the tap dancer with the show," he says. "It was great to be in the spotlight at such a young age." With smaller units of his orchestra, Nat got to accompany Moms Mabley, a top female comedian of the era, and played for Al Hibbler and Sonny Til. Although he auditioned to replace Carmen McRae's piano player, he lost out. "She accepted me, and I had the itinerary in my hand when the guy playing with her decided not to leave. Even so, getting the chance to play for her was a thrill."

In the early 1950s, Nat accompanied Little Jimmy Scott for two years, appearing all over Newark at spots like the Glitter Club, the Key Club, Len & Len's, Hour Glass, Front Room and Wakefield's. He also led Nat Phipps & The Megatones at the Orbit Lounge on Market Street. For a time, Bill "Blues" Johnson handled the vocals. "We called ourselves the Megatones because music was changing," Nat explains. "Jazz was on the wane, so we expanded our repertoire and began singing. The personnel kept changing, but Billy was in it most of the ten years or so we worked together."

Bob Darden, nicknamed "Stix" by a college friend, was the Megatones' drummer. As a protégé of Max Roach, Darden was considered top of the heap during the bebop era. "I met Max as a kid when I used to go to New York," he says. "He liked my playing because he thought it was very soulful—like Art Blakey." After graduating from West Side High School, Darden entered Morgan State University in Baltimore, where he began playing with many of the biggest names in jazz, including Lester Young. "I got to know most of the name musicians, including Max and the guys in Ellington's band, because they stayed on campus when they were working the Baltimore–D.C. area," he notes. "They couldn't stay in the hotels because everything was segregated."

After graduating from Morgan State, Darden stayed in Baltimore for three years, performing with a band led by pianist Paul Bley. For a time the group was the intermission band at Olivia's Patio Lounge in Washington. One night, after backing Lester Young, the famous saxophonist invited Bley's group to join him in Detroit, a highlight of Darden's young career. After returning to Newark, he joined the Megatones. He eventually left music to devote himself to a full-time career in education.

After the Phipps brothers parted in the 1960s, Billy joined Buddy Johnson's band and toured with Ray Charles. By then he was enthralled by bebop, an interest that escalated after Shorter introduced him to John Coltrane's music. On a tip from saxophonist Buddy Terry, he auditioned and won a spot in Dizzy Gillespie's Big Band. "Coltrane was Billy's idol," his widow Barbara says. "When we were first married, we heard that Trane was playing at Len & Len's. So we went to see him. Billy was thrilled. My husband loved Coltrane so much he used to say he would follow him even if Coltrane put lace around his shorts."

Years later, Billy paid tribute to Coltrane when his quartet opened the sixth annual Newark Jazz Festival at the Newark Public Library. Joined by Eddie Wright (guitar), Al Patterson (trombone) and Otis Brown (drums), the group played two Coltrane compositions, *Blue Train* and *Giants Steps*. The program also included tributes to Shorter (*Children of the Night*) and Shorter's Arts High buddy Woody Shaw (*Moontrane*). As Billy later told *Star-Ledger* jazz critic Zan Stewart, he got the gig with Gillespie because he knew *Things to Come*, a lightning-fast tune Gillespie recorded in 1968, backed by an all-star contingent that included James Moody, Cecil Payne, Jimmy Owens and Curtis Fuller.

Billy subsequently toured with organist "Brother" Jack McDuff, a master of the B3 Hammond Organ who appeared often at the Key Club and Sparky J's. He also led his own groups and was active years later with the Newark Jazz Elders, a group of Swing Era veterans, and Amiri Baraka's NewArkestra.

Aside from their musical careers, Nat and Billy Phipps loved nurturing new talent, Nat through his teaching in New York City and at upstate colleges, and Billy through his work in Newark schools, where he taught all instruments. For Billy and Barbara's daughter Lauren that meant accompanying her father and his cousin, Gene Phipps Sr., when they played at schools throughout the city. "Billy taught Lauren to sing like a human instrument," her mother says. "Billy and his group would play and she would improvise."

Billy also taught his granddaughter, Ashley Morse, to play saxophone and counted two nephews, Jimmy Caines, a saxophonist, and Charles Caines, a pianist, among his students. When he died in December 2011, his brother Nat was too distraught to remember much about the service at Trinity & St. Philip's Cathedral or the New Orleans–style jam session afterward at Arts High School. "I was out of it," Nat says. "I think of Billy all the time. Sometimes when I look in the mirror, I think I'm seeing him. We were very close—from the embryo to the end."

Nat still performs in and around Schenectady, where he has taught music and lived for more than three decades. For most of that time he's been a music professor at Schenectady Community College. He and his wife Berta, who met him after she told a friend how much she liked his arrangement of the John Lester tune *Getting Nearer*, marked their fiftieth anniversary in June 2013. Surprisingly, perhaps, none of their three daughters is musical.

With the passing of Billy Phipps, Ernie Phipps, Gene Phipps Sr. and the O'Laughlins, and Gene's brother Harold in retirement, Nat Phipps remains the only older musician in the family who is still active musically.

For years, Gene Phipps Jr., who many musicians say inherited his father's musical talent, played with top-of-the-line artists such as Max Roach, Woody Shaw and Abbey Lincoln. It was, however, a topsy-turvy ride as he battled his addiction. As a young man, Gene Jr. played in his father's band before striking out on his own. He later became a favorite at the Priory on the Friday night bill. More recently he and drummer Bruce Tyler led Tuesday night jam sessions at the DLV Lounge in Montclair. His sister, singer Laranah Phipps, known as La La or Lady Laranah Phipps, has served as stage manager for the Dunbar Repertory Company, a New Jersey Shore-based African-American theater group, and production assistant for the Count Basie Theater in Red Bank. She also has served as cultural arts director at Convention Hall and the Paramount Theater, both in Asbury Park.

The Bey Family

When Ronnell Bey was growing up in Newark's North Ward in the 1960s, music was everywhere—spilling from the family radio and phonograph records and, to her fascination from her mother's siblings singing at the huge house they shared on Chester Avenue. Hardly a day went by when Bey didn't listen to her uncle Andy and aunts Salome and Geraldine—Andy Bey and the Bey Sisters to the rest of the world—rehearse for a show or recording session.

"My mother, Victoria Bey, was a nice little Christian lady dealing with nine children," says Geraldine "Gerri" Bey de Haas. "My father, Andrew Pierce Wideman Bey (better known as A.P.), was a window washer and a Moorish American who embraced Islam. My brother Andy was the architect of Andy Bey and the Bey Sisters," she explains. "He's why we were known for our unique harmonies. He was extremely talented in terms of vocal expression and had perfect pitch."

Just three when he started playing the family's piano, Andy began banging out boogie-woogie tunes at six. A few years later, he began recording on Jubilee. At seventeen, while at Arts High School, he formed the trio with his sisters. While Andy was into pop tunes and jazz, older sister Gerri's main interest was semi-classical music. "My idols were Marian Anderson (The Voice of the 20th Century) and movie stars Deanna Durbin and Jane Powell," she says. As a teenager, she sang in all-state choirs. According to Gerri, Salome had "the most extraordinary voice" in the family. "Salome won a lot of talent shows, including the Amateur Night competition at Harlem's Apollo Theater," she says.

Between 1957 and 1966, when Andy Bey and the Bey Sisters broke up, they recorded three albums, one for RCA and two for Prestige. During that time they spent eighteen months in Europe, where the Blue Note supper club in Paris was home base. "It was a wonderful time," Gerri says. "We were young, so we had a lot of fun." Of all their experiences, she says, the night they were invited to sing at a party at the home of actress Brigitte Bardot and her film producer husband Roger Vadim stands out. "Evidently, Roger Vadim was filming us," she recalls. "We knew nothing about it until Chet Baker's documentary, *Let's Get Lost*, a film about jazz in Europe, came out. There we were."

Like her uncle and aunts, Ronnell felt destined to become a singer. "I guess I was about four or five when I began singing along with the music I heard," she says. "In the beginning I kept it a secret from my family, but once they heard me, they encouraged me." And so, she began polishing her talent with the blessing of her mother, Florence, a friend of Sarah Vaughan's who designed clothes for the famous jazz singer.

By the time her aunts and uncle returned from Europe, Ronnell was old enough to hang out with them. One of those occasions was what she calls "The Night of Nights," when her uncle Andy took her to hear Carmen McRae perform at a New York club, then stopped by the Grande Finale on Broadway to catch Vaughan. "Sarah was *it* in our house," Ronnell notes. "We listened to all kinds of music—R&B, jazz, the Beatles, Laura Nyro—even classical. I even remember hearing *Madame Butterfly*. But Sarah was *it*. That's why going back stage that night was such a thrill. Meeting Carmen McRae was great, but seeing Sarah was *it*."

Years later, she and Andy were invited to sing at a tribute in Vaughan's memory at NJPAC. As *Star-Ledger* jazz critic George Kanzler noted in his recap: "When Ronnell Bey, singing with Frank Foster's Loud Minority Big Band, stretched and held notes with pulsating vibrato on *For All We Know*, she was recalling the Divine One. Just as she was reminding us of Sassy when she playfully skipped into bebopping scat lines at the end of *Black Coffee*." Alone at the piano, Kanzler went on, Andy Bey sang with "amazing resonance and the kind of gloriously rich tonal colors and luxuriously long, time-suspending notes like Vaughan introduced to jazz." Bey, he said, displayed "exquisite virtuosity" on *But Not for Me* and *Embraceable You*.

Like her aunts and uncle, Ronnell Bey has appeared in concerts and theatrical productions all over the world. Because she wanted to act, too, she became a theater major at Arts High School and at Rutgers-Newark, where she earned her bachelor's degree. Her first starring role was at Arts, where she played the lead in *Annie Get Your Gun*. After college she spent several years as a substitute teacher in the Newark school system before deciding to pursue music full time.

By then she had sung sporadically at places like the Peppermint Lounge in Orange. She also was hanging out backstage with her aunt Salome, who was appearing on Broadway in *Your Arms Too Short to Box with God*. "I was always excited to spend time with my aunts and uncle," she reflects. "When I was very young, I can remember doing a cartwheel when they returned from a trip to Europe. I was wearing a dress, so my mother was not very pleased."

By the 1990s, Ronnell's career was slamming. "I played so many gigs in Germany it became my second home," she says. On tour she appeared in Eisenbach in *Play Luther*, a compilation of the works of Martin Luther and Martin Luther King that featured Yolanda King, the civil rights leader's daughter, drummer Max Roach and saxophonist Donald Byrd. Ronnell also appeared in a play about Mahalia Jackson and conducted a gospel workshop for German students. She even made a German beer commercial.

"I also appeared in *Ain't Misbehavin'* all over the place," she says. "We started in New York and wound up in Finland." In Toronto, she appeared with her aunt Salome in *Your Arms Too Short to Box with God*. Her TV credits include *A Thanksgiving Celebration*, made in Canada as a tribute to Queen Elizabeth.

Back home, Ronnell won a role in Amiri Baraka's *The Life and Life of Bumpy Johnson*, for which Max Roach wrote the music. After auditioning at Symphony Hall in Newark, where the play made its debut, she was off to California to perform the piece with the San Diego Repertory. Ronnell also made several CDs, including *The Nearness of You*, on which she's featured with Eartha Kitt and Clark Terry.

Whether she is engaged in conversation with friends or performing, Ronnell is prone to humorous asides, a trait made clear one night in 1998 at the Priory when she was appearing with her uncle Andy on piano and her aunt Salome looking on. "She's sticking her tongue out at me," a surprised photographer said. "I love it!" Wherever she appears, Ronnell either moves her audience to tears or has them laughing until they cry, as she did that night. After back-to-back appearances at the Priory that winter, Chase Jackson, who was in charge of the programming, effused, "When Ronnell's in town, we always have a packed house. People just don't come in twos and threes, they come in groups."

While most of her family has branched out, Ronnell still lives in Newark, where she was born, began her career and raised her family. For the most part, she sticks close to home these days, singing locally from time to time as she recently did at the Priory.

In the late 1960s, after Andy and his sisters went their separate ways, he launched a solo career, working for the next few years with artists like Horace Silver and Gary Bartz, and recording on Stanley Clarke's *Children of Forever* with Dee Dee Bridgewater. In the 1970s, Andy worked occasionally with Grachan Moncur III in bands led by Jackie McLean and Archie Shepp and provided the vocals when Moncur recorded *Shadows* in 1977. "For a good part of it, Andy and I just followed each other," says Moncur.

Andy's work slowed after he turned to bebop. Things began picking up again in the 1990s, when he had several recordings to his credit: *As Time Goes By* (1991); *Ballads, Blues and Bey* (1996); *Shades of Bey* (1998); *Tuesdays in Chinatown* (2001); *Chillin'* (2003); and *Ain't Necessarily So* (2007). His latest CD, *The World According to Andy Bey*, was released in 2013. A decade before, his silky vocals captured the attention of the critics when the Jazz Journalists Association named him 2003 Jazz Vocalist of the Year. In 2005, *American Song*, which he recorded on Savoy Jazz the previous year, garnered a Grammy nomination for Best Jazz Vocal Album.

After touring with her brother and older sister from 1957–66, Salome settled in Toronto, where she performed in nightclubs and appeared in musical theater productions. Known as Canada's First Lady of the Blues, she received an Obie Award in 1972 for her role in *Justine*. In addition to a long list of musical and/or dramatic roles and appearances in benefit concerts as well as in clubs, on radio and on TV, she produced *Christmas Blue*, a CD by Salome Bey and the Relatives, on the Rainbow label. In 1996 she received the Martin Luther King Jr. Award for Lifetime Achievement from the Black Theatre Workshop of Montreal. In 2005, she was inducted as an honorary member of the Order of Canada.

Before her retirement, Salome performed frequently with her daughters, Tuku Matthews and Saidah Baba Talibah Matthews. Tuku, whose work includes singing background for Anne Murray, also is a songwriter. Like their mother, Saidah sings and acts, too. Her 2011 debut album *(S)cream*, what she calls "a blend of rock, blues and raunchy soul," won Toronto's inaugural Soundclash Music Award.

In Chicago, where they have lived since marrying more than fifty years ago, Gerri and her husband, jazz bassist Eddie de Haas, are considered the First Couple of Chicago Jazz. He is well-known for his work with Peter, Paul & Mary, Miles Davis, Chet Baker and Von Freeman. Before their children, Aisha and Darrius, were born, she sang at clubs in and around the city and traveled to Europe with the Free Street Theater. Her theatrical credits include *Don't Bother Me I Can't Cope*, *Hair* and *Showboat*.

Later in life Gerri earned a degree in music education at Chicago State University and began working for the Illinois State Arts Council. Over the years, she has produced more than thirty jazz festivals for the council and on her own, mostly for the South Shore Jazz Festival. "Because of my history, I was invited, through my job, to serve on the National Endowment for the Arts in 1988," she notes. "Our objective was to elevate jazz in America."

The de Haas offspring also sing and appear in theatrical productions. Aisha's credits on Broadway include appearances in *Rent*, *Bring in da Noise*, and *Josephine Tonight!*, the life story of Josephine Baker. Darius made his Broadway debut in *Kiss of the Spider Woman*. Often in demand as a solo artist, he has presented two highly acclaimed tributes (to Billy Strayhorn and Stevie Wonder) as part of Lincoln Center's American Songbook Series. He's also appeared in Lincoln Center's revivals of *Carousel, Rent, Hair* and the twentieth anniversary concert of *Dreamgirls*.

If that's not enough talent in one family, add to the mix cousin Marvin Jefferson, an actor/educator whose work includes *Paul Robeson: A Chautauqua* (a dramatic impersonation of a historical figure) and *The Harriet Tubman and William Still Underground Railroad Walks Across New Jersey*. Jefferson's niece, Cara Page, a poet and multimedia performance artist, is the founder of Deep Water Productions.

Yvette Glover and Family

Yvette Glover's voice knows no boundaries. One moment she's soaring skyward, the next she's basement basso. Like her parents, top entertainers in Newark during the Swing Era, and her son Savion, the world's most heralded tap dancer, she is naturally gifted. And she's ever thankful for it. "Everything I have comes from my God, my Lord and Savior," she tells her audiences.

As with many black artists, Glover's faith is hardly surprising. For years she's been a member of New Point Baptist Church in Newark, where her mother, Anna May Lundy Lewis, served as organist and minister of music for more than a half-century. Born in Jacksonville, Florida, in 1916, Lundy Lewis came north as a teenager to live with her father, Dick Lundy, an all-star Negro Baseball League shortstop who managed the 1946 Newark Eagles world champions.

By then, Lewis was an accomplished pianist, some say a genius, even though she never took a lesson. "I just sat down and started playing," she later revealed. "I was about eight when I started playing in church productions." In 1930s Newark, Lewis was at the top of her game, a star among stars in a city where talent was so abundant that customers had to decide which show to see on any given night. At the tiny Hyde-Away on Halsey Street, where she often played, patrons nearly had to force their way in to get to a seat.

"Everyone who heard her play thought she was by far the best," her friend Miss Rhapsody said. "Anna May hardly had to play a note before you knew who was on piano. She had a God-given talent."

Lewis was new to Newark when she met and married Billy Lewis, a personable young man who played piano and sang in clubs along Broad Street that catered to whites only at a time when the city was still segregated. Black entertainers could be hired, but black patrons were unwelcome. Born in Gates, Pennsylvania, in 1913, Billy Lewis often doubled as an emcee at shows in Newark and at the Jersey Shore, ingratiating himself to the fairer sex. "All the ladies loved my dad," Yvette notes. "He had a big following. He could charm a candy bar. If he had asked, women would have eaten dirt off the floor."

After Billy Lewis joined the Navy during World War II, Anna May accepted an offer to tour with the USO, leaving her three young children—Billy, Yvette and Carlton, called Bunky by the family—in the care of Mrs. Barr, her landlord at 452 Washington Street. Yvette's weekly highlight was taking the 118 bus to New York on Saturdays to sing at a studio where music lovers could perform. "That was my delight," she recounts. "Every Saturday Mrs. Barr would give me exactly the right amount of money for a hot dog, orange drink and a doughnut at Nedick's." Otherwise, things were not going all that well at home. "I don't know why, but Mrs. Barr favored Carlton," Yvette says, "so I was sent to live (nearby) with Minnie St. Clair when I was nine. Everyone called her Mama Minnie. The best part about living with her was getting to march with the Junior Elks and Gay Blades Drum and Bugle Corps. I loved marching up West Market Street around the bend to Bethany Baptist Church twirling my baton."

When the war ended and her parents returned home, the family lived briefly on Crawford Street. But things were not the same and the couple soon split. After her mother became the organist and minister of music at New Point, leaving behind the world of jazz, Yvette joined the choir and became the lead singer. "I wanted to sing because I admired my mother so much," she says. "I had never

heard such wonderful music before." Living with her mother, however, proved difficult, especially because they had been separated
for so long. "I guess I was about fourteen or fifteen when a represen-
tative of (Newark-based) Savoy Records heard me sing and invited
me to travel with Aretha Franklin and other well-known performers," she recalls. "My mother forbade me to go because it was so
rough out there. She didn't want me traveling alone. I wanted to go,
so I can't tell you how angry I was. It took me years to forgive her—
to understand that she was saving me because she wouldn't be able
to go with me."

After her father remarried and moved to Washingtonville, New
York, he got her a summer job in the kitchen of a club where he
was performing. "There I was, back in the kitchen making parfaits,
when my dad asked me to come on stage one night and sing for the
audience," Yvette remembers. "Boy, was I thrilled. I was only sixteen." The song she sang was one she still sings: *Zing Went the Strings
of My Heart*. "I learned a lot from my dad—all the show tunes and
standards," she notes. "At some point in time he began taking me to
clubs with him. That's how I started singing (outside the church).
One time he took me to a place in Keansburg, New Jersey, but I had
to hide in the back because everyone was so prejudiced."

Yvette Glover began "singing for real" in the 1970s as a student at
Essex County College. "Connie Pitts, Pat Tandy, Dave Blocker and
a lot of other great singers from Newark were there, too. We often
had our teacher, Jo Sandra Flint, in tears. She told us we all were
going to go places."

Since then she's traveled halfway around the world with Savion,
who launched his career on Broadway in *The Tap Dance Kid* when
he was ten, and on her own. Her solo career has included a command performance before the king of Morocco in a show headlined
by a well-known singer. "When the king came down off his throne
at the end and handed me a bouquet of three dozen white roses,
the star of the show was livid," she says. "I had gotten the most
applause, but I was too naïve to get it (the headliner's jealousy). I just
wanted to do my best, as I always do."

Yvette's singing was not all the king liked. That became evident, she says, at a traditional Moroccan dinner in the desert. "We sat on the ground and ate lamb and rice out of a big bowl that the servants passed around," she recounts. "It was delicious, but then I saw the king and his aides pointing to me and talking back and forth. He wanted to take me as another one of his wives. When we got back where we were staying, I started packing my bags right away. I was ready to go home."

By the time Savion Glover began a two-year run on Broadway in the all-black cast musical *Black and Blue* in 1989, his mother was singing regularly at clubs in New York and New Jersey. "I used to jam in New York with Linda Hopkins, a star of the show," Yvette says. Always a favorite at the Priory in Newark, she celebrates her birthday there each November, surrounded by family and friends as she presents audience favorites like *What a Wonderful World* and *Misty*. For the past decade, she's also been a regular at Tuesday night jam sessions at Crossroads in Garwood. Before it closed, she often sang at Skipper's.

Known as the "Mother of Tap," she also stages showcases for promising talent like Hillary-Marie and Kevin Wilder and was a driving force behind the 2007 restoration of Newark Symphony Hall, the city's majestic theater on South Broad Street. "Yvette has always been very supportive of the arts in Newark," Philip Thomas, the theater's executive director, said at the time. "She was born here, and we're talking about Symphony Hall—what it could be again, what kind of events it could put on."

Like his mother, Savion Glover loves nothing more than giving back to the community where he was born and raised. No matter where he is in the world, he comes home to Newark to perform at NJPAC as least once a year and assists with other projects, including the Symphony Hall restoration. According to family lore, Savion's grandmother, Anna Lundy Lewis, was first to recognize his musical talent. As the story goes, he was an infant when he began singing along as she hummed various rhythms. Although his older brothers, Carlton and Abron, were musical, too, his talent stuck out.

"When Savion was four," his mother says, "I enrolled him at the Newark Community School of the Arts. He was the youngest student ever to win a scholarship."

While studying at the Broadway Dance Center in New York, where he later taught, the precocious youngster was invited to audition for *The Tap Dance Kid*. In winning the lead role, the hard-hitting young hoofer launched a career as a dancer and choreographer that has taken him to Hollywood, the White House and all over the world. During his shows he dances to everything from jazz to classical music. His goal has been the same since he came to prominence: putting the lost art of tap dancing back on the map. These days he runs the HooFerZ Club on Brunswick Street in Newark, where he teaches new generations of dancers.

One of Savion's fondest memories is the night his grandmother was honored by the Friends of Barbara J. Kukla Scholarship Fund at a jazz competition for public school students at Arts High School, his alma mater. Fresh from a New York rehearsal, he bounded down the aisle of the auditorium to the cheers of a packed house to sit at his grandmother's feet. The event that night became a family affair as Yvette sang *My Funny Valentine* in her mother's honor and Savion Glover dedicated a dance routine to his grandmother.

A surprise was yet to come, a rollicking, foot-stomping piano rendition of *It Don't Mean a Thing If It Ain't Got That Swing* played by Anna Lundy Lewis. For the first time in more than five decades she was performing publicly, interspersing jazz with every other form of music she could conjure up.

"Witnessing three generations of one family performing on the same night was totally incredible," retired Arts High Vice Principal Mary Soriano recalls. "Just seeing Savion's face as he watched his grandmother play for the first time in years made it worth the free admission. It was extraordinary."

4 ♪

Woody and Tyrone

Jazz Genius

The trouble with this country is that everything is new. We don't have any consideration for the past. Just because something is old, you don't just rip it down. You can renovate it instead of ripping it down, and build something new. —Woody Shaw

Woody Shaw never forgot his Newark roots, reaching back time and again to invite friends to record with him on Blue Note or, perhaps, fill a vacant spot in a band with which he was playing. Tyrone Washington, Shaw's childhood friend, found that out big-time when he got a call one night from Shaw while he was a student at Howard University. There was an opening for a saxophonist in Horace Silver's band and Shaw wanted Washington to try out.

This was in mid-1966 when Shaw, who had dropped out of Arts High School to tour Europe, was beginning to emerge on the American jazz scene. Anxious to embark on a career in jazz, Washington successfully auditioned for Silver, then left school to travel with his band. "My mother was very upset when my brother quit college midway," says Washington's sister, Barbara Franklin, a Washington, D.C., attorney, "but Tyrone could not have been happier. His music was what was most important to him."

Washington, of course, couldn't wait to hit the road. Once more, Shaw was by his side, just as he had been when they were growing up in the Hayes Homes housing projects in Newark and attending

Cleveland Junior High School and Arts High School together. Little did either of them know at the time that their coming together at this point in their lives would diverge wildly a few years later. While Shaw went on to become one of the last major innovators of jazz trumpet, Washington made a few promising LPs, then suddenly faded from the scene.

It's been nearly twenty-five years since Shaw exited this vale of tears, but his music remains as fresh and inventive today as when he recorded it in his prime. The proof is in the vast collection of amazing music he bequeathed to his fans, including *Rosewood*, for which he won a Grammy in 1978. Many of the top names in jazz were among his collaborators: Eric Dolphy, Horace Silver, McCoy Tyner, Herbie Hancock, Art Blakey, Jackie McLean and Bobby Hutcherson, to name a few.

While Washington's music is still appreciated by those who remember him as an up-and-coming musician or still talk about *Natural Essence*, the much-heralded LP he recorded with Shaw on Blue Note at twenty-three, he remains an obscure jazz figure. Meanwhile, Shaw went on to become one of the world's premiere trumpeters of all times. His journey, however, turned into a constant struggle to stay true to his music, one fraught with disappointments, health issues, addictions and various frustrations that often accompany life in the public eye.

In essence, Shaw was a straight-ahead musician, a throwback to the trumpet kings he idolized: King Oliver, Jabbo Smith and Louis Armstrong, for whom his son, Woody Louis Armstrong Shaw, is named. He also is a direct musical descendant of Dizzy Gillespie, Miles Davis, Clifford Brown and Lee Morgan. Eclectic in thought and execution, his music, like theirs, was years ahead of its time.

Without taking jazz out of its cultural context, Shaw's vision of what it is and what it should be encompassed everything from Tibetan chants and songs of the central African rain forest to classical Indian musical forms. Music was his religion, but his sense of spirituality also embraced the Chinese martial arts, self-hypnotism and yoga. "I'm walking a similar line," says Woody III, an ethnomusicologist and arts administrator who has traveled the world and, for a time, lived in Vietnam. "In attempting to figure out the universal qualities of jazz, I'm listening to weird stuff and coming to understand the connections my father was trying to make. He didn't want to be boxed in." Shaw never was, refusing to succumb to commercialism or otherwise compromise his artistry. But his devotion to more evolutionary forms of music came at a cost, particularly when work was scarce.

Years after Shaw's career peaked, he came back to Newark to receive his high school diploma at a ceremony at Essex County College. There was no great fanfare that day in the college cafeteria. Bill May, then a music teacher at West Side High School, brought a group of students to hear Shaw and his band play. Liz Del Tufo, then the county director of recreation and cultural affairs, spoke briefly. Shaw also was reunited with Jerome Ziering, his music teacher from Cleveland Junior High. "What I remember most is how Woody just cried when he received his diploma," Del Tufo says.

Given the complexities of Shaw's life, no one in attendance could have comprehended the range of his emotions, perhaps not even himself. On one hand, his son says, his father could be impatient with the importance some people attached to educational degrees. On the other, Shaw himself was a lifelong learner, a man of amazing intellect and thirst for learning that made him better educated than many of those who may have looked down on him as a high school dropout.

Shaw's brilliance shines through in a talk he gave on *Jazz Trumpet History and the Style of Miles Davis* at the University of Pittsburgh in 1977. In the course of little more than fourteen minutes, he packed in a synopsis of the history of jazz trumpet (from Buddy Bolden in the 1880s to himself), played two songs, including a blues tune, shared his take on Davis's *Autumn Leaves* and fielded questions from his audience.

Shaw, whose genius was acknowledged the world over, was just forty-four when he was critically injured in a subway accident in January 1988. According to Amiri Baraka, Shaw was supposed to meet drummer Max Roach that night at the Village Gate in Greenwich Village, but left early when the drummer didn't show up on time. In his attempt to get home on his own, he inadvertently stepped off a subway platform and was hit by an oncoming train, suffering massive injuries. "The whole thing was tragic," says Baraka. "Woody had worn thick glasses all his life and was practically blind by then." Four months later, Shaw died of kidney failure in a New York hospital.

Born in Laurinberg, North Carolina, on Christmas Eve, 1944, Shaw was the oldest of four children of Rosalie and Woody Shaw Sr. His younger brother Pete, a football star at Barringer High School, went on to play pro football with the New York Giants. "Woody Jr. looked just like his daddy," his mother says, recalling how she and her son joined her husband in Newark when Woody was just two months old. Like many Southern young men, Woody Sr. had come north to find factory work and make a better life for his family. He was musical, too, a member of the Diamond Jubilee Singers, a 1930s gospel group. As a boy, he attended Laurinberg Institute with Dizzy Gillespie, its most famous graduate.

As far back as Rose Shaw can remember, her son's musical talent was apparent. By age nine, he had mastered the bugle and was playing in the Junior Elks band. After the family moved from downtown Newark to Hayes Homes, he joined the band at Eighteenth Avenue School. Shaw took up the trumpet at his grammar school teacher's suggestion, skeptical at first he would like it. "Of course, it didn't take me long to fall in love with it," he later said. His prized possession was the trumpet his father bought for him.

At Cleveland Junior High, Ziering encouraged him to study classical music. He did, for a time, but jazz was a more natural calling. "Woody's teachers said he was a genius," his mother says. "He had difficulty seeing (later diagnosed as a degenerative eye disease), so he memorized everything. They said he had a photographic memory, so they skipped him two grades."

"In those days Woody and Tyrone Washington were tighter than tight," says Ron Smothers, who played in the Eighteenth Avenue School band with Shaw. In his book, *The Salt Mine*, Smothers recalls how Shaw and Washington practiced incessantly in the piano room at Cleveland Junior High while their friends played basketball. Even then, their peers appreciated their talent, as Smothers notes: "When Woody and Tyrone came to play, the other kids made a beeline to the music room to hear them. They were that good."

Shaw also had perfect pitch. By the time he entered Arts High, he was writing marching songs for the George Washington Carver Gay Blades, a nationally known drum and bugle corps. Founded in 1957, the group was one of the few primarily African-American units in corps history.

"When we had assemblies at Arts High, Woody played when we all marched in," says Eric Stokes, one of Shaw's classmates. "But he wouldn't play straight. He'd jazz up the songs and bend notes, which would make us all laugh." While at Arts, Shaw formed a popular jazz ensemble with Larry Young Jr. on organ, Billy Brooks (tap dancer Savion Glover's uncle) on drums and Dave Blocker, vocals. He wanted more, so he quit high school to pursue music full-time.

Fame was not far off. By mid-1963, after Shaw recorded with the innovative multi-instrumentalist Eric Dolphy, Dolphy invited Shaw to tour Europe with his band, but died suddenly before their departure. Shaw went on to Paris anyway and wound up performing with many of the top jazz artists living abroad, including Bud Powell, Kenny Clarke and Art Taylor. During his sixteen-month stay, he also made a splash in Germany and recorded with a group that included Young and Brooks, pals from Arts High.

After returning home, Shaw joined the house band at Blue Note and made his solo debut in November 1965 on Young's acclaimed album *Unity* after taking over the trumpet chair with Horace Silver. By the late 1960s, Shaw had worked with many of the top names in the business, including Chick Corea, Jackie McLean, McCoy Tyner and Herbie Hancock. Even so, modern jazz was in decline, prompting him to relocate to California, where he made two albums under his own name and toured with Joe Henderson, Art Blakey and Bobby Hutcherson.

Following his return to New York in 1974, Shaw began recording for Muse, which led to a close friendship with Michael Cuscuna, his producer. "Thus began the happiest and most productive stage of Woody's life," Cuscuna wrote in the 2011 liner notes for *Woody Shaw: The Complete Columbia Albums Collection.* "His artistic identity was fully formed, and he was playing better than ever. In Maxine Gregg (Shaw's manager and mother of his son)," Cuscuna added, Shaw "found love and understanding" as well as the "guidance, skill and insight" he needed "to overcome his reticence to becoming a leader and take responsibility for his career."

In an online biography for *AllMusic,* Matt Collar describes Shaw as a "younger statesman among his admired elders," an heir to the musical legacy of great trumpeters such as Gillespie, Fats Navarro and Clifford Brown. As an alumnus of Art Blakey's Jazz Messengers, Collar continues, Shaw "felt responsible for upholding the integrity and appreciation of the tradition of straight-ahead jazz." At the same time, he was gaining recognition for his unending quest to revolutionize the technical and harmonic vocabulary of his instrument.

After catching the attention of Bruce Lundvall at a midtown New York club called Storyville in 1977, Shaw spent the next four years recording for Columbia, where Lundvall was president. In short order, Shaw's first Columbia LP, *Rosewood,* was nominated for two Grammys, won one and was voted Best Jazz Album of the Year by *Downbeat* readers. Pollsters also named Shaw Best Trumpeter of the Year and No. 4 Jazzman of the Year. The album's name comes from a tune Shaw had written for his parents. The core musicians on it were members of his quintet: Carter Jefferson, Onaje Allan Gumbs, Clint Houston and Vince Lewis. A guest appearance by Joe Henderson made it a blockbuster.

In 1979, Columbia released *Woody III,* featuring a photograph of Shaw with his father and son on the cover. "As far as I'm concerned, *Woody III* is Woody's masterpiece as a player and as a composer/

arranger," Cuscuna says. "Inspired by the birth of his son and new-found closeness with his father (probably a direct result), Woody composed this three-part suite to tell the story of three generations of music."

Amiri Baraka, who wrote the liner notes for the 1979 LP, saw the "widespread critical and popular recognition" Shaw was getting at the time as a metaphor for a black man's escape from the "poverty, ignorance, violence and indifference" of a gritty inner city like Newark. Perhaps, he adds, "there's even a chance (remember that, chance, 'cause this is a lottery for most of us) he (Shaw) might even make a little money."

After Shaw's original quintet disbanded in 1980, he created a new band with Steve Turre on trombone, Mulgrew Miller on piano, holdover Stafford James on bass and Tony Reedus on drums. The group, which disbanded after eighteen months, debuted on *United*, Shaw's final LP. Although the band recorded four albums and Shaw collaborated with trumpeter Freddie Hubbard on two others, his career was in decline. According to Cuscuna, he abhorred being a bandleader. The stress was getting to him.

More than two decades have passed since Shaw's death, but his legacy as one of the music world's most brilliant jazz innovators lives on through the work of his son. "My grandson always tells me he will never let his father's name be forgotten," Rose Shaw says. "So that's what he's doing."

"There's been a serious absence of recognition of the magnitude of my father's legacy," says Woody III, who spends his time assisting with the re-issue of his father's music and making public previously unreleased material. "I don't want people saying how great Woody Shaw *was*," Woody III says. "I want them to understand how he revolutionized the horn, how no one could de-code what he did."

While Shaw won worldwide acclaim, Washington decided to abandon his promising career in jazz after exploding onto the scene in 1967 with *Natural Essence*. To this day, many of his fans wonder if he is dead or alive. For the record, he wants the world to know he's still with us, at peace with himself, but removed from the world of drugs, alcohol and other ills that consumed so many of his peers. Instead of grasping for fame, he decided to turn away from music altogether after becoming a Sunni Muslim in 1968 and changing his name to Muhammad Bilal Abdullah. From that moment, he dedicated his life to Allah. Music no longer was his interest or obsession.

While growing up in Newark Washington was much like other young black men from the projects (low-income public housing), including his friend Shaw. "Back then, we all smoked a little weed and did a little cocaine. It came with the turf," he says. By the time he graduated from Arts High School, where Shaw was two years ahead of him, Washington was an up-and-coming musician on Newark's vibrant jazz scene. Like Shaw, just about anyone who heard him play predicted great things.

All that changed after he and Shaw recorded *Natural Essence* in producer Rudy Van Gelder's Englewood, New Jersey, studio in 1967. By then, Washington had embraced Islam, although he said little about it publicly. Because so many Jewish men were at the helm of the music industry at the time, he says, Muslim musicians were reluctant to reveal their religious identity. He was too, fearing it might jeopardize his career.

From the moment *Natural Essence* hit the airwaves, critics proclaimed it a hit. As one reviewer put it, "You can definitely hear the influence of the soulful, spiritual-search sound of Coltrane and Pharoah Sanders, but this is also the sound of a bunch of excited young kids having fun and swinging hard." What a group of young geniuses they were: Washington on sax, Shaw on trumpet, Kenny Barron, piano; James Spaulding, alto; Reggie Workman, bass, and Joe Chambers, drums. All of them seemed destined for stardom. To some extent, they all achieved it.

After appearing on two other Blue Note LPs with Horace Silver and Larry Young Jr., Washington served as leader on two more: *Roots* on Perception and *Do Right* (Blue Labor). That was about it. "After *Natural Essence*, I started going to the Masjid (temple) and met some dynamite people," he explains. "Their lifestyle was different, and I wanted to be like them. I wanted to help people get to heaven, to save them from the devil instead of playing the horn. So I put it (music) down."

In turning to the Muslim faith, Washington looked to the teachings of Malcolm X for guidance. "I didn't want anything to do with the Nation (of Islam) created by Elijah (Muhammad)," he says. "I had no argument with the white man. I didn't hate anybody. What's good is good, no matter what your color. If it's bad, it's bad. I wanted to get away from playing in bars, surrounded by alcohol, drugs and prostitutes. As a Muslim I didn't have to get recorded. I didn't have to ask radio stations to play my music. I could be myself."

Now in his late sixties, Washington has spent four decades traveling the world preaching the word of Allah. After making his first journey to Mecca in the 1960s, he returned in 2007 and 2009. As a preacher he's also been to Japan, India and Dubai, a long way from Lillie Street in Newark's Central Ward, where he and his siblings, Robert Jr. and Barbara, were raised by their mother after their parents split.

"My brother was anointed musically," his sister says. "I believe he was born to be a musician. By the time he was four or five, he could play anything, so my grandmother bought him a baby grand piano. When my mother had to discipline him, she'd take away his horn for a week. Nothing else. Tyrone was inconsolable." Blanche Bailey, their aunt, says it's hard to remember when her nephew was not consumed by his music. "He used to lock himself in the bathroom and played so long nobody could get in there."

"Even as a teenager Tyrone was a phenomenal musician," recalls Franotie Washington (no relation), a friend of his sister's. "Everyone loved to hear him play." That was true, not just in Newark, but everywhere he went. One of Washington's classmates at Howard, for example, told the story of how he astounded other music majors shortly after arriving on campus. "Who was that?" they wanted to know after hearing the sounds emanating from a practice room where Washington was playing piano.

Washington himself still remembers the moment he became enamored of jazz. "I was walking down a path that led from Fairview Avenue, near the old GE (General Electric) building, to Lillie Street when I heard a guy named B.J. playing Charlie Parker," he recalls. "There was another guy named Kenny who also played (bebop). I don't know what happened to them, but they both had a good, soulful feeling." Soon after, he began pumping nickels into a jukebox at a nearby grocery store to hear Parker play. But Coltrane was his idol. "'Coltrane. New Trane.' That's what Tyrone scribbled on the covers of his notebooks," his sister remembers. "That's how he referred to himself."

By the time Washington entered Arts High, both he and Shaw aspired to careers in jazz. While other black teenagers their age spent their time singing doo wop on Newark street corners, listening to R&B on the radio or playing their favorite LPs, they were captivated by the newer, more progressive, sounds of jazz. They also began hanging out with older musicians who recognized their talent and gave them a chance to sit in at joints like Len & Len's, even though they were underage. Sometimes, after staying out late, they barely made it to school the next morning.

"Tyrone was just like the other guys, into girls and sports," says Wilma Grey, a classmate who now serves as director of the Newark Public Library. "As I remember, he was captain of the basketball team. Woody was more into himself—very quiet. I don't remember him saying much at all." While Shaw was laid back, Washington had the look of a hipster, emulating Coltrane, his hero, to the point where he wore sunglasses in his sophomore class picture. Whatever other interests Washington may have had, music was the focal point of his life. "It was in Tyrone's being," says Eleta Caldwell, another classmate. "His horn was part of him. He had it with him everywhere he went."

Although it's been more than forty years since he put down his horn, Washington's staunchest followers still search out his music. One tune, an amazingly fast romp with Shaw called *Soul Dance*, goes on for eight minutes.

Does he ever regret abandoning a life in jazz? "Never," Washington says, reiterating his rejection of wine, women and song as a personal lifestyle. "I'm not against anybody, but all worldly success must be attributed to the Creator, not the creature. Only Allah and his prophets can save humanity from going to hell."

5 ♪

The Jazz Clubs
On the Scene

*I've had the pleasure of playing with the baddest
jazz cats on the planet. —George Benson*

Running a jazz club, like making a living as a jazz artist, can be
an especially tough go when the economy is pitiful, parking
is at a minimum and customers fear staying out after dark, some
of the reasons why Newark's once-thriving nightlife has just about
vanished. Yet club owners like Greg Salandy, who kept Skipper's
Plane Street Pub in Newark going day and night for nearly five
years before closing in 2012, occasionally give it a shot. "I'm proud
to say we had some really talented people play at Skipper's," Salandy
says. "We had music practically every night, but after working fifteen to eighteen hours every day there came a point of diminishing returns."

Nevertheless, there are some encouraging signs that jazz in the
Newark area is not falling off the ends of the earth. In May 2013,
Dinosaur Bar-B-Que at Market and Mulberry streets began offering jazz on Thursday nights. A month later Kimako's Blues People, run by Amina and Amiri Baraka out of their South 10th Street
home, reopened. In nearby West Orange, a new series of Tuesday
night jam sessions, led by drummer Greg Bufford, began attracting
top-name musicians like drummer T.S. Monk and guitarist Russell
Malone on Tuesday nights at SuzyQue's.

Perhaps the most encouraging sign came in the summer of 2013, when the New Community Corporation (NCC) began renovating the former church that's been home to the Priory, a club on West Market Street that's presented Friday night jazz for two decades. Add to that old standbys like Private Place in Orange, where singers Denise Hamilton and Madame Pat Tandy often perform, and Trumpets in Montclair, where Carrie Jackson stages showcases featuring members of the Newark-based Jazz Vocal Collective, and the jazz scene appears less bleak.

Salandy believes Skipper's might have survived if the economy had been a bit better. But it was not, leaving the Priory as one of the few spots in Newark presenting jazz on a regular basis. Fortunately, organist Radam Schwartz and singer Eugene Goldston, who played each week at Skipper's, found a new gig at the Ideal Bar after Skipper's closed. Other artists, including Jackson, now travel to venues in the Poconos and at the Jersey Shore. "This involves more time on the road," Jackson says, "but if you want to work, that's what you have to do," a striking change from years gone by.

Even after the flight of Newark's middle class in the aftermath of the 1967 civil rebellions, Newark offered live music seven nights a week. Despite the supposed dangers of coming into the city, jazz fans continued to pack the Key Club and Sparky J's. When they folded, it was because their owners, Jeanne Dawkins and William (Sparky) Jacob, died, not because they lacked customers. "In those days, everyone (in the black community) hung out at the Key Club and Sparky's," says Alma Bostick, who worked at the nearby federal building. "The Owl Club and Bridge Club, which had music from time to time, also were popular spots."

When Dawkins and her husband, Walter, opened for business in October 1956, the Key Club was on West Street, just off West Kinney, in a residential center city neighborhood. On weekdays, it was just a bar, but on weekends, it came alive with the sounds of jazz. "Going to the old Key Club was like going to a speakeasy," says Walter Chambers, later a regular at the Priory. "You had to go down an alley and ring a bell to get in because the door was locked. The bartender would let you in."

"The old Key Club was where we (the Rhoda Scott Trio) first played in Newark," recalls saxophonist Joe Thomas. "In those days they had a two-way mirror and you had to be buzzed in. That made a lot of people feel important. It was a fun place. There was no profanity, no arguments or loud voices except when the customers cheered for the musicians. And it was safe. Women could park two blocks away on Halsey Street, walk up to West Street and be perfectly safe."

On nights when there was music, drummer Gus Young, organist Ducky Massey and saxophonist Jimmy Rogers led the house band. From 1958–60, when the club moved downtown to Halsey Street, organist Ernie Scott and drummer Herbert "Geronimo" Johnson took over as musicians-in-residence. After the move to a more central location, business skyrocketed. With the Cadillac Club on an opposite corner, the Key Club went from neighborhood hangout to popular jazz club. When Jacob, once an aide to Mayor Kenneth Gibson, took over the Cadillac in the early 1970s, he changed the name to Sparky J's and implemented a jazz format, making William and Halsey streets The Jazz Corner of the World.

While the new Key Club was a bit larger than the original, it remained a place where the regulars knew each other. In many ways, it was even more intimate because the musicians played from inside the bar, so close they could practically touch the bartenders and customers. "It was like being on stage," says organist Rhoda Scott. "The public saw everything, so the musicians were motivated to show off because the audience was so close."

Singer Betty "Bebop" Carter was fresh off the road from a tour with Lionel Hampton when she became a Key Club favorite. Like Little Jimmy Scott, Hampton's male vocalist, Carter did not have to look far for work. Newark also was where Carter met James Romeo Redding, a bartender at the Owl Club, an after-hours joint on Quitman Street. He became her common-law husband and the father of her two sons. Until they split, they lived in Newark.

By 1976, the Key Club was the second longest-running jazz venue in the New York-New Jersey metropolitan area. Only the Village Vanguard in lower Manhattan, which opened three months earlier in 1956, had been in business longer. Maxine Harvard, who organized the Key Club's twentieth anniversary tribute at Essex County College, believes it survived because Jeanne Dawkins, who took over the management after her husband's shocking suicide, was so highly regarded by her customers. While friends said Walter Dawkins was deeply depressed, it was never determined why he killed himself. Rather than sell the club, Jeanne Dawkins kept it open. "Business remained brisk because Jeanne was exceptionally fair to the musicians, a rarity among club owners at that time," Harvard says.

Except for the music, there was nothing particularly noteworthy about the Key Club. The old venue on West Street, which barely held fifty people, was hardly more than a one-room shack, according to Thomas. Downtown, patrons sat either at the bar or at nearby tables. With City Hall two blocks away, both the new Key Club and Sparky's became hangouts for local politicians. Donald Payne, who became New Jersey's first black congressman, and his brother, Bill, were among the regulars. So were Bob Queen and Connie Woodruff, who wrote about politics and entertainment for the city's black-owned newspapers.

By the time the club's twentieth anniversary celebration rolled around in January 1977, Donald Payne was Essex County's freeholder director, head of the county's legislative branch of government. During the tribute to Jeanne Dawkins at the college, Payne praised her as "someone who has remained positive about the city and helped keep the city's musical culture alive."

The special guest that night was guitarist George Benson, who made a hero-like entrance toward the end of the three-hour program wearing a full-length white fur coat. To the delight of the audience, Benson ran down the center aisle and bounded onto the stage to join his fellow musicians. Harvard says Benson's appearance was kept secret for fear an overflow crowd would show up. In the end, more than 700 people came anyway and the police had to be called for crowd control.

For jazz fans, it was a night to remember, a musical marathon that included performances by Key Club favorites Jimmy McGriff, Ray Bryant, Irene Reid, Lu Elliott, Al Hibbler, Houston Person, Etta Jones, Billy Phipps, Buddy Terry, Sam Williams, Eddie Gladden, Leo Johnson, Ernie Scott and Geronimo. Bryant brought down the house with what *Star-Ledger* critic George Kanzler called "churchy blues," then accompanied Duke Ellington alumnus Hibbler on *Danny Boy*. Person, a Newark resident, played soulful sax, and Jones, always a local favorite, rendered *Don't Go to Strangers*, her signature song. By the time Benson began trading vocals with Reid on his hit tune *This Masquerade*, the standing-room-only crowd was in a frenzy. "After the show, we all went back to the Key Club and locked the doors," Harvard remembers. "George and the other musicians played all night."

Benson was one of many well-known names in music who made the Key Club a draw. Sarah Vaughan generally made it a point to stop by when she was off the road. Dionne Warwick won the club's first talent contest. On nights like one in April 1976, when Rahsaan Roland Kirk was playing at Sparky's and Vaughan was sitting in at the Key Club with Reid, fans often went from club to club. "Irene Reid was my favorite because she was a sultry singer, like Dinah Washington and Billie Holiday," says Paul Dietrich, who stopped by that night. "She really could put on a show." Accompanied by trombonist Steve Turre, Kirk, who was making his comeback after suffering a stroke, crossed the street at intermission, with his newly altered saxophone dangling from his neck, to give the Key Club crowd a free mini-concert.

Most nights, however, fans who could not afford to or chose not to pay the $3 or $4 admission charge at Sparky's simply stayed put at the Key Club where the entertainment was free. Meanwhile, Sparky's was attracting younger fans who didn't mind paying the admission charge. "When Dizzy Gillespie comes into my club, the young people are here because they know where he's been," Jacob said in a 1980 article on the history of jazz in Newark. According to Harvard, who wrote the piece, the roster of talent Jacob hired read like a jazz *Who's Who*, a list that included Earl "Fatha" Hines, Hazel Scott, Horace Silver, Ahmad Jamal and Philly Joe Jones.

Louise Scott-Rountree was one of the many customers who patronized both clubs. "I was fifteen when I met Joe Brown, the bartender at the Key Club," she recalls. "One day, when I was passing by, Joe was outside and invited me in." Before long she was hanging out at the club, smoking, drinking and enjoying the music, even though she was underage. "No one ever questioned my age," she says. "I must have looked older. But all hell broke loose after Sadie Veney (who ran local fashion shows) called my mother and told her she had seen me. My mother called down there and said there would be no Key Club if they served me again." That worked for a while, but Scott-Rountree, who loved hanging out with an older crowd, soon was back to her old ways. "I didn't know anything about bartending, but I was there the day Sparky caught his barmaid stealing glasses," she says. "So he hired me. I was good at it because I had a lot of personality and that made people want to buy drinks."

When Sparky's eventually went out of business, the Key Club was still going strong. Hardly anyone was surprised because they thought Dawkins had far more business savvy than Jacob. As Harvard found, "Sparky was always looking for money," to the point where he would not, could not or did not pay his musicians. Singer Ruth Brown found that out first-hand. Warned by friends that she might not get paid, she brought along a friend, a menacing-looking guy wearing a fedora who was supposedly packing a gun. Needless to say, Jacob anted up.

Even today, more than three decades after the closing of Sparky's and the Key Club, the regulars still have fascinating stories to tell. Dionne Warwick, for example, recalls in her biography how Benson never showed his singing ability in those days "but sure let us know he could play the guitar." Other customers remember Elliott wearing a sleek evening gown as she emerged from the Key Club ladies' room singing a dramatic rendition of *Always Lovers Never Friends* in French. Visions of Sam Williams, who captivated the ladies by singing sexy lyrics, his colorful 1970s-style shirt half-unbuttoned, also linger.

By the early 1960s, the Key Club was a regular stop on the Chitlin' Circuit, a network of black clubs where African-American musicians played primarily for African-American audiences. Following the lead of organist Jimmy Smith, it became known as The Home of the Hammond B3 Organ. For the next decade or so, every major exponent of the instrument—Rhoda Scott, Jimmy McGriff, Richard "Groove" Holmes, Charles "The Mighty Burner" Earland, Gloria Coleman, Dr. Lonnie Smith, Captain Jack McDuff and Smith—played the Key Club and Sparky's.

Rhoda Scott's longtime association with the Key Club goes back to West Street, where she played when she first came to Newark. Downtown she made two of her earliest recordings—*Hey! Hey! Hey!* (1962) and *Live At the Key Club* (1963). Famous for playing barefoot, Scott also was a favorite at the Playbill Lounge. Whenever or wherever she performed, her followers requested *Ebb Tide*, which always brought down the house. Sweeping the keyboards and building momentum with each new run, she made the music come alive in a style so powerful it seemed as if the sea would engulf her audience.

Philadelphia-born McGriff settled in Newark in 1960 after playing at clubs worldwide with Buddy Rich and various Woody Herman aggregations. With Jimmy Smith, a childhood friend, and Holmes, his mentor and teacher, he was a Key Club fixture. Eventually, he opened his own club, the Golden Slipper, two blocks from the Key Club on Branford Place.

As a beloved figure in the community, as well as one of the city's few black businesswomen, Jeanne Dawkins was named Newark's Woman of the Year in 1980. Following her death two years later, her son, Walter Jr., tried to keep the Key Club afloat. "But that didn't last long," Harvard says. "Things were never the same." And so, the club shut down. By then, Sparky's was gone, too. So were the Front Room and Playbill Lounge. Other clubs—El C's, Midas Gold, the Four Leaf Deli, Jasmine's and Mr. Wes's—came and went, leaving jazz fans seeking new outlets. Like Rhoda Scott's *Ebb Tide*, their popularity waxed and waned.

The Priory

Except for vacationing in Florida in winter, Diane Mora and Andy Nelson spend their Friday nights bucking traffic on the Garden State Parkway to get to Newark. Their destination for the seventy-mile trip north is always the same—the Priory on West Market Street, the city's longest-running jazz club.

Mora and Nelson happened on the Priory more than a decade ago after reading about an appearance by singer Etta Jones and saxophonist Houston Person. "Diane was a big Etta Jones fan, and I loved the saxophone," Nelson explains. "So, we came." They've kept coming ever since, even after moving from Bergen County to Lakewood ninety miles away. "There's not much jazz at the shore," Nelson says, "so we come to the Priory."

As longtime regulars at the Priory, Mora and Nelson enjoy the camaraderie as well as the music. "It's like sitting in your living room with all this great music a few feet away," Nelson says. "Everyone knows everyone." No matter that they are among the few whites in the mostly African-American audience. "From day one, the atmosphere has been welcoming," Mora says. "We've made many friends," she adds, reeling off a list that includes Charlie Cann, Walter Chambers, Stan Myers, Richard Whitten, Donnie Mitchell, Jessie Martin and Jimmy Robinson. "I've also learned a lot about jazz."

"The Priory is like a little clubhouse," singer Pam Purvis agrees. "Everyone who comes on Friday night is a regular. It was the same at Skipper's." Situated in the atrium of the old St. Joseph's Roman Catholic Church, the club is operated by the New Community Corporation, a community-based organization founded nearly fifty years ago by Monsignor William Linder and parishioners from Queen of Angels Church. Their goal, carried out project by project, was to rebuild Newark's center city following the 1967 civil rebellions. Since its founding, NCC has built thousands of housing units, opened a nursing home and created a transitional housing facility, job training center and supermarket, among other projects. But it is the jazz program that the community at large knows best.

Considered a Newark jazz institution, the Priory began offering weekly shows in the early 1990s. In the beginning the banquet manager booked Friday night events, which continue to this day. After that, saxophonist Bradford Hayes took over for two years. "I brought in all the local talent like Don Williams, Geary Moore and Leo Johnson," he says. In 1995, after NCC received a $2 million Ford Foundation grant to bring the arts to the community and address health issues affecting minorities, Chase Jackson, an arts administrator, took over. "On the arts side, we had theater programs for young people, art exhibits and lots of music," she says. "In addition to Jazz in the Atrium on Friday nights, we had a jazz listening club, the Jazz Aficionados, that met on Wednesday nights, Gospel Gourmet on the first Saturday of the month and a jazz brunch on Sundays.

"One of our best nights ever," Jackson says, "was when the Jazz Aficionados presented 'Sarahthon,' a posthumous tribute to Sarah Vaughan on what would have been the singer's seventy-fifth birthday." With Ada Vaughan, Sarah's mother in the audience, "it was an unbelievable night," she says. Sounds of Vaughan's music filled the atrium all evening. Between sets, pianist Michael Cochrane played tunes made famous by Vaughan and audience members participated in a contest devised to test their knowledge of her life and career. The following year, the Aficionados presented *A Date With the Duke*, a tribute to Duke Ellington.

For years, Houston Person and Etta Jones were among the Priory's top attractions, appearing there until shortly before Jones died of breast cancer in 2001. "Etta wasn't only a unique jazz singer," says organist Dave Braham, who spent several years on the road with Person's band, "she was the most down-to-earth person I ever knew. Other singers would go in the back during their breaks, but Etta always stayed out there, sitting with her fans. That's part of the reason they loved her so much."

During Jackson's reign, the Priory also was a popular dining spot, attracting patrons to its spacious restaurant for dinner and area business people to its deli at lunch hour. Lunch also was available in the atrium, where Swing Era veteran Floyd "Papa Stoppa" Lang, Corky Caldwell and Ernie Edwards played piano.

After Jackson left NCC, Denise McCoy took over the jazz programming. With the grant money gone and the economy on a downslide, she kept the Friday night programs going on "a string, a prayer and lots of support. We didn't have money to promote our events or for advertising," she said before plans for renovating the club were announced, "but we're still here." McCoy says her moral support comes from people who knew her as a girl growing up in Stella Wright Homes in Newark's Central Ward, NCC itself and the community at large. "To many people in our audiences, I'm just Denise from Spruce Street."

On Friday nights, McCoy gets an assist from sound engineer Fred Simpson and volunteer Mercedes (Sandy) Deskins. Recently, she began hiring rhythm and blues acts on the third Friday of the month to attract younger audiences. Despite the struggles McCoy has encountered, she's kept Friday night jazz at the Priory alive. Having singers like Dwight West and Carrie Jackson present off-night jazz events, for which there is a nominal charge, and hosting annual birthday bashes for singers Jackson and Yvette Glover have also provided a boost. Her go-to musicians include Joe Brown Jr., whose band includes noted guitarist Dave Stryker, Leo Johnson, Rudy Walker and Bradford Hayes.

Jan Carden, a retired Arts High School fine arts teacher, has been singing at the Priory since 2000. "I was asked to sing the first time when my art work was on exhibit as part of a program featuring Newark teachers in the arts," he says. Carden's daughter, Stephanie Battles, who appeared on Broadway in *The Lion King*, often performs with him.

Most nights there's also a wealth of talent in the audience, singers like Joy Foster, Yosko and Rosalind Grant, and musicians like Cornell McGhee, Gerry Cappuccio and James Gibbs III, who help liven things up. To the audiences' delight, Jimmy Robinson, a retired postal worker from Jersey City, and his dance partner, Diane Marie Williams, generally take a spin or two around the atrium. "We love seeing Jimmy and Diane dance," Glover says. "It adds an element of charm to what we do."

After struggling for years to keep things going, McCoy and her crew got a new lease on life in 2013, when the interior of the former church was remodeled and reopened as the Priory Jazz Club and Hall. Bradford Hayes, who was there from the start, Lady CiCi and Don Williams, and Daoud Williams and the Spirit of Life Ensemble, featuring Dwight West, were among the opening acts.

Skipper's Plane Street Pub

When Greg Salandy opened Skipper's in 2007 he had no plans for a jazz club. After tiring of working in administrative positions for companies including Time Warner and HBO, he wanted to open a restaurant and Skipper's Plane Street Pub was it. From the moment Salandy stepped into the place, he loved everything about it, including its brick walls and wooden floors. "It reminded me of places in Europe," he says.

Situated opposite Essex County College on University Avenue, Skipper's was previously known as the VIP and Sidebar. By the time Salandy arrived in Newark, his friend Mike Hamilton, a bartender and part-owner of Hamilton's on Central Avenue, was running it. Hamilton named the place Skipper's for his father, the bartender at McGovern's on New Street, a popular Irish pub. Rather than change the name, Salandy kept it after taking over the lease.

"Historically, Skipper's had been a daytime lunch place," Salandy explains. "I saw the potential for music, but first I needed to establish the restaurant part of the business. In the beginning, Mike stayed on, so we drew a big Irish crowd on Friday nights." Daytime business was brisk, as students from ECC and Rutgers and workers from Prudential and the nearby Essex County courts packed the place for lunch. Nights, however, were a different story. "If we stayed open late, the bartender and I were the only ones in the place," Salandy says. "By 7 p.m., it was completely dead."

Eventually, he saw music as a way to jump-start his business. With the help of his friend and partner, Norman Mann, once a football star at Weequahic High School, all kinds of music became part of the nighttime trade. "Newark was new to me," says Salandy, who was born in Trinidad and grew up in New York. "Norman was instrumental in building the business because he came from Newark and knew so many people from here."

Initially, the club became a rehearsal hall for an R&B group brought in from Mann's church. Word about live entertainment spread and singer Hunter Hayes and saxophonist Bradford Hayes were hired after inquiring about gigs. "Eventually, we booked a Latin band led by Orlando Vega," Salandy recounts. "In January 2008, Jackie Jones became the first female singer to appear at the club."

Within months, Skipper's began offering music nearly every night of the week. Singer Gene Goldston led Monday night jams. Tuesday nights were devoted to the blues, hosted by Dean Shot and Sumyiah. Dave Braham held sway on organ on Wednesday nights. Bands were booked on Thursdays. Singer Denise Hamilton hosted Friday night karaoke sessions, and Sunday afternoons were devoted to jazz with Dave Braham on organ and Greg Bufford on drums. "Goldie (Goldston) was a big help because he knew the business so well," Salandy says. "He is an excellent emcee and has a great voice. He's a true professional. When Radam (Schwartz) came in, the numbers really worked out. Sunday was my best day."

Business took off, but the non-stop action was taking its toll on Salandy. With the club open seven nights a week at its height, he was working double shifts, sometimes eighteen to twenty hours a day. "Sometimes I was so tired I slept in my car," he recalls. "Other aspects of my life were on hold." By expanding his night time business through music, poetry readings and tap dance shows during the week and booking private parties when things slowed on Saturdays, he managed to keep going. But not all programs were equally successful, marginalizing the profits.

Some of Skipper's most profitable nights occurred when singers Yvette Glover and Carrie Jackson headlined the shows or when Amiri Baraka and his wife Amina presented poetry programs, accompanied by Rudy Walker on drums. "They pumped things up by spreading the word and sending out flyers, so they always brought a crowd," Salandy says. Skipper's also was home to shows Glover sponsored, featuring tap dancers Hillary-Marie and Kyle Wilder. As the mother of Savion Glover, the internationally acclaimed hoofer, she is known as The Mother of Tap.

Other area artists who performed at Skipper's include organist Gloria Coleman, guitarist Bob DeVos, drummer Victor Jones, pianist Dr. Lewis Porter from Rutgers-Newark, drummer Cecil Brooks III, trumpeter James Gibbs III and singers Jackson, Pat Tandy, Pam Purvis, Cynthia Holiday, Rosalind Grant and Joy Foster.

Despite Skipper's outward appearance of success, Salandy constantly struggled to keep it going. "We only had a $10 minimum (which patrons said was rarely enforced), but many of my customers were philosophically opposed to paying for music," he notes. "That was one of the challenges I faced." With an exception or two, Salandy's penchant for hiring critically acclaimed artists from outside Newark bombed. "When we brought in (saxophonist) Stanley Jordan, the place was packed," he says, but that occurred largely because Jan Greiner, a promoter who books Jordan, pumped up the crowd as a Skipper's regular. Skipper's also was standing room only when Victor Bailey, the bassist for Weather Report, appeared. Yet when percussionist Steve Berrios, whose musical associations included Mongo Santamaria and Dizzy Gillespie, performed, hardly anyone showed up. Nor did trombonist Vincent Garner of Wynton Marsalis's Lincoln Center Orchestra or hard bop trumpeter Cecil Bridgewater draw much of a crowd.

Nevertheless, the roster of musicians that came to hang out or sit in with their friends at Skipper's was impressive, one that included

Raphael Cruz, a Grammy-award nominee for Best Latin Album; drummer Bernard Purdie, who has backed B.B. King and Aretha Franklin; organ master Rhoda Scott, guitarist Russell Malone, who has toured with Jimmy Smith and Ron Carter; and Newark drummer Tyshawn Sorey, a fixture on the international jazz scene.

With so much good music to offer and a solid menu at reasonable prices—despite exceptionally slow service at times—Skipper's was not nearly as profitable as it seemed, Salandy says. With the Priory just blocks away and Crossroads in Garwood offering Tuesday night jam sessions, competition was stiff. "Unless we had a private party, we were closed on Saturdays because so much else was happening," he says. "There was too much competition."

Matters only worsened when Salandy discovered employees stealing food, dipping into the till and giving away drinks. As if that wasn't enough, he also was deluged by customers demanding freebies. Exhausted as he was from his struggle to survive, Salandy still wonders if he shut down prematurely. For a time, friends like Denise Hamilton, who hosted a jazz benefit to encourage him to start anew, hoped he would re-open, but those dreams fizzled. Skipper's was no more.

LEFT: Promoter Carl "Tiny Prince" Brinson.
(Courtesy of Carl "Tiny Prince" Brinson.)

BELOW: Singer Grace Smith, 1940s.
(Courtesy of Charles Cann.)

ABOVE: Pianist and bandleader Howard "Duke" Anderson, 1990s. *(Author's collection.)*

RIGHT: Hipster Babs Gonzalez, 1940s. *(Courtesy of Honi Gordon.)*

RIGHT: Saxophonist
James Moody, 1950s.
(Courtesy of Honi Gordon.)

BELOW: Newark Jazz Jam.
From left: Herb Morgan,
Al Cotton, unidentified
singer at microphone,
Walter Davis Jr., Danny
Quebec, unidentified
trumpeter. *(Courtesy of
Pam Morgan.)*

Wayne Shorter recording for Blue Note, 1960s.
(Photograph by Francis Wolff. Copyright, Mosaic Records.)

RIGHT: Flyer featuring
Benny Green and
Hank Mobley at the
Blue Mirror, 1950.
(Courtesy of Bob "Stix" Darden.)

BELOW: Flyer for a Friday
night bebop session
at Lloyd's Manor.
(Author's collection.)

EDDIE JARDIM Vice Pres. NEW JAZZ SOCIETY
Newark Chapter, Says: For a fresh conception
of the present Age. Dig

The JAZZ SCENE

Contemporary Life Set To Music

AT

THE BLUE MIRROR
SILVER SADDLE
275 Clinton Ave.   Newark, N. J.

FLORENCE WRIGHT
Presents
The Brilliant Trombonist

BENNY GREEN

Expressing Truth
With

LLOYD TURNER	AL COTTON
DRUMS	BASSIST
HANK MOBLY	JOE MANNING
TENOR	PIANIST

ALSO

★ GEORGE GORDON'S Pianistic Inventions

EVERY TUESDAY NITE
From 8 - 2   19.50 .   DUES 40c

Dig: Carl Ide's Jazz Revue - W.N.J.R. 4 - 6

❧ A BE-BOP SESSION ❧
EVERY FRIDAY NIGHT
At Lloyd's Manor
42-48 Beacon Street, Newark, N. J.

Featuring

AL ARMSTRONG, Trumpet	HENRY DURANT, Tenor
CHINK WILLIAMS, Drums	ART WILLIAMS, Bass
FATS GORDON, Pianoforte	WINDY, Vocals

Lucky Ticket holders receive Prizes of $10.00-$5.00-$2.00

LADIED 50 CENTS   GENTS 60 CENTS

BERNARDO, 43 Crawford Street, Newark, N. J., Printer

ABOVE: Young Woody Shaw in the Blue Note studio, 1960s. *(Photograph by Francis Wolff. Copyright, Mosaic Records.)*

RIGHT: Larry Young Jr. takes a break during a Blue Note session, 1960s. *(Photograph by Francis Wolff. Copyright, Mosaic Records.)*

Lee Morgan, trumpet, and Herb Morgan, saxophone, at a 1960s Blue Note recording session. *(Photograph by Francis Wolff. Copyright, Mosaic Records.)*

Woody Shaw with his parents, Woody and Rosalie Shaw. *(Courtesy of Sony Music Entertainment)*

LEFT:
Grachan Moncur III during his composer's residency at the Newark Community School of the Arts. *(Courtesy of Grachan Moncur III.)*

BELOW:
Walter Davis Jr. recording for Blue Note, 1960s. *(Photograph by Francis Wolff. Copyright, Mosaic Records.)*

RIGHT: Sarah Vaughan and her friend Doris Robinson at the Picadilly, early 1940s. *(Collection of Doris Robinson. Courtesy of Walter Chambers.)*

BELOW: Sarah Vaughan, early in her career. *(Collection of Doris Robinson. Courtesy of Walter Chambers.)*

Miss Rhapsody singing with Johnny Jackson's High Society Orchestra, 1940s.
(Author's collection.)

687 GLITTER CLUB
687 SPRINGFIELD AVE.   NEWARK, N. J.
Bet. 18 & 19th Sts.   ES 2-9533

Proudly Presents

LITTLE JIMMIE SCOTT

SAVOY RECORDING ARTIST

"Evening In Paradise"   "Motherless Child"

PLUS **NAT PHIPPS**

TUES. - WEDS. - THURS. - FRI - SAT.

SUNDAY   MATINEE 7 P.M. - TIL

Weekly Specials- TUES. "Party Nite"   WEDS. "Miss Glitter Club"
                                        LADY WITH MOST PERSONALITY
                                        SELECTED MISS GLITTER CLUB
THURS. JAM SESSION   ANDY 'Mr. Continental' HOLLINGER, your host

TOP ENTERTAINMENT & MODERATE PRICES ALWAYS

RIGHT: Flyer advertising Jimmy Scott and Nat Phipps at the Glitter Club, 1950s. *(Courtesy of Bob "Stix" Darden.)*

BELOW: Sarah Vaughan with a group of friends at a Newark club, 1950s. *From left:* Ralph Jackson, Doris Robinson, Vaughan, Ann Robinson, Ella Moncur, Ernest Robinson and Clifford Jackson. *(Collection of Doris Robinson. Courtesy of Walter Chambers.)*

Jimmy Scott singing with the Megatones at the Glitter Club. *From left:* Ed
Lightsey, Scott, Nat Phipps, Bob "Stix" Darden. *(Courtesy of Nat Phipps.)*

Jimmy Scott later in his career. *(Author's collection.)*

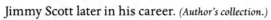

The Brady Hodge Orchestra at the Masonic Temple, c. 1958. *From left: Front*, Bobby Porter, congas/vocals; unidentified; Joe O'Laughlin, saxophone; Harold Van Pelt, saxophone; unidentified; Brady Hodge (white jacket). *Rear*, Stash O'Laughlin, piano; Charlie Davis, bass; John Turpin, drums; Hank White and Dave McDuffie, trumpets. *(Courtesy of Harold Van Pelt.)*

Saxophonist Gene Phipps Sr. (center), with Gus Young and the Heat Waves at the Coleman Hotel, 1950s. Lander Coleman is at the microphone. *(Courtesy of John Hamilton.)*

Calvin Hughes and his Swinging Gents at the Terrace Ballroom, with Hughes on trumpet and singer Fanny Douglas at the microphone. *(Courtesy of Cynthia Holiday.)*

Calvin Hughes on trumpet (center), with Teddy Ritchwood's Nomads of Swing, late 1940s. *(Courtesy of Cynthia Holiday.)*

ABOVE: Organist Rhoda Scott, early in her career, with bartender Jimmy Caldwell at the Playbill Lounge. *(Courtesy of Rhoda Scott.)*

BELOW: The Rhoda Scott Trio at the Torch Club on Clinton Avenue with owner Rose Dibella, 1960s. From left: Rhoda Scott, Joe Thomas, Dibella and Bill Elliott. *(Courtesy of Joe Thomas.)*

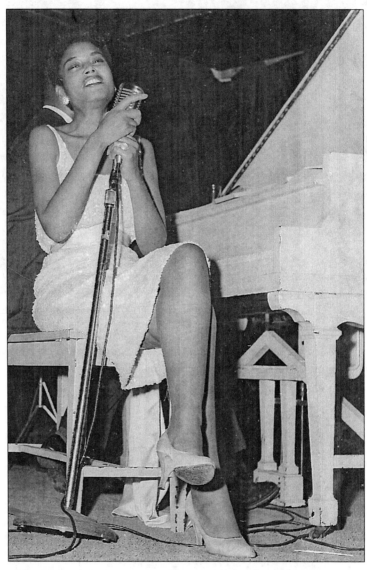

Abbey Lincoln singing at Teddy Powell's Lounge on Broad Street, 1958. *(Courtesy of John Hamilton.)*

6 ♪

The Vocalists

Singing for Their Supper

When I sing, trouble can sit right on my shoulder
and I don't even notice. —Sarah Vaughan

For a small city, Newark has produced more than its fair share of singers whose names are instantly recognizable: Sarah Vaughan, Jimmy Scott, Whitney Houston, Queen Latifah, Dionne Warwick, Gloria Gaynor, Cissy Houston, Connie Francis and Melba Moore, to name a few. Add to that, house singer Gwen Guthrie; R&B artist Linda Hayes; Madeline Bell, star of Broadway's *Black Nativity*; Gerri Grainger, a Sammy Davis Jr. protégé; and Honi Gordon, who recorded with Charles Mingus as a teenager, and it's a pretty awesome list.

But fame and fortune are far different things. While Whitney Houston, Newark's most celebrated singer, rocketed to fame with her first LP, other talented singers never made the leap. Scott, for one, waited forty-plus years for celebrity to come knocking. Gordon had such a unique style that jazz fans never quite knew what to make of her, despite inspiring reviews.

Though revered in and around Newark, blues singer Carrie Smith spent years traveling the world seeking wider acclaim. For most of her career, she was a hit, some say a cult figure, all over Europe while relatively unknown in the United States. In the late 1970s and early 1980s, patrons crowded the streets outside Newark's Key Club to hear Lu Elliott, a Duke Ellington alumna, and blues singer Irene Reid do their thing. Their talent, too, outweighed whatever prominence they enjoyed.

Singers carrying on Newark's rich jazz tradition today, and there are many, include Carrie Jackson, Yvette Glover, Lady CiCi, Pat Tandy, Gene Goldston, Cynthia Holiday, Antoinette Montague, Pam Purvis, Denise Hamilton, Ronnell Bey, Jackie Jones, Dwight West, Jan Carden, Yosko, Hollis Donaldson, Daille Kettrell and Lynette Sheard. Here's a look at the lives and careers of those who were either born in Newark or made the city their home at some point, starting with the incomparable Sarah Vaughan.

Sarah Vaughan

More than twenty years have passed since Sarah Vaughan, Newark's legendary jazz icon, succumbed to lung cancer at her home in Hidden Hills, California. Yet hardly a day goes by in the city of her birth without the sounds of Sassy's songs streaming over the airwaves at WBGO. "Sarah Vaughan was embedded in this community," says poet Amiri Baraka. "She was always a part of it. I can remember pointing to her house on Avon Avenue and saying, 'That's where Sarah Vaughan lives.' I was thrilled just to be walking on the same street." Even in death, Vaughan remains an unforgettable figure in Newark jazz history, forever the hometown girl who made good after dropping out of Arts High School.

Although Vaughan was world famous, she always enjoyed coming home to Newark. Years after she left school, for example, she stopped by Arts High to encourage a new generation of students to live their dreams. "Our students knew who she was and appreciated her music," says Hilton Otero, the principal at the time. "When she arrived, the kids gave her a royal welcome." Vaughan was not scheduled to sing that day, but couldn't resist riffing with the school band. For students and teachers alike, that brief interlude remains an indelible memory.

Signs of affection for Newark's favorite singer still abound. After Vaughan's death in March 1990, the 3,000-seat concert hall at Newark Symphony Hall was named for her and the street adjacent to the New Jersey Performing Arts Center (NJPAC) and Military Park was renamed Sarah Vaughan Way. In 2012, she was inducted into the New Jersey Hall of Fame.

A year later, in the summer of 2013, Vaughan was one of the key figures represented in *A Tribute to Newark Jazz Clubs*, a mural unveiled on Hawthorne Avenue in the city's South Ward created by artist Gladys Barker Grauer and a team of assistants that included students and supporting artist Melanie Stokes. It is part of the Newark Public Art Program, an initiative dedicated to creating works of art that manifest the spirit of Newark in public spaces.

"This sure is something," Ada Vaughan, the singer's ninety-six-year-old mother, told the crowd after arriving from California for the Sarah Vaughan Jazz Festival in 1991. That series of events included the street-naming ceremony in front of NJPAC and a concert at Symphony Hall. "Sarah Vaughan was our hero," Mayor Sharpe James said at the time. "We want her memory and indelible legacy to remain a part of our city's rich history and renaissance." In 1999, NJPAC installed a bronze plaque commemorating Vaughan's life and career along its Walk of Fame.

Vaughan's standing as a hometown icon was never more evident than at her 1990 funeral service at Mt. Zion Baptist Church, when several thousand mourners lined Broadway in the city's North Ward to bid her farewell. It was a spectacular home-going event as the Rev. Granville A. Seward took the theme for his eulogy from two of Vaughan's most famous songs: *Send in the Clowns* and *Someone to Watch Over Me*. Afterward, Vaughan was carried to her final resting place in Glendale Cemetery in a glass-enclosed, horse-drawn carriage.

During a career that spanned more than five decades, Vaughan won every award jazz had to offer. Year after year she topped the *DownBeat* and *Metronome* polls for Best Female Vocalist. Two of her recordings, Tadd Dameron's *If You Could See Me Now* and the LP

Sarah Vaughan With Clifford Brown, made the Grammy Hall of Fame. In 1989, the National Endowment of the Arts presented her with its highest honor, the Jazz Masters Award. Not bad for a girl who dropped out of school in her junior year to give the big time a shot.

Vaughan was in her mid-teens when she became the talk of the town among jazz musicians who considered her a rare talent. "That girl can sang," trumpeter Jabbo Smith told his friends after she popped up one night at the Picadilly Club on Peshine Avenue. Vaughan was underage, but no one cared. She could *"sang,"* so she was allowed to go on despite the possibility of the cops shutting down the place. Pop Durham, who owned the Alcazar on Waverly Avenue, also looked the other way when Sarah begged him to sing.

As pillars of Old First Mt. Zion Church on Thomas Street before the congregation split, Jake and Ada Vaughan knew nothing of their daughter's after-dark escapades. To them, she was simply a shy teenager who played the organ for the junior and senior choirs at church. Nor did they suspect she was club hopping when she was supposed to be doing homework with friends. When one of them stopped by one night, a befuddled Mrs. Vaughan wanted to know, "Where's Sarah? I thought she was with you."

Church friends remember Vaughan's father picking at his guitar when they gathered at her house on Brunswick Street to listen to records, but they knew nothing either about her singing at nightclubs. "That's why we were so surprised when we heard Sarah was going to sing at the Apollo," said Phyllis Brooks, whose grandfather was their pastor. "Sarah and her mother sang in the gospel choir at church, but I don't remember hearing Sarah sing a solo."

As the story goes, Vaughan didn't sing the first time she and her friend Doris Robinson entered the Amateur Night Contest at Harlem's famous Apollo Theater in 1942. Instead, Vaughan accompanied Robinson, who won the $15 second prize and split it with her. After shaking off a bout of nerves, Vaughan won top prize on a subsequent visit. More importantly, she received a weeklong return engagement, opening for Ella Fitzgerald, and caught the eye of bandleader Billy Eckstine, who became one of her closest friends.

Eckstine, in turn, introduced her to Earl Hines, who fired his vocalist so she could sing with his orchestra. By then, she was eighteen.

A year later Vaughan went with Eckstine after he formed his own orchestra. Charlie Parker and Dizzy Gillespie were in it, too. "I thought Bird (Parker) and Diz were the end," she once said. "I think their playing influenced my singing. Horns always influenced me more than the voices." That's well-taken because Vaughan was more musician than vocalist, endowed with a four-octave range that could soar from the basement to the heavens as if she were a horn.

With Billie Holiday and Ella Fitzgerald she became celebrated as one of the world's greatest jazz singers, reaping every prize there was along the way, beginning with the Esquire New Star Poll Award in 1945. A string of hits followed on Musicraft, after which she went solo in 1946, recording *Tenderly, It's Magic* and *East of the Sun and West of the Moon*, as well as the Tadd Dameron classic *If You Could See Me Now*. In 1947, after she married George Treadwell, a saxophonist who abandoned his musical career to become her manager, Vaughan signed a long-term contract with Columbia. For the next five years she barely left the studio, churning out hit after hit, most of them jazzed-up pop tunes. Ironically, perhaps, she was voted Best Female Jazz Vocalist six years in a row (1947–52) by *DownBeat* and won *Metronome* jazz polls from 1948–52.

Longing to return to her jazz roots, Vaughan signed an oddball contract with Mercury that allowed her to make pop hits on the main label while singing jazz on EmArcy, its spinoff. The brass at Mercury got to pick the numbers on one side of her 78s, while she was free to make the flip-side selections. Many of these tunes, like *Make Yourself Comfortable, Misty* and *Broken Hearted Melody*, her biggest hit, topped the charts.

Vaughan went on to record for Roulette in the early 1960s, winning accolades for her recording of *Perdido* with the Count Basie Band. Subsequently, she returned to Mercury, where she spent the next few years. For the rest of her career, she was with Pablo, working with Count Basie and Oscar Peterson, recording two Duke

Ellington albums and one featuring Brazilian music. When she toured Brazil in 1977, Maplewood filmmaker Tom Guy went with her. The following year he produced *Listen to the Sun*, a documentary based on her tour.

Though Vaughan spent most of her life in the public eye, she remained a Newarker through and through. No matter how many records she turned out, how much money she made or how many awards she won, she never forgot the place where she was born and grew up. Although she could be mercurial at times, causing critics to label her aloof and difficult to deal with, she was perfectly at home with her inner circle, a group that included Bert Gibson, Ella Moncur and Annabelle Reeves. In their company, she was just one of them.

"Sarah was one of the most down-to-earth people, I ever met," says Charlie Cann, now in his nineties. "I met her through Ella Moncur (wife of Savoy Sultans bassist Brother Moncur). One night in the late 1940s, Ella Moncur, who was a friend of my sister's, rang the bell at three in the morning. Sarah and Treadwell were with her. They decided to stop by after closing up a club on Broadway."

At the time, Vaughan and Treadwell, the first of her three husbands, were living at 21 Avon Avenue in Newark in a house they shared with her parents. "By then, Sarah was famous," Cann says, "but she was just like anyone else. My sister Bert knew she liked hot dogs, so she cooked some up and we sat around, ate and talked. As I recall, Sarah brought along her own bottle. I think it was cognac."

From then on Cann was one of Vaughan's staunchest supporters. "Wherever she sang, I was right there," he says. "I never remember Sarah singing anywhere at a club in Newark except at the Key Club, where she and all her friends liked to hang out. They'd hand her the mike while she was seated at the bar and she'd sing."

Cann also was in the audience when Vaughan performed with the New Jersey Symphony Orchestra at Symphony Hall in 1980, and at the reception in her honor following the show. Brooks, Sarah's childhood friend from church, also was there that night. "I laugh now, when I think back to when we were in the choir together at my grandfather's church," Brooks said. "We didn't even know Sarah could sing. Boy, were we wrong!"

Jimmy Scott

When Jimmy Scott played Newark clubs in the 1950s, his voice was so ethereal many of his female fans went nuts. As the stories go, some of them went so far as to throw silver dollars at his feet. A few years later, when Scott recorded *I'm Afraid the Masquerade Is Over*, his followers practically wore it out.

Scott's first gig in Newark was with Lionel Hampton's orchestra at the Adams Theater. "I was invited back," he says. "A year or so later, I returned and decided to stay." That was the start of Scott's love affair with Newark as well as the start of his solo career.

Because of his boyish appearance, Scott was billed as Little Jimmy Scott well into his career, a name he detested. "'Gates' (Lionel Hampton) gave me the name," he told David Ritz, his biographer. "I was twenty-eight, but he told the audience I was sixteen." Scott's appearance resulted from a hormonal condition that stunted his growth and maturation. Nevertheless, it often made him all the more attractive to women who considered his androgynous voice a turn on. Even good-looking Quincy Jones couldn't match his magnetism. "Jimmy is the one who always gets the girls," Jones told friends. "They all love him."

Born in Cleveland on July 27, 1925, James Victor Scott, the third of ten children, began singing in church. In his teens, he broke into show business performing with comedian Tim McCoy. Before signing with Hampton in 1948, he traveled with Caldonia's *Revue*, a show headed by his friend and mentor Estelle "Caldonia" Young. Now in his late eighties, Scott still credits her for showing him the ropes.

After leaving Hampton's band, Scott returned to Cleveland, where his career stagnated. By then he had split with his first wife and married Billie Holiday's second cousin, who encouraged him to move to New York to further his career. They did, and he soon began singing at clubs in New York and recording for Savoy Records in Newark. Like many Savoy artists, he fell victim to Herman Lubinsky, who recorded Charlie Parker, Miles Davis and Fats Navarro in the early 1940s but had a reputation for cheating his clients. Despite Scott's stellar reviews on *Everybody's Somebody's Fool, I've Been a Fool* and *I Wish I Didn't Love You So*, Lubinsky cheated him, too. "That was a mess," Scott says. "Don't ever mention his name. He did everybody in, especially Big Maybelle. He really did her bad."

During the time he spent in Newark, Scott enjoyed an extended stay at the Glitter Club on Springfield Avenue with the Megatones, a quintet led by Nat Phipps. He also sang at spots such as Teddy Powell's Holiday Inn bordering Weequahic Park. His running buddies were some of the hippest musicians around—drummer Herbert "Geronimo" Johnson, James "Smokey" McAllister, a popular emcee and dancer who also owned a barber shop, and singer Babs Gonzalez, one of bebop's earliest proponents.

Scott's first brush with success after he went solo was with *I'm Afraid the Masquerade Is Over*, a haunting tune he recorded for Roost, another small label. Record sales, however, were not nearly enough to propel him to stardom. Before long, he found himself back in Cleveland, bouncing from job to job for the next twenty years as a bus boy, short-order cook and waiter. To free up his nights for an occasional gig, he took a job at a home for the elderly. Caring for people who live in agonizing pain, he told Ritz, put his own condition in perspective. Later, he worked at a hotel.

After an unsuccessful comeback on Atlantic with a recording called *The Source*, Scott spent the next five years in obscurity. Then, in 1972, Atlantic invited him to record again. He did, but once again, there was no brass ring, "no comeback, no deals and few performances," as Ritz put it. His career shot, Scott lived off his disability check for the next few years.

Following a failed third marriage, Scott returned to Newark in the early 1980s. During that period Henrietta Parker, who worked for New Jersey Network, became his manager, but they split when they didn't see eye to eye on her ideas to further his career. In early 1985, Scott married Earlene Rodgers, a friend from years before.

Days later she called WBGO, urging the jazz radio station to play more of her husband's music.

"I knew Jimmy's name, but I thought he was dead," recalls Dorthaan Kirk, who took the call. "After we began playing Jimmy's records again, the phone began ringing off the hook, so I talked to 'Big P' (disc jockey Bob Porter), and he thought we should present a comeback concert. We did, at the Mirage, a downtown hangout on Broad Street. We also began taking Jimmy around to places in New York City and around Newark," which led to a gig at New York's Blue Note in May 1985.

Scott performed sporadically for the next few years at places like the West End Café on New York's upper West Side and the Ballroom, where he opened for Johnnie Ray. He also recorded *All the Way with Jimmy Scott: For Whatever the Reason.* Then, to his surprise, he got the break he had been so desperately seeking when he sang at the funeral of his friend Doc Pomus at New York's Riverside Funeral Home in March 1990. On the spot, Seymour Stein, the head of Sire Records, offered him a five-album deal. With Stein's support and backing from Warner Brothers, Sire's parent company, Scott suddenly became a cult figure in his late sixties, as well as a Grammy nominee for *All the Way.* Offers to perform in clubs, on records and on movie tracks poured in. "Madonna claimed he was the only singer who could make her cry," Ritz says. "Liza Minnelli said all other singers should kiss his feet."

Scott also became the subject of a documentary, filmed in part at 175 Prospect Street in East Orange, where he lived on the twentieth floor of a high-rise apartment building. "With the film crew coming and going, it was pretty exciting," says Dale Colston, a neighbor who often exchanged niceties with Scott on the elevator. By then, Scott was traveling the world with his band, Jazz Expression.

Once again, however, trouble was brewing in Scott's personal life. His marriage was crumbling, which led him to return to Cleveland in 1997 and divorce in 2001.

Nevertheless, New Jersey remained on his play list. In April 2006, for example, he opened the Cape May Jazz Festival, where he was honored for many years in music, a tribute that included taped accolades from Harry Belafonte, Diane Reeves and Nancy Wilson. "Scott's voice doesn't have the falsetto-like, aching purity of his prime years," critic George Kanzler wrote, "but like Sinatra in his waning years, he retains the ability to phrase and shape a song in his unique, glacially slow, supremely dramatic behind-the-beat style."

Whatever success Scott has enjoyed through the years, his search for love and acceptance has been a sometime thing. Friends like David Ritz, for one, point to the torment confronting him most of his life. "Some people say this is because of Jimmy's physical appearance," says Jeanie McCarthy Scott, who married Scott more than a decade ago. "But I think it's mainly because of the loss of his mother (who died in a car crash when he was thirteen) and the lack of cohesiveness in his family. All some of his relatives did was hit him up for money."

Others, including family members, see things differently, pointing to Scott's heavy drinking as one of the key factors affecting his personal relationships. "That's a part of Jimmy his fans rarely see," one friend says. "When he's performing, he's a great guy. When he's not, you never know. He'll tell you otherwise, but I think he's chased away most of the people closest to him—wives, family members, managers and friends. He always seems to be searching for happiness that eludes him."

But that, too, seems to be a thing of the past. "Jimmy's been clean and sober for more than ten years now," Jeanie Scott says from their home in Las Vegas. Nearing ninety, Jimmy Scott still performs occasionally. In addition to being nominated for a 1992 Grammy as Best Male Vocalist, he was named *Swing* magazine's No. 1 vocalist in Japan for four straight years (2000–2004) and received the National Endowment for the Arts Living Jazz Legend award in 2007 at the Kennedy Center for the Performing Arts. Several cities have honored him, including Cleveland and Newark.

Among other accolades, Scott was cited in 1985 by Blue Note Records for excellence in jazz. Even now, awards come his way. In October 2013, he was inducted into the Rock and Roll Hall of Fame in

Detroit. "Jimmy still sells out," his wife says. "There are plans now for a show in his honor here in Las Vegas featuring a lot of big stars."

Lu Elliott

Born in Suffolk, Virginia, Lu Elliott was brought to New York, where she was raised and educated, at age three. Her initial musical experiences and training were in the Baptist church, where she was a soloist in the choir.

According to jazz critic Nat Hentoff, Elliott began improving as a singer after she met her husband-to-be, Horace Sims, a singer and guitarist who lived in Newark and led a local group called the Afro-Cubanaires. "In a chance for seasoning, which is now seldom available in evolving singers," Hentoff wrote, "Elliott learned a great deal through working with (1940s) big bands, among them those of Benny Carter, Duke Ellington, Lucky Millinder, Erskine Hawkins and Eddie Heywood."

"That's about the best training you can get," Elliott said, following the release of *With a Little Help From My Friends: Lu Elliott*, her second LP for ABC Records. "It was my friends who made it possible for me to get this far. I'll never forget them," she said, singling out Dinah Washington and comedian Nipsey Russell as particular inspirations.

Washington was the one who urged Elliott to tour Australia, where she played prestigious club dates and appeared on television in 1967. During her travels, she cut her first LP for ABC, *Way Out from Down Under*. For a moment at least, it put Lucy Elliott—her full name—on the map. "This chick can really sing," Washington said after hearing Elliott perform. "She can become a star, if only someone will help her."

Hopes for success were high after Elliott's manager, Louis Zito, signed her to ABC Records and she recorded *Way Out from Down Under*. Reviewer Gene Lees called Elliott "a very big talent," possessing incomparable "intonation, control, range and dynamic breadth." Yet her career never took off, as he and other critics had predicted.

Although several of them claimed she had "arrived," she never got nearly as far as they thought she should.

After marrying Sims and moving to Newark, Elliott appeared at Las Vegas nightclubs and Newark-area venues such as the Key Club, where she and Sims sometimes performed together. They considered the club, run by their friend Jeanne Dawkins, their refuge, a welcoming place whether they were on stage or on the sidelines supporting friends including Irene Reid, a sock-it-to-'em blues singer, or Sam Williams, Newark's sex symbol of the day. While wider recognition was hard to come by, Elliott's name or photograph often appeared in the *New Jersey Afro-American*, a black weekly, in columns written by editor Bob Queen, her upstairs neighbor on South Sixteenth Street.

In 1981, after eighty-five-year-old blues singer Alberta Hunter collapsed during a performance at the Cookery in lower Manhattan, Elliott became her replacement, supported on piano by Robert Banks and bass by Jimmy Lewis. *New York Times* critic John Wilson called Elliott an able choice to take over for Hunter, who was in the midst of a three-year run at Barney Josephson's University Place club. In his review, Wilson praised Elliott's renditions of Duke Ellington's *Mood Indigo* for its "calm, controlled projection," *Sophisticated Ladies* for its "warm serenity" and *It Don't Mean a Thing* for its "finger-snapping groove."

In later years, Elliott was in and out of Columbus Hospital in Newark. Ever strong and upbeat, she insisted on walking visitors to the elevator outside her room, even on the day before cancer finally claimed her life. I know because I was one of them.

Carrie Smith

Until she stole the show at the Nice International Jazz Festival in 1976, Carrie Smith's ability to mesmerize her audiences was a world-class secret. That changed at La Grande *Parade du Jazz* after she attracted crowds larger than superstar Sarah Vaughan. Describing

Smith as "the popular hit of the entire festival," one critic called her performance "spellbinding."

Heavily influenced by Mahalia Jackson and Bessie Smith (no relation), Smith possessed a wide-ranging repertoire and superb sense of showmanship. Tall and statuesque, she was in control of every note she sang, weaving in bits of blues and jazz history between numbers. Breaking into *Gimme a Pigfoot*, one of her idol Bessie Smith's signature songs, for example, she invited the crowd at Nice to "take a trip with me to Harlem," then transported her already-adoring audience to church with a reverent rendition of *Come Sunday*.

"I don't know where she's been or why she's taken so long to make her presence known, but Carrie Smith has arrived like a blast of tropical heat," critic Rex Reed wrote in the *New York Daily News* after hearing Smith sing. "It warmed the cockles of my heart just to be in the same room with her magnetic voice."

"Some enterprising European promoter ought to tour Miss Smith soon, before she becomes too expensive," another critic said. Someone did, which made Smith a headliner on the European jazz festival circuit for nearly thirty years.

While Smith's rich contralto evoked memories of blues empress Bessie Smith, her style was clearly her own. "She knows a great many of Bessie Smith's blues and other songs, but she is no imitator of the Empress," Eric Townsend wrote in *Jazz Journal*, a British publication. "There is some influence of Bessie, but what you hear is Carrie Smith, a really individual singer."

Born in Ft. Gaines, Georgia, a tiny town sixty miles south of Atlanta, Smith came from a musical family. "Both my mother and father sang and my uncle played the piano and taught me to sing," she said. By age seven she began singing at church. A year later her family moved to Bergen Street in Newark, where she attended Avon Avenue School. As a young woman, Smith joined Abyssinian Baptist Church on West Kinney Street in Newark, where she sang in the choir. "That's where we met," says the Rev. Charles Banks, then a musician at Abyssinian.

When Banks founded Greater Harvest Baptist Church at 15th Avenue and Hunterdon Street, Smith went with him. She also joined the highly regarded Back Home Choir formed by Banks and his brother, the late Bishop Jeff Banks. As a soloist, *I Want to Walk With Jesus* was her go-to hymn, a number she later recorded. As a Baptist preacher, Charles Banks saw nothing wrong with Smith singing the blues. "If I'm singing a love song to my girlfriend," he says, "I may sing Ray Charles' *I Can't Stop Loving You*. There is a time and place for everything."

Smith's career outside the church began developing in the late 1960s, when she moved to Las Vegas to act as a personal assistant to singer and actress Juanita Hall, who starred on Broadway in *South Pacific*. "One night Juanita let me sing in the lounge of the place where she was working. Because everyone received me so well, I got the idea that perhaps I could do this professionally," Smith said.

At the urging of WNJR disc jockey Mark Allen, who heard her sing at Greater Harvest, she was invited to present a gospel concert at Town Hall in New York City. That event led her to travel with ragtime piano player Big Tiny Little's band. Trumpeter Al Hirt hired her after hearing her sing with Little's band at his New Orleans nightclub. After spending nine years on the road, winning a raft of favorable reviews as her portfolio grew, Smith returned to New York, where she joined pianist Dick Hyman and the New York Jazz Repertory in *A Tribute to Louis Armstrong* at Carnegie Hall. After appearing at the Kennedy Center in Washington, D.C., for a salute to W.C. Handy, the father of the blues, she was off to the Soviet Union on a State Department tour.

Until she was discovered at Nice, Smith had not recorded. By festival's end, she had signed a contract for her first LP on the French Black and Blue Label, backed by Doc Cheatham, Vic Dickenson and Panama Francis. Several other albums followed. One of Smith's greatest thrills came when the city of Newark and county of Essex selected her as the first artist to appear in a series of "Celebrating the Arts in 1983" shows at Essex County College. "Believe me," Smith promised Mayor Sharpe James, "nobody is going to be disappointed." From the moment she arrived on stage, decked out in brilliant pink plumage topped by a feathery headdress, nobody was. From the opening note, she had the hometown crowd mesmerized.

In 1989, Smith co-starred on Broadway with Ruth Brown and Linda Hopkins in the award-winning musical revue *Black and Blue*. Set in the 1920s, the show also featured old-time dancers Bunny Briggs, Jimmy Slyde and Lon Chaney (the hoofer, not the actor), along with teenager Savion Glover. After *Black and Blue* closed in 1991, Smith traveled nonstop for several years, running from country to country and gig to gig. During the first half of 1994, for example, her schedule included concerts all over the United States, from Florida to Hawaii, as well as several trips to Europe. She even visited Lapland.

Throughout her career Smith was just as at home in small nightclub settings as she was singing to thousands of fans on a European hillside. "How many of you have had the blues?" she would ask before breaking into her foot-stomping, hand-clapping routine. In New York, she became a favorite at top spots including the Blue Note, Eddie Condon's, Michael's Pub and Sweetwater's. When Smith opened at Carlos I on Manhattan's East Side in the 1980s, her friend Eartha Kitt was in the audience. Months before, they had co-starred in *Blues in the Night*, a traveling show that played colleges and theaters all over the South. Clem Moorman, Smith's old friend from Newark, was the music director.

Closer to home, Smith played area clubs, including Trumpets in Montclair and the Priory in Newark. She also received the Carter G. Woodson Foundation Award for artistic excellence and commitment to her community. Smith's last performance was on September 4, 2004, at Essex County College, where she took part in *Newark Stars on Parade for Newark Students*, a benefit sponsored by the Friends of Barbara J. Kukla Scholarship Fund. She was in failing health, but no one would have guessed. The show was long and each performer, other than headliner Gloria Gaynor, had been asked to do one number only. But Smith's fans demanded an encore—and got it. She still knew how to captivate an audience.

Months later Smith entered the Actor's Equity Home in Englewood, New Jersey. Her only trip back to Newark came in September 2006 when singer Antoinette Montague, her friend and caregiver, presented a tribute to her at the Newark Museum, imploring Smith's fans to "show appreciation for a lady who has done her best to preserve America's authentic music." They complied, filling every seat in the museum's Billy Johnson Auditorium. Smith, in her Sunday best, sat up front, accepting the well-wishes of her friends and fans. The performers that day included Charles Banks and Robert Banks (no relation), poets/writers Amiri and Amina Baraka, singer Catherine Russell and her mother, bassist/singer Carline Ray, Smith's accompanist for many years; saxophonist Joe Thomas and singers Yvette Glover, Myrna Lake and Mable Lee (of Broadway's *Bubbling Brown Sugar*). Newark music educator Inez McClendon was the emcee.

After suffering several strokes and enduring various other ailments, Carrie Smith died on May 20, 2012. She was buried from Bethany Baptist Church in Newark, where the pastor, the Rev. M. William Howard Jr., gave the eulogy.

Eugene (Goldie) Goldston

Gene Goldston's music is all about the lyrics. Like Jimmy Scott and Nat King Cole, he's a balladeer, a romantic whose every word adds specific meaning to his songs. When he performs beautiful standards like *What Are You Doing the Rest of Your Life* or *You Don't Know What Love Is*, each word is delivered impeccably.

Goldston, who recently turned eighty but looks years younger, began singing with the well-known Hall Johnson Choir at Bethany Baptist Church when he was nine. As a teenager he returned to North Carolina, where he was born, to study music at Laurinberg Institute on a basketball scholarship. Upon his arrival, he began singing in the choir. Even then, his velvety baritone had a sultry, seductive quality to it. After graduating from Laurinberg, Goldston spent three semesters at North Carolina College before returning to Newark, marrying and spending two years in the Army (1953–55), part of that time in Germany. Upon his return to Newark, he worked at an ice cream factory, then got a job at City Hall after Kenneth Gibson became mayor.

Goldston began singing again in his late thirties. His first gig was at Mr. Wes's across the street from Hallmark House, where he lived. "When Bill Harris, an organist from East Orange, came in, he encouraged me to work there, too," he says. Chink Wing, a former big-band drummer, then the city's head of recreation, was another mentor, as was "Chops" Jones, a local musician who worked with Wing at City Hall.

Goldston also counts organist Big John Patton and saxophonists Gene Phipps Jr., Buddy Terry and Leo Johnson among his closest buddies. Early in his career, Johnson served as host for Wednesday night jam sessions at Mr. Wes's. "When Leo left, I took over," Goldston says. "I sang a lot of ballads because Wesley Weaver, who owned the place, loved Frank Sinatra. He was a Frank Sinatra freak."

Through the years Goldston sang at clubs along the Eastern Seaboard, but preferred sticking close to home. His smooth style and gracious way with a crowd made him a favorite performer and host at Sparky J's, Len & Len's, the Maize (at the Robert Treat Hotel) and Skipper's. One of his extended engagements was at the Renaissance Cafe on Mulberry Street, where singer Carrie Jackson did the booking. "(Pianist) Tomoko Ohno and I opened it up," he says. "We stayed there a year and a half."

In June 2008, Goldston began gigging at Skipper's. "By then, I had retired from it all," he says. "I was trying to enjoy my golden years when a friend introduced me to Greg Salandy, the owner, and Norman Mann, Greg's business partner." Before long, Goldston was back working again, singing and hosting Monday night jam sessions at Skipper's with Dave Braham on organ and Greg Bufford on drums. "When Dave found it difficult to get there because of other obligations, Radam Schwartz came in," he says. "When Greg moved to Finland (for a short stay), Victor Jones replaced him."

Goldston could have hung it up in the summer of 2012, when Skipper's closed, but decided to remain active because he was having so much fun. Since then, he's run weekly jams, with Schwartz on organ, at the Ideal Bar on Frelinghuysen Avenue in Newark.

7 ♪

The Organ Masters

Gettin' Funky

To me, guitar cuts through it all;
it carries more than organ. But organ
has got more guts. —Wes Montgomery

From the late 1920s through the early 1940s, Newark was what poet Amiri Baraka calls a "ticklers' town," home to piano players Donald Lambert and Willie "The Lion" Smith, who played a fast-paced style of music influenced by ragtime called stride. The city was, as well, a hangout for their competitors.

While Lambert, who spent the early part of his career in Newark, was reclusive, rarely straying from his permanent gig at Wallace's in Orange, Smith was a larger-than-life character who spoke Yiddish, traded barbs with customers, chomped on cigars and always wore a derby. Cutting contests—cut-throat competitions to determine who was best—often included Fats Waller, the crown prince of stride; Art Tatum, a blind musician from Ohio who made his mark in Harlem; and James P. Johnson from New Brunswick, whose mother taught him to play piano.

Smith's entry into the jazz world dates to 1920, when he was with Mamie Smith's Jazz Hounds, the band that made *Crazy Blues*, the first blues recording by a Negro singer with Negro accompaniment. Even after the fascination with stride piano faded in the 1940s, he continued performing.

Over the years, Newark also produced many talented piano players, including Jay "June" Cole, Corky Caldwell, Robert Banks, Duke Anderson, Bill Harris and Erskine Butterfield. Butterfield, who recorded on Decca and hosted a radio show on WOR in the early 1940s, was known as "The Singing Vagabond of the Keys."

By the 1960s, jazz organ was Newark's newest rage. According to organist Radam Schwartz, the Hammond organ became popular when Waller played an A100 on a late 1930s recording. In the 1940s the more complex B3 model began popping up on sessions like Jackie Davis's *Saturday Night Fish Fry*. By the mid-1950s so-called "organ rooms" proliferated in many parts of the United States, thanks to the pioneering efforts of Jimmy Smith, Richard "Groove" Holmes and Bill Doggett. In 1956, *Honky Tonk*, Doggett's huge hit, topped the charts.

By then, every city on the East Coast that had a sizable black population had at least one organ club. Newark's most popular spots were the Key Club and Sparky J's, which took over the old Cadillac Club at Halsey and William streets. From the 1950s on, the Key Club was "The Home of the Hammond B3 Organ," the spot where the best organists played, namely Smith, Holmes, Earland, Jimmy McGriff, Rhoda Scott, "Captain" Jack McDuff, Freddie Roach, Gloria Coleman, Grant Green, Dr. Lonnie Smith and Big John Patton.

Newark also was home to jazz-fusion innovator Larry Young Jr., an Arts High School graduate who recorded extensively on Prestige and Blue Note in the 1960s. Scott, who is still active in Europe, where she spent most of her career, remains hugely popular in Newark, where she made her mark early on. With Schwartz, Mel Davis, Dave Braham, Dan Kostelnik and Akiko Tsurga, she is among the most prominent Hammond B3 players active in the Newark area.

Jimmy McGriff

While many of his contemporaries were accompanied by drums and guitar only, Jimmy McGriff, the master of the funky blues, generally had a horn or two up front. As critics, including one from

Rochester concluded, he could get a "helluva lot of music out of his groups, making them sound like a much bigger band."

McGriff also loved promoting promising female saxophonists like Lilly White, who played with him from 1990–94, and Diane Ellis, who toured the West Coast with his band after graduating from Bradley University in Chicago in 1979. "When I met Jimmy, he was the headliner at the Apartment Lounge in Chicago," Ellis says. "I was his opening act, but he let me sit in because he liked my sound." Traveling from gig to gig with McGriff's band, often in a beat-up old blue van, was quite an experience, she says. "I was just a kid and there was a lot going on, so I was scared sometimes, but Jimmy always looked out for me. He was my protector and my mentor."

Born April 3, 1936, McGriff grew up in the Germantown section of Philadelphia. In 2008, after struggling for years with multiple sclerosis, he was buried there from the Harold Davis Memorial Baptist Church, where his mother was a member. In Newark, McGriff was a fixture at the Key Club, where he performed from the 1960s through the mid-1980s, and briefly ran a 350-seat supper club called the Golden Slipper.

On opening night at the Golden Slipper in November 1970, McGriff brought in three tenors, a trumpet, congas, drums, timbales and a rhythm section. Always a big thinker, he anticipated the day he would expand his business to Philadelphia, before moving on to Cleveland, Detroit and Chicago. He never got that chance because his Branford Place club, where he recorded *Black Pearl* and *Love Ain't Nothin' But a Business Goin' On* in 1971, went out of business a year later.

"Jimmy loved playing Newark," says Maxine Harvard, McGriff's manager for more than two decades. And Newark loved him back, packing every spot where he performed. One of his last gigs, after being stricken with MS, was at the Priory, where he tore up the house on his modified version of the Hammond B3, despite the limitations of his disease. Urged on by longtime fans, he offered up familiar tunes like *Teach Me Tonight* and *Lil Darlin'*, thrilled by his audience's response.

"Jimmy was just a sweet man," Harvard says. "He loved challenging his musicians and friends, but he was very kind to people. He cared about them and what happened to them. He was a man's man, who loved drinking beer and playing pool with his friends at a motorcycle club."

During his fifty-plus-year career in show business, McGriff performed throughout the United States and frequently toured Europe. As one of music's most prolific recording artists, he was a leader or sideman on more than 100 LPs, including *A Tribute to Count Basie*, *The Best of Hank Crawford and Jimmy McGriff* and *Let's Stay Together*, a jazz-funk interpretation of the theme from *Shaft*, the Isaac Hayes hit from the movie of the same name.

McGriff's first hit, *I've Got A Woman*, was an instrumental version of the Ray Charles chartbuster. Another LP, *About My Girl*, established him as "a fiery blues-based organist, well-versed in gospel and fatback groove," while *Blues for Mister Jimmy* made him "one of the finest examples of blues-based jazz."

One of four children of Beatrice and Harrell McGriff, James Harrell McGriff came from a musical family. His mother's cousin was saxophonist Benny Golson. Harold Melvin (of Blue Notes fame) was so close to the family he called McGriff's mother "Aunt Bea." "When my husband picked at the piano, Jimmy would join in," McGriff's mother says. "Before he could reach the pedals, he could play the organ. He could play a lot of other instruments—drums, vibraphone, saxophone and bass—but he liked the organ best."

Raised in church, McGriff attended services with his maternal grandparents as a boy. "When I couldn't go, I'd send him to Sunday school at the church next door to where we lived," his mother says. "It was so close to our house I could hear him when he played hymns for Sunday school classes." In his teens, McGriff began playing upright bass in clubs in South Philadelphia. "He was underage, but my husband and I knew nothing about it at first," says Mrs. McGriff, now in her mid-nineties. "Later on we'd go see him all the time. By then my husband was so proud his chest stuck out when Jimmy came around the corner."

After graduating from high school, McGriff completed a stint in the Army as a military police officer, then became a Philadelphia motorcycle cop. By then, his childhood friend Jimmy Smith was gaining notice on Blue Note. Intrigued, McGriff took up the Hammond B3 after another friend, "Groove" Holmes, played at his sister's wedding. After taking lessons from Holmes, he studied under the GI Bill at Juilliard and the McCombe School of Music in Manhattan. Privately, he came under the tutelage of Jimmy Smith, Milt Buckner and Sonny Gatewood. Anxious to create his own groove, McGriff followed a path pioneered by Holmes, modifying his B3 by adding synthesizers to incorporate the sounds of other instruments and tinkering with the speakers to obtain a fuller timbre.

During the 1970s McGriff produced some of his best work, namely *Stump Juice* (1975), *Red Beans* (1976) and *Outside Looking In* (1978). In between gigs in the United States, he was a favorite in Europe, where he often collaborated with Dr. Lonnie Smith as "The Organ Summit"—two organs backed by drums and a horn player. He also worked in a two-organ format with Jimmy Smith, touring the United States and Japan on the Philip Morris Jazz Tour.

But the East Coast was where his heart was, as he indicated after being honored on television by the New Jersey Division of Travel and Tourism. "New Jersey has always had a special warmth for me," he wrote in a letter of appreciation. "It was the place (Trenton), where I began my professional career and it seems to be the place where my music is especially well-received." At the time, he was trying to get *Jersey Bounce*, a tune written by Newark's Bobby Plater, adopted as the state song.

In the 1980s, McGriff brought saxophonist Hank Crawford into his band, drawing raves from coast to coast. "Musically, they were meant for each other," says guitarist Bob DeVos, who joined them in Los Angeles and came back to New Jersey, where he was from, with them. "Instead of one star, we had two," DeVos says. "Each of them had his own following." But DeVos never heard them speak a word to each other. "When Hank talked to me, Jimmy would listen in and vice versa. I was the middle man, but I never knew why."

"We worked all over the place," says drummer Don Williams, who traveled with McGriff on and off for forty years. "We played clubs and festivals all over the United States and in Europe, at places like Marian's in Switzerland and Ronnie Scott's in London. We also toured Japan for the Blue Note Series."

In his later years, McGriff's wife Margaret became his manager. Married in 1992, they had met twenty years before when she was a barmaid at the Golden Peacock on Clinton Avenue in Newark. "Jimmy used to practice there," his widow says. "One of the tunes he played was *The Worm*. It became the theme song for a movie called *The Rounders*, starring Matt Damon." Early in their marriage McGriff was diagnosed with MS, a debilitating disease that eventually affected his ability to work. But he kept playing, even after being confined to a wheelchair.

In 2005 he headlined an organ jam in his honor that attracted 1,200 music lovers to the African American Education and Cultural Center in downtown Newark. Sponsored by the city's Department of Recreation and Cultural Affairs and WBGO, the show featured many of McGriff's old friends, among them Dr. Lonnie Smith, Trudy Pitts, Gene Ludwig, Don Williams, David "Fathead" Newman and Houston Person. DeVos was the music director. "This concert is a gift to the people of Newark and to all who love jazz organ," the guitarist said at the time. "We are honored to pay tribute to Jimmy McGriff." Three years later, after spending his final days in a South Jersey nursing home, McGriff was gone. "Music was Jimmy's life," his wife says. "I think he just gave up once he couldn't play anymore."

Ellis, the saxophonist who toured with McGriff years before, was among those who played at a concert in his memory at his mother's church the night before his funeral. "From the time I was starting out, Jimmy and I remained friends," says Ellis, a Chicago teacher known as "Lil Sax." "When he came to town I'd go to hear him play. We'd go to dinner and hang out."

During the jam session at the church, Ellis and Chris Foreman, an organist whose sound often is compared to McGriff's, played several of McGriff's best-known tunes, including *Teach Me Tonight*, a staple wherever McGriff played. Months later, Don Williams led a second concert in McGriff's memory at the Priory. Ellis and Foreman flew in from Chicago for that one, too, joining guitarists Geary Moore and Eric Johnson on the bill. "Jimmy was a great bandleader," says Ellis. "To this day, I'm thankful to him for teaching me so much."

Rhoda Scott

Jazz organist Rhoda Scott has enjoyed a reputation as an international superstar since moving to France more than forty years ago, but she remains a hometown favorite in Newark, where she launched her career in the early 1960s. "Rhoda's just a phenomenal musician," says arts administrator Philip Thomas, who has presented Scott in concert at Newark Symphony Hall, where he was executive director, and at other spots around town. "She's a legend."

That's why more than 600 fans turned out for Jazz Vespers at Bethany Baptist Church in February 2013 to hear Scott play *Ebb Time* and other tunes she made famous at Newark clubs years ago. That April many of the same folks turned out at a jazz jam at Newark's Terrace Ballroom honoring Thomas. Scott was the star attraction. "She was the centerpiece," Thomas says.

That's the way it's been during the nearly four decades Scott commuted between Newark and France, where she settled in 1968 after marrying French actor and nightclub owner Raoul St. Ives. Scott first played Newark in 1959 with Joe Thomas and Bill Elliott at the old Key Club before becoming a favorite at the Playbill Lounge in Newark and the Peppermint Lounge in nearby Orange. "Being at those places in those days was like being at a big house party where everyone knew each other," says Sally Carroll, one of Newark's first black female police officers. "Newark was swinging, and everyone was like family."

"We were always there together—the bartenders, the music and the public," Scott says. "We always shared a certain convivial spirit."

That, and the energy she puts into her music, is what makes it party time every time she performs. "You can tell Rhoda's always having a ball," says Gladys Howell, a friend since childhood. "She enjoys being with her friends. Even when she had big engagements In Europe, she always brought her musicians over to play with her."

Born in 1938 in Dorothy, New Jersey, a speck on the map in Weymouth Township twenty-five miles west of Atlantic City, Scott was one of seven children of the Rev. Winfred Scott, an African Methodist Episcopal minister, and his wife, Amanda. "I was told I could reach up to the piano and replicate the songs I heard my mother play in church when I was very young," she says. But it was the organ, which she began playing when she was eight, that fascinated her. With the parsonage nearby, she got to practice whenever she wanted. "I didn't want to scratch the foot pedals, so I always took off my shoes and played barefooted," she says. That's the way it's been ever since.

As a child, Scott's world turned upside down when her mother died at thirty-eight. "My father promised my mother he would keep us together, and he did," she says. Keeping that promise, however, meant frequent moves until the family settled in Riverton, New Jersey, where her father served as pastor of Mt. Zion AME Church from 1955–59. By that time Scott was about to strike out on her own. "I think my style differs from other organists because of the influences I experienced throughout my life and the aesthetics I embraced," she says. "My mother played Hawaiian songs, my father classical music. Although blues and spiritually based, my music is more influenced by classical music."

Until his death years ago, Scott's father made education paramount in his children's lives. She and her siblings attended several schools as they moved from place to place in South Jersey, but that never hindered their ability to learn. Three of her brothers and sisters went on to earn doctorates, while she received a master's degree from the Manhattan School of Music and is about to complete her second master's degree in jazz history and research at Rutgers-Newark.

Scott's proclivity for popular music as a child came from listening to the radio. "When I was a kid, I could play all the soap opera themes," she says. She never learned to dance because she was always playing the latest hits at dances for her friends. At seventeen, she joined a band led by Lee Smith, a choir member at her church. After begging off at first, she took the gig. To her amazement, she knew all the standards the group played—blues, pop and Broadway tunes. Eventually, her repertoire grew to more than 1,000 songs, including her own compositions and arrangements.

Originally called Lee Smith's Satellites, Smith's band became Lee Smith's Hi-Larks after Larry O'Neal joined as vocalist. Scott was a two-fer. "Lee didn't have to hire a bass player because I played bass with my feet," she explains. Despite the Hi-Larks' popularity, Smith's weekday job at Campbell's Soup limited the band's ability to travel, which led Scott and O'Neal to form their own group. One of their first gigs was at the Hat Box in Elizabeth, where saxophonist Joe Thomas and drummer Bill Elliott came looking for a replacement for organist Dee Dee Ford. "I didn't want to leave my responsibilities with Larry," she says, "but we decided that I could learn a lot by working with musicians who had much more experience than I had."

Scott was twenty-one when the Rhoda Scott Trio, featuring Thomas and Elliott, first played the old Key Club in Newark. From the start, their trio was a hit. When the club moved downtown, patrons often lined up outside, waiting to get in. Once the barstools filled, the interior was standing room only. Just about everyone came to listen, Scott says. "There was a lot of sporting life and a lot of professional people. The Sunday matinee was an institution. All the church folks came out, including ladies who wore beautiful hats. Before going to their nighttime gigs, the musicians came by and sat in. When I run into George Benson nowadays he always tells me how he used to come to listen to me in Newark. Back then, Dionne Warwick, who wound up marrying Bill Elliott, our drummer, would come in from time to time and sing a few tunes with us."

Eventually Scott decided to further her studies at the Manhattan School of Music, playing solo gigs to pay her tuition. When one of her teachers suggested she study in Paris with Nadia Boulanger, whose protégés included Quincy Jones, she jumped at the chance. That experience, however, was hardly ideal. "She (Boulanger) was heavily into classical music and couldn't understand where I was coming from," Scott says. "To me, she was from another planet." What Scott did take away from their time together was a passionate approach to her music, the idea that each note should be played "as if it was the opening to a grand symphony."

During her time in France in 1967 Scott fell in love with the French culture and people. After returning in February 1968 at the invitation of record magnate Eddie Barclay, she met and married St. Ives. With her talent and his connections as a nightclub owner, her international career soared. Critics called Scott "a complete talent." Later in her career she began presenting concerts with Campanella, a vocal group backed by a 200-voice choir that sang songs such as *Steal Away* and *Down By the Riverside* in English.

"I didn't realize that Rhoda was such a star until I went to visit her when she was headlining a show in Paris at the Olympia," her friend Howell says. "It was a big to-do. Rhoda's dressing room was a two-room suite, and there were flowers and champagne all over the place. After the show, a long line of fans waited outside for autographs. Rhoda not only signed every one, she made a personal connection with every fan. That's just the way she is with everyone."

Sandy Ford, a friend from St. Mark AME Church in East Orange, met Scott when Scott became the church organist. "I was still at East Orange High School when Rhoda began taking me to Sunday matinees at the Playbill Lounge in Newark," Ford recounts. "She was awesome. I loved to hear her sing. Rhoda's always been the same since I was a child," Ford adds. "She's very caring, giving and compassionate. When my father died, she played at his funeral."

Scott's remained just as close with her musician friends. Drummer Victor Jones, a pioneer of acid rock, was a teenager when he traveled to Europe to accompany her the first time. Three years later, at twenty-two, he went with Stan Getz. When Scott played the Olympia in 2001, Joe Thomas was on stage beside her. Saxophonist Leo Johnson also recorded with her in France. For several years, drummer Steve Phillips accompanied her all over Europe. As one of the world's most prolific musicians, she's made more than 100 records, mostly on her friend Eddie Barclay's label.

Early in her career, Scott also played for birthday parties in Haiti when Jean-Claude "Baby Doc" Duvalier was in power. On one of the trips, she and her husband adopted two infants, a boy, Virgile, and a girl, Eugenie. Following her husband's death in 2008, she began spending more time in New Jersey after enrolling at Rutgers. She still spends summers and holidays in France, playing places like the Meridien Hotel in Paris and relishing her role as a grandmother. Whenever there's an organ jam in Newark, look around. Scott's apt to be there, too. If not, check her out at St. Mark AME Church, where she directs the Senior Inspirational Choir.

Larry Young Jr.

While critics often proclaim Larry Young Jr. the master of jazz fusion, opinion is divided as to whether Young played it because it came naturally or because he saw it as a path to commercial success.

Young's contemporaries, like Jack McDuff, who considered him the "Coltrane of the Organ," take the former view of his exploration of formerly uncharted musical territory. That's demonstrated by a story Rhoda Scott tells about the night the three of them played a Newport Jazz Festival gig at Carnegie Hall in New York. "While McDuff and I were waiting to play, we decided to have a drink at an outside bar," Scott recalls. "When a lot of people suddenly came rushing out of the hall, Jack wanted to know, 'Is there a fire or something?' The stage manager replied, 'No. It's Larry Young playing.' I think that was McDuff's way of saying that Larry was so far ahead of everybody no one understood him. People were waiting for the chitlin' and blues sound, and Larry had gone way beyond that."

Michael Cuscuna, founder and president of Mosaic Records, which reissued Young's complete works on Blue Note, sees things differently. "It was not in Larry's DNA to come up with fusion," says Cuscuna, a friend from the days when he was a college disc jockey in Philadelphia and Young was playing there in a trio. "I think he saw it as a way to be successful, that it came naturally to other guys, but deep down in his heart he knew what he was doing was contrived."

Whatever the case, Young was a musical genius, someone to be reckoned with when he played. "My father was untouchable, and he was feared," says Larry Young III. "Other musicians were afraid to take the bandstand when he was in the house. He was smooth and gifted, with a double-octave range in one hand that blew everyone else away."

Born October 7, 1940, in Newark, the same month and day as poet Amiri Baraka and drummer Jo Jones, Young was the son of Agnes McCoy and Larry Young Sr., who also played organ professionally. Young Sr. owned clubs in Newark, including the Parisian Lounge and Shindig, where Larry Jr. took up organ as a teenager and practiced incessantly at his father's insistence. After Young began playing with rhythm and blues bands at clubs in Newark and Elizabeth, he tacked "Jr." on to his name to distinguish himself from his father. Aside from their shared interest in music, father and son were two very different men. "Larry Jr. was just a big, jolly kid," says saxophonist Leo Johnson, "but his father was a demanding man." "My father had no childhood," says Larry Young III. "My grandfather was very controlling. He ruled with an iron hand. My father had to practice all the time. Practice and practice."

Pianist/organist Richie McCrae has similar recollections. "Larry taught me a lot, but his father didn't want him to teach anyone anything," says McCrae, who frequently visited the Young household on Clinton Avenue. "He was one mean sucker. But Larry Jr. was a great guy, a genius. He had excellent technical skills on the organ and was very creative. I loved to sit and hear him work things out."

Friends like McCrae also remember how Young's father refused to let him play sports at Arts High, despite his imposing size—six feet, six inches and packing more than 250 pounds. Instead, Larry Jr. immersed himself in his music, studying classical piano before turning his attention to jazz organ. Fortunately, he grew to love it.

Scott started hanging out with Young and his cousin, Jimmie Smith, who later played drums with Erroll Garner, after hearing Young play at the Savoy in Elizabeth. "He was fabulous, even though he was nineteen years old," she says. "He used to tease me about playing the pedals because he didn't use them that much." While organists like Jimmy Smith and Jimmy McGriff stuck to soul jazz, fusion became Young's bag. He played soul jazz, too, but his style gradually became more closely aligned with bebop than blues. "Once he hit the keyboards he was gone," says his son, who played bass with his father for the first time as a teenager at a spot called Bill's on Bergen Street in Newark. "I didn't know what he was doing, so I had to look to the guitarist for instruction. My father was playing fusion, and I was lost."

By the time Young signed with Prestige in 1960, he was pretty much a cult-like figure, gigging around Newark with friends Woody Shaw, Eddie Gladden and Buddy Terry. "We all grew up together and were associated with each other musically and personally all our lives," says Terry. "I was at South Side High, while Larry, Eddie and Woody were at Arts. The fact that all four of us were 'juniors'— Woody Shaw Jr., Eddie Gladden Jr., Larry Young Jr. and Edlin Terry Jr.—was another common bond."

While Young's unique gift was acknowledged worldwide, staying employed proved problematic, especially as his style became more ethereal. "Gloria Coleman tried to get him a gig at the Key Club but was told his style was too far out," organist Radam Schwartz recalls. By the time Terry, Shaw, Gladden and Young collaborated on *Natural Soul* in 1968, Young had a string of LPs to his credit. The one best known was *Unity*, written by Woody Shaw and recorded on Blue Note in 1964 with Shaw, Elvin Jones and the front line of Horace

Silver's band. Critics hailed it as one of the finest jazz albums ever, a prelude to *DownBeat* naming Young a Talent Deserving Greater Recognition on Organ two years later.

Early in his career Young also recorded with Shaw in Europe. He later made six albums as a leader on Blue Note, after recording on Prestige with tenor saxophonist Jimmy Forrest, best known for his No. 1 hit *Night Train*. Somewhere along the way, he changed his name to Khalid Yasin, which he used on some of his recordings. His credits as a sideman include his work with Jimi Hendrix on *Nine to the Universe*, a jam session released after Hendrix's death in 1970, and *Bitches Brew* with Miles Davis (1969). With guitarist John McLaughlin and drummer Tony Williams, Young also was responsible for some of the earliest fusion experiments, unique for their heavy percussive emphasis and use of guitar and synthesizer-like effects. *Love, Devotion, Surrender* (Columbia, 1972) is a prime example.

After working with McLaughlin and Williams on various projects through the mid-1970s, Young joined drummer Lennie White's group and recorded an album called *Spaceball*, featuring Larry Coryell, on Arista in 1976. When it didn't sell, he was hugely disappointed, faulting Arista for failing to promote it properly. Demetrius Jones, who owns a salon in South Orange, was one of Young's friends who thought he deserved better. "Larry was the absolute master of the organ," Jones says, "yet he never reaped the rewards lesser musicians enjoy."

Jones, who came to Newark from Harrisburg, Pennsylvania, met Young there one night at a club on the Chitlin' Circuit. "The first time I heard Larry play, it was so intense I wound up walking out," he recalls. "He made me realize what you can do with sound—how it can take your mind and body anywhere you want it to go. After I moved to Newark, our friendship developed and I became Larry's chauffeur. We went everywhere together. He was a very lovable guy, talkative, yet soft-spoken, not boisterous."

Just about everyone who knew Young loved him, yet tales about his increasingly strange behavior abound. "I can remember when the door opened one night while I was playing at the Cadillac Club and this huge guy wearing a turban—before Lonnie Smith—came in," says guitarist Bob DeVos. "It was Larry. I was in awe, inspired to be playing in the same room with him." One of the weirdest tales comes from organist Robert Banks who remembers seeing Young dressed in a hooded robe while standing on a hill in Central Park in New York for hours on end. "He just stood there doing nothing from early in the morning until the early afternoon," Banks recalls. "He was just out there—way out there."

"A lot of guys were fighting demons," Young's son says when asked about these incidents. "I think he just went wild from being underneath his father so much. Take the drugs away and he was a gentle giant, a very reticent man who was always smiling." More than thirty years after his death, questions about the circumstances surrounding it remain unanswered. "My father had been missing for two days when he was found under a tree in Orange Park," Larry III says. "His ID and a check from Warner Brothers, an advance to go to California and record again, were gone."

Young was just thirty-seven when he died. The official cause was pneumonia, but his son still questions the circumstances. Meanwhile, Larry Young III, who served twenty one years in the Navy and works in information technology, has established a website in his father's honor. For a short time, he also ran Larry Young's, a club on Branford Place in Newark. "I don't mind when people argue whether my father was the greatest organist ever," he says. "I'm just proud that his work is remembered." It is, through Young's recordings and, most recently his induction in 2009 into the Jazz Organ Hall of Fame with Fats Waller, Wild Bill Davis and Jimmy Smith. Rhoda Scott, who was honored at the ceremony, told the audience, "I knew them (the honorees). We met together in organ battles. We exchanged feelings and sounds and gimmicks. We loved to play together." Asked afterward about Young, she said: "Larry was a sweet soul. He was so humble one had to wonder if he realized how great he was."

Radam Schwartz

When other jazz organists were performing at the Key Club in the early 1980s, Radam Schwartz was often across the street at Sparky's J's playing piano with saxophonist Jimmy Ford. Today he is one of the few full-time organists on the Newark scene. From 2008 until its closing in mid-2012, Schwartz led the Sunday jazz sessions at Skipper's. More recently, he's worked weekly jam sessions with singer Eugene Goldston at the Ideal Bar.

"I've never worked alone," Schwartz says. "I've always been a sideman." He's also a much-in-demand accompanist for singers including Pat Tandy, Cynthia Holiday and Carrie Jackson, and a jazz historian, having earned a master's degree in jazz history and research from Rutgers University in 2012. The theme for his dissertation was the history of jazz organ, a review of various styles from the 1950s on.

Schwartz was playing piano when he joined Ford's group at Midas Gold in Newark in 1977. Until then, he had been playing with Ford and other bands in the New Brunswick area. Born in New York City, he grew up in Brooklyn and Queens. In his youth he studied clarinet and saxophone, then doubled on sax and organ in a school band called Quince Honey. "I was playing a Farfisa, a cheap version of the Hammond B3," he recounts. "I paid $90 for it, including the speakers."

Schwartz had little interest in jazz until he began listening to Miles Davis with a friend. "I also remember listening to Paul Quinichette on an LP in my uncle's collection," he says, "but I didn't think much of it. I was into more modern stuff." After graduating from Rosedale High School in 1971 he enrolled at Long Island University and started going to jam sessions in Brooklyn and other places that had jazz. Despite his increasing interest in playing keyboards, he had no formal training on organ or piano until he won a scholarship for a summer session at the Berklee College of Music in Boston. "LIU had no jazz program, so I decided to stay in Boston and enroll at Berklee for another semester," he says. He wound up working odds jobs, including one at a vegetarian restaurant, while playing in area bands.

After returning home, Schwartz was accepted at Hofstra University, where he completed his bachelor of arts degree in 1974. "I was a liberal arts major, but I also took a course in composition with Ellie Seigmeister, a highly regarded classical composer," he says. While at Hofstra, he became serious about becoming a jazz musician and wrote his first tune, *Old Shoes*, one he still plays.

After earning his college degree Schwartz moved to a loft on Chambers Street in Greenwich Village where he worked as an elevator operator between gigs. In the late 1970s, he moved to New Brunswick, New Jersey, to study piano with Kenny Barron and composition with Robert Moevs at Rutgers. "I was playing with the Neo Bop Crisis Committee at a street fair in New Brunswick when I met Jimmy Ford," he recounts. "Jimmy's group was the act before us. I thought they could really swing." Ford, a Swing Era veteran of Jimmie Lunceford's orchestra, liked what he heard, too, and invited Schwartz to join his group. "We played a lot of black-owned clubs along the East Coast and for dances sponsored by groups like the Masons and Elks," Schwartz says. When Ford began playing in Newark, Schwartz went with him. "Midas Gold was our regular spot," he says. "It was a hangout for cops, so we always had a good audience. We also played for dances at the Terrace Ballroom (in Newark) and the Coronet Ballroom (in Irvington)."

Schwartz soon began studying jazz piano with Duke Anderson and playing with Anderson's New Jersey State Contemporary Orchestra on a grant from the National Education Association. "Duke's gigs were a mix of Swing Era and bebop tunes," he says. "It was a great experience because I got to play with guys like (saxophonist) Jimmy Anderson, (trombonist) Grachan Moncur III and (trumpeter) Leslie Ford. Thanks to saxophonist Harold Van Pelt, we had superb arrangements. Harold was the one who got me into Sparky J's. We played there three or four times a week—Tuesdays through Thursdays and for Sunday jam sessions. All the cats, like (drummer) Eddie Gladden and (pianist) Mickey Tucker, sat in. On our breaks, I would go over to the Key Club, but I wasn't playing organ yet. I was still playing piano."

Schwartz rekindled his interest in jazz organ in the early 1980s at a jam session Tucker led at Cheryl's on Central Avenue. "Mickey invited me up to play the Hammond B3, but I didn't know anything about it, so I kept hitting wrong notes," he recalls. "The whole time Leo Johnson and Eddie Crawford, who were playing with Mickey, were laughing at me." Soon after, he began hanging out at organ sessions, bought a portable organ called the Viscount and began gigging with Johnson at Mr. Wes's. That led to a Monday night job with trumpeter Charlie Mason and Crawford at El C's in East Orange.

On weekends, Schwartz played at the Jersey Shore with pianist Alan Watson. Chico Rouse and Tommy Lavella, who toured nationally with organist Charles Earland, also were in the band. "Here I was playing with guys who were associated with one of the greatest B3 players of the era (Earland), when I hardly knew anything," Schwartz says. But he was getting there. While working in Newark with the husband-wife team of Don Williams and Lady CiCi, he met Arthur Prysock. At the time Williams was Prysock's drummer. "Arthur hired me after I auditioned for him at Fat Tuesday's," Schwartz recalls. "I spent the next eighteen months traveling with him all over the country. Because he sang ballads, I had to learn the bass pedals."

In 1986, Schwartz met Tandy while playing with Jimmy Anderson at Jackson's Manor in Jersey City. They've been working together ever since, performing on cruises and at clubs along the Eastern Seaboard. "Pat's a jazz singer, but she can sing anything—from the blues to show tunes—whatever the audience wants," he says. "She's got great intonations and a great repertoire."

From 1986–97, Schwartz led the house band at the Peppermint Lounge with drummer Don Williams and guitarist Geary Moore. From 2008–12, he led the Sunday matinees and Monday night jam sessions at Skipper's. For more than fifteen years, he's also been part of the Tuesday night jam sessions at Crossroads in Garwood.

Schwartz supplements his income by teaching organ and piano and accompanying singers like Cynthia Holiday with whom he made a CD; Yvette Glover and Carrie Jackson. He's also toured with Della Griffin, Irene Reid and Eddie "Lockjaw" Davis and led his own band. From 1996 to 2006 he was with the CB3 Band, led by drummer Cecil Brooks III. Schwartz also has hit the national charts as a leader, most notably with *Blues Citizens* on Savant, which reached No. 9. His current group is Conspiracy for Positivity.

Today, Schwartz is a much-in-demand musician despite a diminishing market and a changing atmosphere for aspiring musicians. "Many of my students have never visited a club," he says. "All they want to know is how to get into a college classroom. That's changed the entire tableau. How can they become jazz musicians if they've never set foot on a bandstand?"

Dave Braham

Jazz organist Dave Braham has done it all—toured with Houston Person and Etta Jones, played locally with Don Williams and Lady CiCi, led his own groups, including a Latin jazz band, and taught music to thousands of elementary school students.

While Braham has fond remembrances of his days on the road, he was never enamored of the daily grind that goes with traveling from city to city year after year. For a while it was fun, he says, but eventually he became bored. "How much TV can you watch?" How many novels can you read? We worked nights, so there was nothing much to do all day."

And so he turned to teaching full time and performing on nights and weekends, not just for the financial security but to improve his lifestyle. "I was working all the time," he says, "but I wanted to teach—something else I loved." And so, he says, he's had the best of two worlds, teaching elementary school music for the past twenty years in Orange, East Orange, Newark and Union Township by day and playing professionally after school hours. "This way, I get to spend time with my family as well as play and teach music."

Born in Uniontown, Pennsylvania, not far from Pittsburgh, Braham began playing trumpet, guitar and piano in elementary school. At thirteen, he joined a pop band and expanded his musical interests to the organ. As his interest in music grew, he began haunting bars and clubs in black neighborhoods around Pittsburgh on a circuit that brought organists like Jack McDuff, "Groove" Holmes and Gene Ludwig to town. "There were a lot of playing opportunities," he says, "even for an underage, self-taught teenager."

Before long, Braham had a gig every Friday night, which got him ejected from the marching band at South Uniontown High School. "I was missing practices because I got home so late and didn't have time to rehearse," he explains. After earning a degree in music education at Penn State in 1976, Braham taught for a year, then became a full-time musician, attracted by the chance to make a living playing organ. Work was plentiful in Pittsburgh, where he lived for four years, as it was after he moved to New Jersey in 1982.

Braham's bags were barely unpacked when blues singer Irene Reid hired him to accompany her four nights a week at a club in Harlem. Encouraged by saxophonist Billy Phipps, Braham also became a regular at weekly jam sessions in Newark at El C's. Phipps also introduced him to pianist Corky Caldwell, who was playing with Lady CiCi and Williams. "I began subbing for Corky, then took over his spot when he left their band," he says. It marked the beginning of a thirty-year-plus association that included guitarist Geary Moore as the band's original guitarist.

"We've worked together since Dave came off the road with Houston and Etta," says Lady CiCi (Cheryl Williams). "Dave's not only an incredible organist and keyboard player—pianist too—he's what I call a singer's accompanist. Instead of running away with a tune, he provides the structure, the tempo, coloring and style the singer wants." Her husband, drummer Don Williams, describes Braham as a musician who is "easy and comfortable to work with" and possesses a vast musical repertoire. Braham feels the same way. "After working together for so long, we don't even have to say much to each other," he says. 'We just get out there and do our thing."

Working with Person and Jones was just as enjoyable, he says. "Houston is one of the greatest musicians I've ever worked with, and Etta one of the greatest jazz singers of all times, even though she didn't seem to know it. She was that humble." Nevertheless, he tired of traveling. "I loved what I was doing, but it was a constant scramble to keep working," he explains. "Houston was especially adept at finding new gigs. Sometimes he'd spend the entire day on the phone, calling ahead to promote the band. But that wasn't for me."

Braham's first teaching job after leaving music full time was in Orange, where he taught for two years before moving to the East Orange school system for the next five years. In Newark, his first job, which he found "very rewarding," was at George Washington Carver School, where he taught the fourth through eighth grades. His transfer to Arts High School in 2005 was a different story. "I wanted to teach instrumental music, but those spots were filled," he explains. "They already had a band director, so I wound up teaching classes like music appreciation, which was not for me."

Braham gave it a go for two years, then took a job in nearby Union Township, where he teaches all fifth-grade students before they move on to middle school. It's an ideal situation, he says, especially because he loves working with low-income children. "Union isn't as big as Newark," he says, "but there are a lot of similarities in the student population. Most of my students are black and come from poor or low-income families. It's important for kids to have music in their lives and to make music of their own because it's such a satisfying thing. It's fundamental to American life."

Outside the classroom Braham performs locally, mostly with Jazz Just-Us at places like the Priory. He also was a regular at Skipper's, where he led weekly jam sessions. Like his students he always is learning, having taken up Latin jazz in recent years. "My friend Willie Rodriguez wanted to learn piano, so we traded lessons," he explains. That led to the formation of a Latin jazz band. "For a time, while Latin jazz was hot, we played weekly at area clubs," he says. Recently he began playing on Tuesday nights at SuzyQue's in West Orange with drummer Greg Bufford.

8 ♪

All in the Family
Jazz Is Their Thang

*All ensemble music is enriched by a close
collaboration between, and familiarity
among, players. —Goerie.com*

If families that pray together stay together, what about families
that make music together? In Newark, that means jazz artists like
The Gordons, a 1950s singing group composed of George Gordon
and his children, and the husband-wife teams of Don Williams and
Lady CiCi and Bob Ackerman and Pam Purvis. "Music was the *most*
important thing in our lives," says Honi Gordon, who began singing professionally with her brothers at twelve and still performs
occasionally. "Our family's love of music made us closer. Starting
with The Gordons, here's a look at how their love of all things musical has shaped the lives and relationships of these three families.

The Gordons

Honi Gordon and her brothers, Richard and George Jr., were in elementary school when their father, a gifted composer and lyricist
who wrote much of their material, brought them to New York to
record for the first time. By the time Honi was in her early teens,
The Gordons, as they were known, were seasoned performers, having collaborated with many of the top names in jazz.

As a master musician, George Gordon Sr. had many friends in the music business, including Dizzy Gillespie, Charles Mingus and legendary jazz pianist Mary Lou Williams, who frequently visited the family's home on South Seventh Street in Newark. "They were just my father's friends," Honi says. "Singing was just something we all did. When musicians like James Moody and Babs Gonzalez needed a place to stay, they came to live with us." Gonzalez, who was down and out during one stay, was forever thankful, sending George Gordon a note that read in part: "I want to thank you and Mert (Gordon's wife Meredith) for letting me stay with you in January and February. There are not many people left that help people when they're broke but trying."

George Gordon's decision to have his children sing bebop at an age when their peers barely knew a tune or two, was unheard of at the time. So was scatting their way through the tunes he wrote for them to sing. Honi was fourteen in 1952, when she and her brothers made their first LP with Mingus on Debut, a small independent label. It was so well-received they were invited to work with scat singer Eddie Jefferson. During that period, they also worked with Gillespie, Williams and Lionel Hampton.

When The Gordons broke up a few years later, Honi kept recording with her father's friends. On *Honi Gordon Sings*, her only solo LP, she was backed by the eclectic Jaki Byard on piano and George Duvivier on bass. Recorded in 1962 on Prestige, the album leads off with her improvisation of *Strollin'*, one of her father's best-known compositions. "It takes an exceptional singer to perform such material," Sidney Falco wrote in the liner notes. "This is Miss Gordon's first LP and her first recording outside the context of the family vocal group. And it seems to me that one of the most pertinent things to say about the recording is that it is courageous. She presented each song with the poised assurance that can only come from a complete grasp of the craft."

For whatever reasons, and there are probably many, Honi Gordon's album never went far. After its release, she never recorded again, despite assurances from Prestige that she was star material.

At twenty-four she "retired" from the recording industry. Instead of hanging it up completely, she kept singing, appearing everywhere from Carnegie Hall to St. Peter's Lutheran Church, which serves New York's jazz community. Her father often accompanied her until his death in the mid-1980s.

Honi Gordon never became famous, but the critics loved her. "She knocked my socks off when a friend dragged me to Jazz Vespers at St. Peter's," one of them said after she appeared there in the early 1970s, calling her "supremely gifted." Soon after, she appeared at Carnegie Hall and at an Easter Sunday concert with Duke Ellington and his Big Band Orchestra at Symphony Hall in Newark. The money wasn't bad—$150 for the Carnegie Hall gig—but hardly enough to make a living on, so she became a graphic designer at Bamberger's after studying art at Arts High School, and continued singing during off-hours.

From the 1970s on, she was closely associated with *Mary Lou's Mass*, the sacred concerto written by Mary Lou Williams. When Williams performed her critically acclaimed piece, Honi often shared the bill. Those performances throughout the New York area came to an end when Williams died in 1981. Thirty years later, Honi sang part of the *Mass* at Fordham University, when Geri Allen reprised Williams' role on piano. Although her career has slowed in the ensuing years, she sings from time to time at civic and social events and at Memorial West Presbyterian Church in Newark, where she's been a member for many years. Whenever she performs, she brings down the house.

Lady CiCi and Don Williams

Whenever Lady CiCi sings, someone is sure to request *At Last*, an audience favorite she belts with the best of them. That includes Etta James, whose version made the tune one of the most popular hits of all times. Like James, CiCi—real name Cheryl Williams—has a big voice, though she's also prone to sing richly textured ballads like *Misty*.

CiCi started singing in school and church choruses, but didn't perform professionally until her children were old enough to leave home alone at night. By then, she had graduated from Fairleigh Dickinson University and was teaching sixth grade at Nassau School in East Orange. Lionel Richie was her inspiration. "When I heard him sing *Easy Like a Sunday Morning* one night in 1977, I had an epiphany," she says. "The lyrics touched me so deeply I decided to pursue a career in music."

CiCi's first stop was the Peppermint Lounge in Orange, where she began hanging out at Monday night jam sessions. "At first, I just watched and listened," she says. "When I finally got up enough nerve to sing, I asked Calvin Ridley, the bass player, what to do and he told me to speak to Bill Harris, the band leader." Harris graciously invited her to the bandstand, where she sang *Days of Wine and Roses*. "When Bill asked me for a key, I had no idea what to say," she remembers. "But he saw that I was serious and helped me."

Before long, she was a jam session regular, so well-received that saxophonist Coy Shockley suggested she take lessons with composer and arranger Duke Anderson. "I studied with Duke for about a year, then went with Corky Caldwell," she notes. "I learned so much I used to say I was studying at the Duke Anderson and Corky Caldwell academies of music."

In 1978, her life changed forever when she met drummer Don Williams, her husband-to-be. "We just hit it off and have been together ever since," she says. By then, she had played her first professional gig with saxophonist Jimmy Ford at the Pines Manor in Edison and had sung at private parties with Anderson and Caldwell. Soon after, she began working with trumpeter Billy Ford. "I had the chance to go to Europe with Billy's band, but I didn't want to give up teaching, so I passed it up and decided to wait for another opportunity to go," she says. By then her growing repertoire included jazzed-up versions of *Summertime* and *This Can't Be Love*, tunes she still sings.

By 1979, she and Don Williams, who led the house band at Midas Gold, were a team. When he left town to tour Europe with Arthur

Prysock—a gig that lasted fifteen years on and off—she took over for him, performing as Lady CiCi and Company with Caldwell on piano and Geary Moore on guitar. While she held the fort at home, Don Williams crisscrossed Europe with Prysock and organist Jimmy McGriff. She was still teaching but had a reputation by then as a much-in-demand singer at clubs all over Newark, performing on weekends at spots like Sparky J's, the Club Eleganza, Mr. Wes's and the Playbill Lounge.

"In 1982, Don and I formed our own group, Jazz Just-Us, with our friends Dave Braham on organ and Geary Moore on guitar," CiCi says. "Then, in the mid-1980s, I began traveling with Don, opening shows for Arthur and Jimmy." That eventually led her to tour Europe. "In 1992, we (Jazz Just-Us) followed Arthur into the Hillside Inn, a resort in the Poconos. Not only was it a great gig, it lasted until they closed the place ten years later."

Williams, which may surprise his fans, started his musical career as a tap dancer, not as a drummer, the instrument for which he became well-known. "I was two years old when I started dancing and good enough at it for my mother to enroll me at the Joe Michaels Dance School at the Mosque," he says. "In those days, Michaels had a TV show on Channel 13. One of my partners, Reggie Williams, and I appeared on it and in dance recitals for several years. We called ourselves the Williams Brothers."

Williams' interest in playing a musical instrument was piqued at Newark's Broadway Junior High School. "I auditioned to play trumpet in the school band, but didn't make it," he recalls. "Another opportunity came along when Mr. Schwartz, my teacher, encouraged me to play drums for the Variety Club. I always loved watching the Masonic Drum and Bugle Corps march up Prince Street when I was a kid, so I tried out and became a member." From day one, playing drums was his passion. "But I was fourteen when I started out—old for a drummer," he says. "Other kids had been playing since they were eight. I had to quickly learn what they already knew."

Fortunately, he was a quick study. Although he had no drum set at home, he practiced incessantly on a drum pad, a piece of wood covered with a thick rubber cover. "I learned all I could by watching other drummers on TV," he notes. His hard work paid off. Within six months, he was good enough to play in the school band and orchestra. "We'd play John Philip Sousa songs when the kids marched in for Friday assemblies, and we performed in scaled-down musicals like *Oklahoma*."

Williams wanted to go to Arts High School after graduating from Broadway Junior High, but missed the audition when his grandfather died and his family went south for the funeral. After attending Central High School for a year, he tried out again at Arts and was accepted. "In those days you had to maintain a B average or get kicked out of school," he says. "Thankfully, I had a smart sister who helped me with my homework."

A year after graduating from Arts, nineteen-year-old Williams was drafted by the Army and sent first to Vietnam and then to Okinawa, where he attended ordinance supply school. "Until then, I hadn't done anything professionally," he says. "Then I began performing with a band that played three nights a week at the Officers' Club. All of us were making more money playing music than we were paid by the Army."

After returning home, he got a job at Marlo's, a bar on Lyons Avenue in Irvington, where he played with a group led by Tom Campbell, his sister's boyfriend at the time. "I always say that my friend Bob Stewart, our saxophonist, put me on the map," he says. "Bob was the one who introduced me to Jimmy McGriff. (Drummer) Eddie Crawford asked me to sit in for him one night when he and McGriff were playing at the Golden Peacock on Clinton Avenue. I wound up playing the whole night."

Williams began touring the United States with McGriff in late 1969. "I was with Jimmy on and off for forty years, until just before he died," he says. In later years, saxophonist Hank Crawford also was in the group. "We had some wonderful years together. Some of my clearest memories include the gigs we played at clubs in Austria, as well as the Umbria and North Sea jazz festivals. Sometimes, when we played the Key Club and Playbill Lounge at home, it was almost spiritual. That didn't happen every night, but every so often we hit another level. It was awesome."

Williams also led weekly jams sessions at the Peppermint Lounge for several years. After the club folded, he and Radam Schwartz, who took over for him while he was on the road, moved the sessions to Crossroads in Garwood. He also sings occasionally. "I used to sing as a kid when I was tap dancing," he says. "Dave Braham, our organist with Jazz Just-Us, started me singing again. I just try to have fun and not goof it up."

"Don loves to have a good time," says singer Yvette Glover. "There's a certain charm about his singing." Audiences also can count on Williams to lob a few jokes his wife's way when they perform. "I love doing things like calling CiCi 'Ida Mae,'" he says, chuckling at the thought. "It's all impromptu," CiCi adds. "Don always catches me off guard, so I just follow his lead."

Pam Purvis and Bob Ackerman

Pam Purvis was totally into theater as a college student at North Texas State in the 1960s. Although she had sung in her high school chorus, the stage was her consuming interest. All that changed after she won a full scholarship to the American Academy of Dramatic Arts in New York and began taking singing lessons with one of her professors. That inspired her to become a singer.

Purvis's first gig was as a singing waitress during her student days at a place in Manhattan called Hilly's. "It was a great job," she says. Not only did she meet future celebrities Bette Midler and Steve Martin, she also got a chance to sing a tune or two every night. "One night," she explains, "a woman came in and sang *When Sunny Gets Blue*. That was my first encounter with a real jazz singer, and I was mesmerized." Ironically, although she never learned the woman's name or saw her again, she became a jazz singer.

After graduating from the academy in 1969, Purvis landed a singing waitress job in Dallas (her hometown), which gave her the chance to perform with professional musicians for the first time.

"Before long, I was hanging out with Dwight Conyers, the guitarist, and learning the Great American Songbook," she says. She also began sitting in at the King's Club in the old Adolphus Hotel, one of the fanciest spots in town. After being hired at King's and working there for eighteen months, she spent a year on the road with a pop/cover band that traveled all over the South, then came north again to tour the Northeast with another band. "We were doing tunes like *The Lady is a Tramp* and *Foggy Day*," she notes, "but occasionally I'd sing a jazz song like *Misty*. Once I got the bug, I loved it."

Soon after her return to the New York area in 1974, Purvis got a Wednesday night gig at Gulliver's, the once-famous West Paterson, New Jersey, jazz club run by Amos Kuane. Backed by Jim DeAngelis, Ron Naspo and Gene Favatella, she was a hit from day one, especially with Bob Ackerman, the Irvington-born saxophonist who was in the audience most nights after playing in the orchestra at the Paper Mill Playhouse. Purvis didn't know it, but Ackerman wanted to ask her out. Nor did he know she was just as interested in him. But she was. So she took the initiative and invited him to meet her one night at the Village Vanguard to hear Elvin Jones. "I fell in love with Bob that night," she says. "We didn't even drive to New York in the same car, but after the show we met at the Riverboat Café and talked to five in the morning." Six months later they became partners for life, musically as well as personally. With their Blue Skies band, they have been a fixture on the New York–New Jersey club scene ever since, playing places such as the Blue Note in Manhattan along with many jazz clubs in the Newark area. Their longest gig, which lasted more than four years, was at the Headquarters Hotel in Morristown.

Ackerman's love of music, both jazz and the classics, dates to his childhood. "I loved listening to Louis Armstrong, Bessie Smith and a lot of classical music on the old Victrola my grandmother had in her basement," he recalls. "Her sister, my aunt, was a big jazz fan. By the time I was ten, she'd taken me to Jazz at the Philharmonic. By then I'd also seen all the big bands, including Basie and Ellington." Somewhere along the way, his aunt also bought him a piano.

Ackerman began studying alto saxophone as a fifth-grader at Union Avenue School in Irvington. "The music director taught me to read music, and I was very good at it," he says. "I went through all the books right away." By the time the spring concert rolled around, he was featured on *Saxophobia*, what he calls "a real Paul Whiteman-style tune."

By then Ackerman also was into bebop. "The father of a friend who played drums hipped me to it when I was about nine," he notes. "I can remember having a lot of friction at home when my parents found out that the music I liked was played mostly by black guys." By the time Ackerman was thirteen, he was playing with the Irvington Symphony Orchestra and had formed his own trio and big band. "I remember a jazz band coming to my school," he says. "There were a lot of community activities then that have fallen by the wayside. Now, there are no music classes, and kids are left to hang on the streets."

While at Irvington High School, Ackerman began working two and three nights a week at area bars. "I was underage and paid under the table," he recalls. "My parents had no idea what I was doing." One of his fondest memories is the night in 1957 when he was working at Johnny Capo's around the corner from the Mosque. "Around 11 p.m., the door opened and in came all the guys who were part of Art Ford's jazz band at the theater—Gene Krupa, Lester Young, Ben Webster, Coleman Hawkins, Roy Eldridge and Count Basie. Billie Holiday, too. They were all drinking at the bar and partying, but I was too shy to go over and talk." Around the same time he got to play with Cozy Cole, the famous jazz drummer, at a gig in the Bronx and trumpeter Chet Baker "somewhere in Newark." Still a kid, Ackerman also was hanging out at places like Sugar Hill, where he saw Art Blakey, Mary Lou Williams and Dizzy Gillespie's Big Band.

While studying classical flute at Montclair State College, Ackerman continued gigging in and around Newark. During the summers he played at spots in the Catskills with pianist Horace Parlan. As a college student he also performed in the Paper Mill Playhouse orchestra for a year. Later, he earned a master's degree in music education at Columbia University.

Following their marriage in the fall of 1975, the Ackermans spent the next three years on the road, playing clubs and hotels throughout the Midwest and South. "That's when Pam began playing keyboards," he says. "I taught her the bass parts, so I could fill in on horns. It also helped her with her vocals." In the mid-1980s, while living in Dallas, the couple spent three months each year touring Europe. At home, they played with quintets in the Dallas area. "We came back to New Jersey in 1986 because we had a recording contract with Black Hawk," Ackerman says. "It wasn't our first LP, but *Heart Song* was the first one we made on a major label. I wrote the compositions and words that Pam sang."

Over the years the couple became entrenched in the Newark-area jazz scene, playing at Gulliver's, the Maize at the Robert Treat Hotel, the Priory and the Headquarters Hotel. "Unfortunately, we returned to New Jersey when many of the clubs were closing down and work was less plentiful," Purvis says. "But we were lucky because Bob's saxophone repair business took off. That allowed us to buy a house on McGotty Place in Irvington, next door to the house he grew up in." In mid-2012, the couple moved to Bethlehem, Pennsylvania, where Ackerman still runs his business and Purvis gives piano lessons. They continue to perform in New Jersey and Pennsylvania.

9 ♪

The Saxophonists

Wailin' in Sax City

I always think of music as interior decoration.
So, if you have all kinds of music, you are
fully decorated. —Wayne Shorter

Newark has a reputation as a city that's produced an inordinate number of piano and organ players. Rarely, however, has it been acknowledged as "Sax City," even though it has been home to many gifted saxophonists, especially when bebop was the music of the moment. Wayne Shorter, Ike Quebec, James Moody and Hank Mobley all came from Newark. So did Buddy Terry, Leo Johnson, Joe Thomas and Herb Morgan.

Known in his youth as "The Newark Flash," Shorter went on to win nine Grammys during a career that's spanned more than six decades. Quebec, one of Blue Note's earliest recording stars, doubled as the label's chief talent scout in its early years, while Moody's souped-up version of the classic *I'm in the Mood for Love* put him on the jazz map for eternity. Early in his career, Mobley, known for his mellow, laid-back style, led weekly jam sessions in Newark at the Picadilly.

Stories about legendary jazz artists Charlie Parker's and John Coltrane's forays into Newark abound. Jazz enthusiast Ben Mosley, for one, tells of the night he and Al Clayborne, his boyhood pal, drove Parker home to New York. "Al and I were leaving the Blue Mirror on Clinton Avenue when Bird (Parker) asked us what time the last train to New York left Penn Station," Mosley recounts. "We offered to take him to Penn Station and wound up driving him all the way to New York in Al's 1954 Buick. I don't remember much of the conversation because we were so excited to be in Bird's company."

In addition to hanging out at jazz clubs throughout the city, many Newark musicians took lessons at Dorn & Kirchner's, a music repair shop at Springfield Avenue and High Street (Martin Luther King Boulevard) that rented and sold instruments. Founded in the 1920s, the store moved to Union, New Jersey, after the 1967 civil rebellions. Saxophonist Bob Ackerman still remembers the day when he and a group of teenagers from West Side High School that he describes as "hoodlums" stopped by the store. "They were wearing oversized coats, but I didn't know they were stealing stuff," he says. "When we got outside, they said, 'Hey, do you want a clarinet?'" Fortunately, for Ackerman's sake, they weren't caught.

In 2003, when *Star-Ledger* reporter Guy Sterling brought together the Newark Jazz Elders—a band of veteran musicians that included several of Newark's most seasoned saxophonists—Leo Johnson, Buddy Terry, Joe Thomas, Connie Lester and Harold Van Pelt were in it. "I brought these guys together because they still had something to offer," Sterling says. "I didn't get them out of mothballs. Most of them were still playing, but they were underestimated, underrated and under-reported." At the time, Sterling envisioned the day when the Elders, given their talent and years of experience, would achieve a level of fame akin to the New Orleans-based Preservation Hall Jazz Band, but that idea faded when the economy tanked in 2007. Here's a look at some of Newark's most noted saxophonists, starting with Johnson, the Elders' music director.

Leo Johnson

Born in Daytona Beach, Florida, in 1939, Leo Johnson came to Newark in the late 1950s. After serving in the military in Europe with an Air Force band, he returned in 1961 and has been a mainstay on the city's music scene ever since.

Johnson's first steady job as a musician was in early 1962 with organist Specks Williams at the Blue Note on Branford Place. "I stopped in one night and Specks invited me to play with him," Johnson recalls. "Until I joined them, Sticks was working with drummer Kenneth Pollard as a duo. Soon after I joined, Barbara Sharpe, who was singing in Broadway shows, became our vocalist."

The foursome wound up playing all over Newark at places like Robbie's at Park Avenue and North 13th Street and Wilfred's Lounge on Lyons Avenue, then became the house band for Tuesday night jam sessions at Len & Len's. "Everyone came to play at Len & Len's," Johnson says, reeling off a list that includes Woody Shaw, Tyrone Washington, Eddie Gladden, Larry Young Jr., Herb Morgan, Jimmie Smith (the drummer), Benny Golson, Hank Mobley, Johnny Griffin, Julian Priester, Paul Chambers and Walter Davis Jr. Between stints with Williams, Johnson played with Chico Mendoza's band at Wakefield's on West Market Street and Billy Ford and the Thunderbirds around town. He also recorded with Mendoza on the Ocho label.

In mid-1965, Johnson joined organist Bill Doggett, whose recording of *Honky Tonk* topped the charts in 1956. "All Bill's fans wanted to hear was *Honky Tonk*," Johnson says. "I know because I had to play it every night." Johnson was on the road with Doggett in Pittsburgh when organ master Jack McDuff first heard him play. A year later, McDuff invited Johnson to audition and hired him, a job that found Johnson traveling the East Coast organ circuit. Newark's Key Club and Cadillac Club were two of the stops.

Looking back, Johnson sees 1970 as a turning point in his career. With several years of experience under his belt, he decided to form his own group. Through the years he's led many quartets and quintets bearing his name. Initially, he had Mike Melillo on piano, Roy Cummings, bass; Eddie Crawford, drums, and Charlie Mason, trumpet. In those days, their favorite haunts were spots like the Cadillac Club and Playbill Lounge.

After graduating from Essex County College with a degree in music, Johnson continued his studies at Rutgers-Newark. Then, with twenty-seven credits to go, he left to play in Europe. "I was out of school for twenty-two years before I returned," he notes. But he eventually re-enrolled, earning an undergraduate degree, then a master's degree in jazz history in 2003.

Most of Johnson's in-between years were spent on the road with organists Jimmy McGriff and Rhoda Scott. For a time, he also was Jimmy Scott's music director. He recorded two albums with McGriff: *Stump Juice* with Buddy Terry, Joe Thomas and Jesse Morrison, and *City Lights* with guitarist Jimmy Ponder. He also recorded with Rhoda Scott in Paris.

Johnson got a major career boost early on when Sonny Stitt was in town. Although Stitt wasn't in the best of health, he invited Johnson back to his room at the Robert Treat Hotel after his performance. Handing his horn to Johnson, he implored the younger musician to "show me what you've got." Though hesitant at first, Johnson complied. "'You can play,' Sonny told me afterward," he says. "I can't tell you what a great moment that was for me."

In 1994, Johnson began teaching theory and woodwinds at the Newark Community School of the Arts, a job he held for almost twenty years. In the late 1990s he served as director of the Rutgers Mosaic Ensemble, a student group that performed at campus functions. Johnson presently teaches jazz appreciation and world music at Essex County College, where Richard Alston, the department director, is producing a documentary on his life and career. "Teaching is gratifying, especially when I see people who have never heard jazz before learning about it and enjoying our classes so much," he says. In addition to other activities, Johnson remains a favorite on the Newark jazz scene.

Joe Thomas

Like many of the Elders, Joe Thomas's career in music dates back more than sixty years, to his days at Oliver Street School in Newark's Ironbound section, where Wayne Shorter was two grades ahead of him. "Those were wonderful days," Thomas says, reflecting on how great he felt to see his mother's pride when he played *Begin the Beguine*, his first solo, at a school assembly. "At first I was more interested in hanging out in the playground than playing music," he says. "But my older brother Frank played saxophone and kept encouraging me to play, too. Eventually I did. That was my initiation."

Thomas took a few lessons on flute in elementary school but learned to read and write music on his own. One of his fondest memories at Oliver Street dates to the days when he and Shorter practiced together in the school playground. "It was just the two of us," he says, "and it was a lot of fun. It was the thing we loved to do most."

After graduating from East Side High School, Thomas joined a trio that played at the Palm Garden in Asbury Park, then signed on to tour the South. "We got as far as Portsmouth, Virginia, when the band broke up and I got stranded," he recounts. "That's when I decided to join the Army." After his discharge, he got back into music in 1955 as a member of Specks Williams' band. "We played places like the Brass Rail on Plane Street (University Avenue) and Len & Len's," he says. "Then I formed my own band, the Joe Thomas Nite-Liters. We played all over Canada for three years. One night Bill Elliott and I went to see Dee Dee Ford in Buffalo," he relates. "There were problems with her band and she wound up stranded, so she asked us to join her. We did, but we weren't getting along with her, so we approached Rhoda Scott to form a trio." With Elliott on drums and Thomas on sax, they became the Rhoda Scott Trio, one of the most popular groups in the New York area.

"I think half of Newark was in the audience when we played Count Basie's club in Harlem," Thomas says. "People would line up outside to get in because so many of our fans from Newark came to see us." After playing together for two years, Scott left to further her musical studies in Paris. Meanwhile, Elliott married Dionne Warwick, who sang backup with her aunt Cissy Houston on the Rhoda Scott Trio's first recording, *Hey! Hey! Hey.* Along the way, Thomas went to Paris to record three LPs with Scott, including *Live at the Olympia*. Steve Phillips, an old friend from the Oranges who played in Europe with Scott, was the drummer.

Later in his career, Thomas stuck closer to home. El C's in East Orange was one of his favorite spots, as was the Priory at St. Joseph's Plaza. Thomas also joined singer Carrie Smith on several Caribbean cruises. More recently he has performed at North Reformed Church in Newark, where he is a deacon, and with the Newark Jazz Elders. "I've got great memories," he says, "but getting work now is tough. All the old places are gone, and there's little money out there to support live performances. That's why groups like the Elders are so important."

Conrad "Connie" Lester

Alto saxophonist Connie Lester's colleagues describe him as "a natural musician," self-taught but so admired by older musicians that they invited him to play with them at clubs in Newark long before he was old enough to legally enter a bar. Born in Roselle, New Jersey, Lester started coming to nearby Newark to take tenor saxophone lessons at Dorn & Kirschner's music store while he was still in school. Before taking up saxophone, he played clarinet, which he picked up from his brother, a member of the school band.

After switching to saxophone he began performing with Gus Young, a well-known roots-of-jazz drummer, at Conlan's Bar on Washington Street in Newark. "I learned a lot by playing with older guys like Gus, Clem Moorman, Chops Jones and June Cole," he says. "I wanted to emulate them, so I listened to everything they played." Like many saxophonists, Illinois Jacquet's *Flying Home* was one of his favorite tunes. "All the guys who played saxophone were doing it," he says. "We also played a lot of blues and show tunes at places like Billy's Tavern in Elizabeth, the Washington Bar in Newark and Tyler's Chicken Shack in Rahway. All the acts from New York used to play Tyler's. I co-led a band there for a while."

While Lester often led his own groups, none of them bore his name. "My reputation was as a sideman," he says. In the late 1960s and early 1970s, he began backing organists Jimmy McGriff and Larry Young Jr. One of his most important gigs, in 1967, was with McGriff at the Felt Forum at Madison Square Garden.

During that stage of his career he began recording, making *My Soul People* on Prestige, and *All That's Good* and *Mo' Greens, Please* on Blue Note, the latter with organist Freddie Roach. He also was closely associated with pianist/organist Specks Williams. "We made an LP produced by Charlie Parker's wife Doris that featured Joe Carroll singing bebop," he says. "I also traveled with Specks to Bermuda, where we worked for two months."

Lester also toured with Roach, a popular Newark organist, on a circuit that took them from Pittsburgh and Harrisburg to Utica, New York. But traveling wasn't his bag. With two daughters at home to support, he quit the road and began playing locally at venues in and around Newark. "That was OK," he says, "because the money I was making on the road wasn't all that good."

After returning home, Lester took a job at L'Oreal of Paris in Clark, where he worked for thirty-six years. "That's a funny thing," he says, "because a lot of musicians look down on you if you work a day job. If you don't play music full time, they don't think you're a real musician." Not that it mattered all that much to him, for he remained in great demand on weekends and holidays. "Through the years, I was always working," he says. "I played with a lot of groups and worked with a lot of great musicians, including Pepper Adams and Roy Haynes." He also backed some of the era's best-known singers, including Arthur Prysock and Etta Jones. Lester's longest gig was with organist Alvin Valentine at the Top Club on 125th Street in Harlem. "We played there two years straight," he says. "It was popular because it was just around the corner from the Baby Grand and the Apollo Theater. All the people who went to the shows would stop by afterwards."

Now in his eighties, Lester still practices daily and still plays publicly on occasion. Full time or part time, music is his life.

Edlin "Buddy" Terry Jr.

The squib under Buddy Terry's photograph in the 1959 South Side High School yearbook reads like the story of his life: *Usually found playing jazz in a nightclub. Edlin is noted for his warm smile and genial jokes. He digs John Coltrane, Cannonball Adderly, Miles Davis and Sonny Rollins.* Terry was seventeen when those prophetic words appeared in *The Optimist*, South Side's annual publication. More than fifty years later, they still ring true. Terry still hangs out in nightclubs on occasion, still loves telling jokes and still digs all the cats, like Trane and Miles, who were among his musical mentors.

Clearly a prodigy, Terry was barely out of knee pants when he and Woody Shaw began hanging out at bars and clubs all over Newark, blowing the competition away. "Even at fourteen, Woody could play his butt off," he says. Whatever the call—rapid-fire bebop, fluid blues or ballads—the two friends more than met the challenge. Before taking up flute and saxophone, Terry played clarinet at Newark's Charlton Street School, where he learned to read music and belonged to the orchestra.

"Newark abounds in musical talent," says Terry, who also counted organist Larry Young Jr., his Charlton classmate, among his running buddies. As a young teenager he began playing with the Jazz Correspondents, a group composed of brothers Willie and Brad Hutcherson, Dennis Moorman and Rod Clark. Except for Dennis's sister, Melba, who sang with the band while attending Arts High, the members were all from South Side. She became the celebrated singer Melba Moore.

"We were all in the school orchestra," says Willie Hutcherson, who alternated with Moorman on bass and keyboards and credits John Coppock, their music teacher, with encouraging them to play together. "We started out as the Jazz Correspondents, then became the Jive Five." In his youth, Woody Shaw also was in the group for what Hutcherson calls "a quick minute. Little did I know that Melba would achieve such great success," he adds. "At one point, I wanted to kick her out of the band. She wanted to sing *Foggy Day*, and we wanted to play rock and roll. In those days, young musicians were able to sit in at any one of a number of bars on Washington Street, as we often did." Before long, he says, his brother Brad, a drummer, and Terry were gigging all over Newark.

"Buddy and I used to play the matinees at Len & Len's on Warren Street," says Brad Hutcherson. "Melba and Dennis were with us then." Another one of Terry's initial gigs was at Sugar Hill, a popular downtown club that attracted top musicians from New York. He appeared there with a group that featured Melba and Dennis's cousin, Wilson Moorman Jr., on drums.

During his senior year in high school, Terry contemplated joining the Army. Instead, he married Georgianna "Nell" Smallwood, his high school sweetheart, three weeks after graduation and embarked on a career in music. Terry and his wife didn't have to hire a band for their reception. "All the cats from Newark played downstairs in the Blue Room at 188 Belmont Avenue (the Masonic Temple)," he says. By then he had taken part in jam sessions in and around town and played a few professional gigs.

"I was about fourteen when Woody and I began going all around Newark to gain experience," he reflects. "We wanted to learn more, but we realized right off that we were far ahead of most of the guys." Those early gigs were at places like Fredericks' Lounge on Boston Street and Len & Len's, where he and Shaw got to play with all the hot young cats on the scene, including Lou Donaldson, Pepper Adams, Sonny Redd and Kenny Durham. In his late teens Terry began fronting organ groups led by Dayton Selby, Dee Dee Ford, Rhoda Scott, Freddie Roach, Floyd "Papa Stoppa" Lang and Specks Williams. Roach later chose him to play tenor on *The Freddie Roach Soul Book*, the organist's first album on Prestige.

By then, Terry's apartment in the Stella Wright Homes on Spruce Street, where he lived for nearly four decades while raising his family, had become a second home for jazz pianists Horace Silver and Jaki Byard. In 1961, he began traveling, first with Ford as far as Buffalo, then to Canada with Duke Ellington alumnus Cat Anderson. "After I joined Rufus Jones (who had been with Max Roach), I got

Woody in the band," he notes. "We played Birdland, then traveled the circuit to places like Pittsburgh and Harrisburg." The following year he went with trumpeter Billy Ford and His Thunderbirds. Ford, who graduated from Central High School in the mid-1930s, was the inspiration behind the 1958 hit *La Dee Dah*, a catchy cha-cha-like tune.

Terry was part of what he calls "The Clique," a group of musicians who didn't have to promote themselves. Once they played, offers poured in. In 1966 he performed briefly with Lloyd Price, then joined Lionel Hampton. "Hamp's band was going to Europe," he says. "He needed a sax player, and I was it. I wanted to build a resume, so I was trying to play with everyone I dreamed of playing with. I went with Hampton because Clifford Brown (the great trumpet player) was with him."

"My experiences with Hampton's band exposed me to a great deal of traveling," Terry notes. "We toured the Eastern section of the United States, from Buffalo to Miami, and throughout Europe. You can't buy this kind of experience. You have to live it." He subsequently spent two years on the road with Ray Charles and belonged to bands led by Art Blakey, Dizzy Gillespie, Charles Mingus and Duke Pearson. He also became a prolific recording artist, cutting more than thirty LPs as a sideman with Blakey, Joe Morello and Harold Mabern, as well as on his own. His name as a leader appears on a half-dozen albums, starting with *Electric Soul* in 1967. In 1972–73, Terry hardly left the studio, making three LPs on Mainstream: *Awareness*, *Pure Dynamite* and *Lean On Him*. All three won critical acclaim. "Buddy Terry has been overlooked unfairly," one critic wrote. "Nobody writes or talks about him, but these three albums represent the highest order of spiritual jazz and deep funk." Joined by childhood friends Shaw, Young, Eddie Gladden and Joe Thomas, Terry made *Natural Soul* in 1968. It includes *Don't Be Mean*, a tune he wrote and recorded with Hampton.

While teaching music at Essex County College in the mid-1970s, Terry joined the Duke Ellington Alumni Band, led by former Ellington bassist Aaron Bell, the music department chairman. For the next few years he played with several older-style bands, appearing with Sy Oliver at the Rainbow Room in New York and with the Heart of Basie Band. He also began doing Broadway shows—*Broadway Comes Uptown* with Gregory Hines, *Sophisticated Ladies* with Cab Calloway and *A Raisin in the Sun*. As an original member of the *Saturday Night Live* band, he found working with John Belushi and Steve Martin "wild and crazy times."

At home in Newark, Terry was the bandleader when Gladys Knight & The Pips appeared at Symphony Hall and played in shows starring Teddy Pendergast, Phyllis Hyman and Kool & The Gang produced by Teddy Powell. By the mid-1980s he was traveling less, playing occasionally with the Basie band, while turning his attention to an outreach ministry he began after becoming a licensed preacher. He subsequently spent eleven years at Maxwell's, a popular bar in Hoboken, with Dave Post's Swingadelics. After suffering a stroke a week before Christmas in 2009, Terry eventually made his comeback with Post at the Priory.

Harold Van Pelt

Wherever he goes, Harold Van Pelt takes his music with him. Early in his career that meant playing with the 753rd Army Air Force band at military bases in the United States, performing with small groups in Detroit—where he lived for two years—and in Newark—where he was born and raised—and traveling the road with bands led by Joe Morris, Sticks McGhee and Annie Laurie.

Now in his eighties and a resident of Clearbrook, a central New Jersey community for residents over age fifty-five, Van Pelt recently reorganized the Jazz Vanguards, a group he formed years ago in Newark. "All of the musicians live nearby," he explains. "Our first performance was at Princeton University. Now we're playing at senior citizen events in the area where I live." Like the original Vanguards, the new ensemble, with Cindy Parker handling the vocals, plays a lot of music Van Pelt writes and arranges, including *In Spite of It All*, for which his wife Alice wrote the lyrics.

Born in Newark in 1930, Van Pelt began playing baritone saxophone as a teenager at Newark's Robert Treat Junior High School, studying first with his uncle, Don Anthony. "I really looked up to him (Anthony)," says Van Pelt. "I also learned a lot from Danny Quebec (saxophonist Ike Quebec's nephew), who lived around the corner from me and was playing at Dodger's Bar & Grill on Bedford Street." After graduating from junior high, Van Pelt continued his studies at Arts High School. "Phil Rayfield, who later played piano with Red Rodney, was in my class and Achilles D'Amico, a cousin of jazz clarinetist Hank D'Amico, was our teacher," Van Pelt says. "After hearing me, Mr. D'Amico made sure I was in one of his classes."

After dropping out of school to join the Army, Van Pelt played in the Army-Air Force band. "In those days there were three duties: a parade band, a concert band and a jazz band. Elvin Jones, Dwike Mitchell and Willie Ruff were in the jazz band, but that was pretty steep," Van Pelt says. "I was a novice gaining experience, so I was in the parade and concert bands." To gain further experience, he joined a group that played for social events off-base and at the Officers' Club. Van Pelt's next stop during his two years in the military was Alaska, where he played in a band led by pianist Earl Van Dyke, who later performed with Martha and the Vandellas at Motown. After completing his military duty, Van Pelt moved to Detroit, where he performed in small jazz groups for two years. During the day he worked for an auto company. At night and on weekends, he played at clubs with small groups.

After moving back to Newark, Van Pelt joined the Brady Hodge Orchestra, which played for social events at the Terrace and Wideaway ballrooms. From time to time, he also played with units led by Duke Anderson and Ernie Ransome. In the late 1950s he went to work in the cable shop at Western Electric in Kearny, performing locally for the next five years until Joe Morris offered him a chance to travel with his jazz band.

"When I got the job with Joe, my wife was good enough to go along with the idea," he says. "That was a blessing because she was left alone to handle our son." After joining Morris's band in the early 1960s, Van Pelt spent six months on the Southern circuit. Until then, he knew little about the state of racial affairs in America. All that changed when the band was stopped by the Mississippi State Police. "They were looking for drugs," he explains, "so they took all of our instruments and the seats out of the car. They didn't find anything, so they let us go." Things got worse when the band got to Montgomery, Alabama, then in the throes of the bus boycott. "It was like a vacant city," Van Pelt says. "Not one person was on the street or anywhere. Anyone who was black either walked to work or piled into a car with their friends. If they did that, the police would stop them, maybe arrest them."

After returning to Newark, Van Pelt began working in the insurance industry, spending the next twenty-five years with companies including Lincoln Life of St. Louis. But music was his main interest, leading him to form jazz quartets and quintets that played the Key Club, Teddy Powell's Lounge, the Golden Slipper and Sparky J's. "I always hired local guys like saxophonist Jimmy Anderson, Grachan Moncur III and Woody Shaw," he says. "I met Woody through Jimmy Anderson when I needed a trumpet player. Hank White couldn't make it, so Jimmy recommended Woody. He was a young guy, but he played with us a lot."

In the 1970s, Van Pelt joined a band led by Joe Thomas that played for the next two years at the Four Leaf Deli on Bergen Street in Newark. "We had a lot of great guys in the band, including Leo Johnson on tenor, Gene Phipps Sr., alto; Bill Hartman and Leslie Ford, trumpet; Steve Turre, trombone; Mickey Tucker, Jiggs Chase and Billy Gardner, piano; Bobby Forrester, organ, and Eddie Gladden and Eddie Crawford, drums," he says. "Everybody contributed, but Joe did most of the arranging and I did most of the writing." After leaving the band, he formed the Jazz Vanguards, a group that included Melvin McRae on tenor; Rodman Bostick, trumpet; Robert Pickett, piano; and Cornell McGhee, trombone. "Cornell was just starting out," says Van Pelt, "but he was terrific." For the next six months, they played on and off at a tiny spot called Jasmine's on Lock Street, off Central Avenue in Newark's Central Ward.

Over the years Van Pelt has played just about every club in the Newark area. He's also written more than seventy songs, and is still at it. "It's what I love best," he says, "so I keep doing it."

10 ♪

The Advocates

Other Voices

*What has served me best, I hope, is that I
learned about the music not from books but the
people who created it. —Dan Morgenstern*

Absent the contributions of those who recorded, promoted or captured the essence of Newark's jazz history via the written word, the world would know little about those who made New Jersey's largest city so musically important.

The irascible Herman Lubinsky, founder of Savoy Records, is one such luminary. Even members of Lubinsky's family do not dispute stories of how he cheated those he did business with, yet, without Savoy, jazz fans the world over would never have known the early works of Charlie Parker, Miles Davis and Little Jimmy Scott. Lubinsky's contribution to jazz—flawed as it may be—was, nevertheless, enormous.

Jazz lovers owe a debt of gratitude to Dan Morgenstern, another seminal figure in jazz history. As editor of *DownBeat* for many years, Morgenstern, a frequent Grammy winner for his liner notes, wrote about every major figure in jazz. Subsequently, in his position as director of the Newark-based Institute of Jazz Studies, he guided the work of thousands of jazz researchers and historians.

Bob Porter, the host of *Portrait in Blues* on WBGO since the station's inception more than thirty years ago, is a member of the Blues

Hall of Fame. In producing and re-issuing more than 200 albums, mostly on Prestige and Savoy, he introduced fans to many previously unrecorded artists while recording the early works of musicians like Parker, Davis and Dexter Gordon for generations to come.

Here's a closer look at how several jazz stalwarts—Carl "Tiny Prince" Brinson, Maxine Harvard, Dorthaan Kirk, Stan Myers and Philip S. Thomas—influenced Newark jazz history.

Carl "Tiny Prince" Brinson

For nearly forty years (1949–86), jazz musicians and fans looked forward to reading *After Hours*, a weekly magazine co-founded by native Newarker Carl Brinson. Until his retirement in his early nineties, Brinson, better known as Tiny Prince, also produced a similar publication called the *Black News Mirror*. "Anyone who wanted to know who was playing where, who was sick or had died or what was happening in Newark politics, looked to Tiny for that kind of information," says saxophonist Joe Thomas, who wrote for the *Black Mirror* in the early 2000s.

Like Bob Queen, editor of the *New Jersey Afro-American*, Brinson spent his career chronicling life in black Newark, turf he knew well because his grandfather, Alfred C. "Pop" Gibson, owned the Radio Inn on Halsey Street in the late 1920s and 1930s. In those days everyone who was anyone in Newark flocked to the Radio Inn to hear Newark's most popular singers and musicians perform. Rosie Jones had the house band. Emma Hawkins and Miss Rhapsody often headlined the shows.

Born May 12, 1918, Brinson was a year old when his mother died. Afterward he was raised by his grandparents, who lived across the street from his grandfather's business. As a child, Brinson was surrounded by music. His uncle, Danny Gibson, was a popular Swing Era drummer who belonged to the Savoy Dictators and led the Del Mar Boys at the Del Mar Bar. His aunt, Regina Gibson, was a dancer.

After graduating from the Robert Treat Junior High School on Norfolk Street, where the new Science Park High School stands,

Brinson attended Central High School. "There weren't many things for black kids to do in those days," he says, "so we all took up lindy hopping. We began hanging out on weekends at the Savoy Ballroom in Harlem because that was the place to be. We didn't dance at first. We just watched until we began to catch on. It was forty cents to get in, but we used to go early on Saturdays or Sundays because we were afraid they would raise the prices for the main attraction. That's how I got to meet Duke Ellington and Count Basie. They used to come in once a year."

Brinson's crowd, all kids from Jersey, included an Italian girl from Bayonne, another white girl whose father owned a 5 & 10 cent store (a lucrative business in years gone by) and Buster Jamison from Jersey City, one of North Jersey's best dancers. "We wouldn't let the boys from New York take advantage of the girls," he reflects. "We'd drive them away. Being from New Jersey was the important thing. Not race."

Brinson was still underage when he began hanging out at Newark clubs or, at least, tried to. "If I went anywhere where my Uncle Danny was playing, he would point a finger at me and tell me to go home," he says. "I wanted to hear the music and see what all the excitement was about." Being Pop Gibson's grandson was an advantage because it gave him an inside track into Newark social and political life. Eventually he landed a job writing for the city's black newspapers, the *New Jersey Afro-American* and the *Herald News*. "I never asked for a job," he says. "When one of the regular columnists went on vacation she asked me to substitute for her for two weeks, so I did. The editor liked how I wrote and asked me to stay on."

During his many years in publishing, Brinson was known as Tiny Prince. They called me 'Tiny' because of my size," he explains. "'Prince' came after I started writing because someone thought I should have a better name for my byline. I was a sharp dresser, so they started calling me 'Tiny Prince.'"

When Hugh Addonizio ran for mayor of Newark in 1961, Brinson became one of his key advisers in the black community. Because he knew so many musicians and had strong family ties to Newark's jazz community, Brinson also began helping promoters Henry Graham and Teddy Powell bring acts to Newark. Graham operated an auditorium on Belmont Avenue, now Irvine Turner Boulevard, that ran jazz events, including teenage canteens and dances for black middle-class social groups. Powell owned Teddy Powell's Lounge on Meeker Avenue.

A decade after co-founding *After Hours* with Harry Webber, a photographer for the *Afro-American*, Brinson joined Addonizio's campaign. After Addonizio's election in 1962, Brinson became the city's human rights chief. Most of that time he also was employed part time as a salesman at Dan Esposito's Oldsmobile dealership on Central Avenue in Newark, a prestigious job for a young black man. "I was no flunky cleaning cars in the back of the place," he asserts. "I was on the floor," almost unheard of at a time when many of his friends held menial jobs.

If that weren't enough to keep him busy, Brinson spent his spare time delivering *After Hours* to clubs and bars in the Newark area. Because the publication was free, he and Webber depended on advertising to sustain it. With the help of employees such as Barbara Thompson and Marcia James, circulation gradually rose from 2,500 to nearly 9,000 copies each week.

In the beginning, *After Hours* operated out of an office building on Branford Place near Hobby's Delicatessen. "The guy that rented me the office said I was the first black guy to lease space downtown," Brinson says. "He liked me, so he gave me a chance." Then again, lots of people liked Brinson. That's true, he says, "because I'm the same way my grandfather was. I'm respected because I always treated people fairly."

Maxine Harvard

Even after managing some of the top jazz artists in the business for thirty-plus years, Maxine Harvard wonders why she was so passionate about jazz during her high school days in Rochester, New York. Little did she surmise that she would someday manage the careers of Jimmy Scott, Jimmy McGriff and Freddy Cole, Nat King Cole's brother. "I really don't know why jazz had such an appeal to me," she says, "especially as a white girl growing up in a very conservative Jewish family."

Harvard's interest in jazz blossomed as a student at Westside High School, where she played piano in the orchestra, learned acoustic bass and joined a friend's jazz band. After graduating from Ithaca College and arriving in Newark, she began hanging out after work at the Key Club, where she met many of the musicians, including McGriff and jazz pianist Ray Bryant. "I also became good friends with Jeanne Dawkins (the owner) and (singers) Irene Reid and Lu Elliott," she says. "Name any jazz musician from that era and they probably played the Key Club."

Harvard's involvement in the world of jazz began in the early 1970s after she became the community relations director at the newly opened Essex County College. In 1976, she organized the Key Club's twentieth anniversary celebration at the college. Held in the Mary B. Burch Auditorium, the event was billed as "A Tribute to Jeanne Dawkins and the Key Club." Because seating was so limited, George Benson's appearance as a special guest was omitted from the publicity, Harvard says, "but the word got out and we had to call the police for crowd control." During her time at ECC, she and Dr. Aaron Bell, the music department chairman, organized many jazz events on a grant from the National Education Association. "It was something J. Harry Smith (the college president) wanted us to do," she says. "So Aaron and I cooked up a lot of things. I can remember bringing in Duke Ellington groups and (saxophonist) Lou Donaldson."

With Jimmy McGriff and Dorthaan Kirk of WBGO, Harvard organized the city's first Newark Jazz Week. By then she was director of editorial services at Blue Cross/Blue Shield of New Jersey. To pump up interest in the weeklong series of jazz events throughout the city, she wrote a detailed history of jazz in Newark that appeared in *Metro-Newark*, the Chamber of Commerce magazine.

Titled *Keeping a Great Jazz Tradition Alive and Well in Newark*, the piece contained many interesting nuggets of Newark jazz history.

In the 1980s, Harvard became Jimmy McGriff's manager and booking agent. "When I first met Jimmy, disco was the big thing," she says. "He had stopped playing, but I kept bugging him to start again. Eventually, he taught me everything I needed to know about booking and managing musicians." After working out of Cranford, New Jersey, Harvard moved her business to Glendale, Arizona. Today she runs a full-service booking and management agency, working with high-visibility musicians at venues around the world. In addition to Scott, McGriff and Cole, she has represented Hank Crawford, Mary Stallings, Ed Reed, Bobby Broom and the Deep Blue Organ Trio.

Dorthaan Kirk

"Bright moments." That's how Dorthaan Kirk answers her phone and greets friends, words coined by her late husband, the legendary saxophonist Rahsaan Roland Kirk. For him, the words personified his upbeat outlook on life, despite being blind from early childhood and suffering a stroke as a young man that claimed his life at age forty-two. "Bright moments are like makin' love on a leaky water bed at a Holiday Inn," he would say, displaying a sense of verbal ingenuity similar to his musical genius. Or "like eating pork chops, French fried potatoes, watermelon and candied yams in a Kosher restaurant." For his wife the use of "bright moments" is simply a matter of how she wants other people to feel.

After her husband's death, Dorthaan Kirk began building her own career in music at WBGO, Newark's jazz radio station. Through the years, she's also devoted her time to keeping her husband's memory alive. "Rahsaan was meant to come through my life, for whatever reason," she told his biographer, John Kruth. "I wouldn't be doing what I'm doing today had I not met my husband. I'd probably be in Los Angeles, retired from the Department of Social Services, havin' a good time with my pension. Instead, I'm here in Newark, New Jersey."

Kirk joined WBGO at the invitation of founder Bob Ottenhoff, when the station was as new to the Newark community as she was to radio. As a bonus, she brought along her husband's vast record collection since WBGO had no collection of its own at the time. As the face of WBGO, she's staged hundreds of jazz events in and around Newark as director of special events and communications. She also oversees the WBGO Kids Jazz Series, manages the station's art gallery and is responsible for the on-air music calendar and public service announcements.

Over the years, Kirk has introduced thousands of children to the rudiments of jazz, bringing well-known jazz artists to Newark for concerts geared to their age level. Adults can attend only if accompanied by a child. With the support of the Agnes Vargas Foundation and longtime sponsors, including the Prudential Foundation and PNC Bank, Kirk was able to expand the 2013 season to ten concerts—five in the spring and five in the fall.

Kirk credits Emily Wingert, who founded Trumpets, the popular Montclair jazz club, with sparking the idea for the concerts. "Emily thought the series should be based in Newark because she wanted urban kids to learn about jazz and enjoy it," she explains. "At first we (WBGO) provided the space, but eventually Emily and Nancy Barry, who ran the Unity Concert Series in Montclair, came to me and we took over. Once we got funding, the program grew quickly.

"At the concerts, kids learn about the elements of jazz and why it is a reflection of our community, our nation and our world," Kirk says. "Our first criterion is to make sure the programs are not over their heads." She also has been the guiding force behind the Jazz Vespers Series at Bethany Baptist Church, where she is a longtime member. "Dorthaan has been a key person responsible for the success of Jazz Vespers at Bethany," says the pastor, the Rev. M. William Howard Jr. "The caliber of musicians who perform and who return over time is due directly to her long-standing credibility and good relations with the performers. Some have called her 'Newark's First Lady of Jazz.' She is undoubtedly the 'First Lady of Jazz Vespers.'"

As part of her work at WBGO, Kirk also interacts closely with the New Jersey Performing Arts Center, a partnership she developed when Philip Thomas was the center's vice president for arts education. "There were few opportunities for young people to hear jazz, so Philip and I collaborated on NJPAC's Jazz for Teens initiative," she says. Sponsored by Wells Fargo, the program gives young musicians an opportunity to deepen their understanding of jazz by learning its history and participating in jam sessions and concerts alongside professional musicians. "Jazz for Teens is important because it teaches discipline," she says. "Some of the young people who participate are our musicians of tomorrow."

Kirk's latest project, Dorthaan's Place, is a series of jazz brunches at NICO Kitchen + Bar at NJPAC. Launched in November 2012 as part of the first James Moody Democracy of Jazz Festival, the program was renewed for a second season in 2013. "There are no words to explain how I felt when John Schreiber (president and CEO of NJPAC) came up with the concept of Dorthaan's Place," Kirk says. "I was amazed to think that people would pay to hear music at a place named for me."

In August 2013, Kirk and poet Betty Neals spent five days at the Café Stritch in San Jose, California, for a tribute to Rahsaan Roland Kirk's pioneering work as a jazz musician. Neals performed her well-known poem *Theme for Eulipions*, taken from the title of a Kirk composition. The celebration also featured a documentary on Kirk's life and performances by former sidemen including trombonist Steve Turre. "It probably was the greatest week of my life," Dorthaan Kirk says.

Stan Myers

Jazz historian Stan Myers still hasn't forgiven himself for passing up the opportunity to walk Billie Holiday back to her hotel room after she appeared at a downtown jazz club in Newark more than fifty years ago. Although he gave it some thought, he was reluctant to approach the legendary singer after seeing her sing at Sugar Hill, a Broad Street club. "When I saw her walking down the street, I should have walked with her back to the Douglas Hotel, where she was staying," he says. "It was just around the corner. But I didn't, and I'm still sorry."

By then, Holiday's voice was practically shot, Myers says. "It was strained, nothing like the old Billie. But that didn't really matter. Just saying I was in the audience listening to Billie Holiday was enough for me." Myers first heard Holiday sing at the Apollo Theater in New York, where Symphony Sid, a popular radio personality, was the emcee. "Billie was messed up (high on drugs) that night and everyone knew it, but Sid tried to cover up for her," Myers remembers. "He kept telling us she wasn't up to par because she'd had dental work."

Bob "Stix" Darden, the drummer during Holiday's weeklong gig at Sugar Hill, doesn't remember her using drugs. "All I remember is that she was very quiet and kept to herself," he says. "She was cordial if approached, but not very talkative." The stint at Sugar Hill was Darden's second time backing Holiday. A few years before, he was part of a group led by Thelonious Monk that played for her at the Tijuana Club in Baltimore. "Billie was easy to work with," Darden says. "So was Monk. We just got together and did our thing."

Myers also saw Holiday sing at Teddy Powell's Holiday Inn in Newark. "That was the best of the three performances I saw," he says. "She was more in control."

A Newark resident his entire life, Myers has been a fixture on the Newark jazz scene since the early 1940s, when he began listening to his brother's records. "As a result, I became a big fan of Louis Armstrong, Count Basie, Duke Ellington and all the big bands," he says. Smitten by the music, he learned more about it by listening to the radio and the riffs wafting from the Villa Maurice, a Swing Era tavern next door to his family's house on Washington Street. "There was no air-conditioning in those days. When it got hot in the summer, the owner of the bar opened the door, so we could hear everything."

By the time he was sixteen or so, Myers began sneaking into old Third Ward clubs with friends from South Side High School. Sometimes they got in. Sometimes they got caught. With the United States about to enter World War II, the city's jazz clubs were filled with factory workers listening to music to escape their otherwise monotonous lives.

For Myers and his underage friends, the challenge was finding a way to get into places like the Picadilly on Peshine Avenue without being detected so they could hear Clem Moorman, Melba Moore's stepfather, and the Picadilly Pipers. One of his favorite spots was Fredericks' Lounge on Boston Street, where James Moody reigned over the jam sessions. It's also where saxophonist Ike Quebec, credited in jazz annals with bringing an array of talent to Blue Note Records, often sat in. "Sometimes we'd get turned away or thrown out," Myers says. "If we were lucky, we'd get to stand in the back where we could mix with the crowd and not be noticed. Once in a while someone would ask us for our draft cards."

As he grew older, Myers began attending events sponsored by black social and civic groups in the Terrace Ballroom at the Mosque Theater. With its two bars and terraced seating areas, it was one of the city's most popular settings for concerts and dances. "I saw Duke Ellington there, but I really wasn't into big bands," Myers relates. "I took to the small groups because I liked the rhythm and beat." When bebop came in, his new haunt was Lloyd's Manor, where Kenneth Gibson, who became Newark's first African-American mayor in 1970, was one of the aspiring young musicians sitting in on saxophone.

In those days, many well-known musicians and bands also played the Savoy Ballroom on Springfield Avenue. "That's where I saw Bird—Charlie Parker—the first time," Myers says. "Dizzy Gillespie and Fats Navarro also played the Savoy. Instead of recording, they came to Newark to play because the musicians were on strike during the war. The (recording) studios were shut." Aware of his growing knowledge, friends who had questions about jazz, came to Myers for answers. "Just ask Stan," they would say.

In the early 1960s, Myers began emceeing Sunday afternoon jam sessions at the Loft, an upstairs space on Shipman Street. "A lot of up-and-coming guys like Woody Shaw and Tyrone Washington used to come by to jam," he recalls. His role as a jazz historian expanded to radio announcing in 1992 after he began mentoring students at Seton Hall University in South Orange, where his daughter was a student. "The black students wanted a mentor for their program on WSHU, so I began making up the playlists and writing the scripts," he says. "Before long, I had my own show." After serving as a volunteer at WBGO, he became the station's overnight host. "I played everybody, all the top names in jazz," he recounts. "So I had a chance to meet many musicians. Guys like Clark Terry would call in, then come to the station to sit in. Bill Cosby also was a listener. I met him when he came to Newark to help with our fund drive."

Myers currently hosts a Sunday afternoon radio show on WFM 88.7 at William Paterson University in Wayne. He also hosts programs at Ramapo University in Mahwah and Tuesday night jam sessions at Crossroads in Garwood. He spends Friday nights at the Priory, where he's among the regulars. A longtime trustee of the New Jersey Jazz Society, he emcees its events and is on the selection committee for the society's American Jazz Hall of Fame.

Philip S. Thomas

Five years before NJPAC opened in October 1997, Philip S. Thomas was working behind the scenes as vice president, shaping an unparalleled arts education program for young people and their families. During his tenure at the center, thousands of New Jersey children, including students from practically every school in Newark, benefited from it.

When Thomas began his tenure with NJPAC in 1992, he was one of its first employees, bringing with him a wealth of experience as founder of the Newark-based Carter G. Woodson Foundation. That program provided nationwide exposure for African-American artists, bringing performers like Ruby Dee and Ossie Davis face to face with the masses. Black Culture on Tour in America, another component, promoted and packaged shows that generated wider audience appeal for Amiri Baraka, Terri McMillan, Sweet Honey in the Rock and Stepping into Tomorrow, a two-woman show featuring the daughters of civil rights leaders Martin Luther King Jr. and Malcolm X.

"All of this was in the 1980s, before Martin Luther King Jr.'s birthday became a national holiday or Black History Month became an institution," Thomas says. "That was the state of black arts at the time. A lot of what we did had a Newark focus. A lot of artists we booked, like Sweet Honey in the Rock, had never performed in Newark before. We presented them at almost every venue in the city, including Essex County College, Rutgers, the Newark Museum and Newark Public Library. It was a beautiful marriage between our organization and the city."

Blues singer Carrie Smith, who grew up in Newark, was one of the artists often booked by the foundation. Roy Haynes, the legendary jazz drummer, was another client. "I've always been someone who appreciated jazz," Thomas says, "so the first thing I did after forming the foundation was create the Rufus Reid Jazz Residency, a music training program for high school students." It was based at William Paterson University in nearby Wayne, where Reid ran one of the nation's most respected college-based jazz programs.

By creating the residency, Thomas was laying the groundwork for Jazz for Teens, which he established a decade later at NJPAC. Pianist Steve Colson and trombonist Steve Turre were the program liaisons. Guest artists included saxophonist Benny Golson, trombonist Dick Griffin and Take Six. Meanwhile, "On Stage in New Jersey" brought popular jazz artists to venues throughout the state. In Newark, McCoy Tyner and Jackie McLean appeared at Essex County College and Carmen McRae packed the house at the Terrace Ballroom at Symphony Hall. Abbey Lincoln was presented at the Grant Avenue Community Center in Plainfield, Jimmy Heath at Bloomfield College and Roy Haynes at another venue outside the city.

After his arrival at NJPAC, Thomas began cultivating Jazz for Teens, a training program for young musicians similar to the Rufus Reid Residency. Reid, WBGO's Dorthaan Kirk and Art Martin, then president of the International Jazz Educators Association of New Jersey, were his advisers. "Our goal was to train the next generation of jazz musicians," Thomas says. "The teachers were some of the best around: Mike Ledonne on piano; Mark Gross and Bruce Williams, saxophone; Ron Jackson, guitar; Ralph Peterson, Yoron Israel and Dion Parson, drums; Andy McKee, bass; Earl McIntyre, trombone; Valery Ponomorev, trumpet, and Dina Derosa and Roseanna Vitro, vocals." Trumpeter Bryan Lynch, the first artistic director, was succeeded by saxophonist Don Braden.

To expose NJPAC to the broader community and vice versa, Thomas also instituted a series of family concerts featuring artists such as Bobby Hutcherson, Jimmy Heath, Kenny Garrett, Hilton Ruiz, Bobby Sanabria, Eddie Palmieri and Ray Barretto. Between 1997 and 2003, several young artists—including pianist Sergio Salvatore, trumpeter James Gibbs III and drummer Rory Quince, along with other trainees from the Jazz Institute of New Jersey—were featured at family shows. Quince also got to open for Kenny Garrett.

When Thomas became executive director of Newark Symphony Hall in 2007, one of his first endeavors was a tribute to Kirk. Ron "Slim" Washington, WBGO's Sheila Anderson and Stan Myers hosted the event, which featured an array of Newark-based talent, including the Newark Public Schools Super Band directed by Bill May. Also on the bill were the Spirit of Life Ensemble, Carrie Jackson and Her Jazzin' All Stars, Jason "Malletman" Taylor with tap dancer Maurice Chestnut, Steve and Iqua Colson, the Rufus Reid Quartet, dancers Deborah Mitchell and Karen Calloway-Williams, Savion and Yvette Glover, Antoinette Montague, and Don Williams and Lady CiCi. The Jazz Marathon Ensemble, which also performed, was composed of Gibbs, Sherry Winston, Al Patterson,

Cornell McGhee, Chris Brown, Dion Parson, Cecil Brooks III, Melvin Davis and Bradford Hayes. "This was a seminal event in Newark jazz history," Thomas says.

During his tenure at Newark Symphony Hall, which came to a close with his retirement in 2012, Thomas often worked with Rhoda Scott. "Rhoda is probably the finest organist alive," he says. To showcase Scott's diversity, including her classical roots, he presented a three-part program featuring her in concert in 2001. The first show was part of WBGO's Kids Jazz Series at Newark Symphony Hall, followed by a sacred music concert featuring Scott and Courtney Bryan at Newark's Bethany Baptist Church. The culminating event was an organ jam at the Terrace Ballroom featuring more than a dozen musicians.

Scott returned the favor by headlining a Jazz Jam presented by Symphony Hall trustees in Thomas's honor in April 2013. Among the many praises that came his way that day, trustee board vice president Marion A. Bolden, with whom Thomas worked when she was executive superintendent of Newark public schools and he was at NJPAC, had this to say: "Not only is Philip Thomas a nationally recognized arts administrator, he has been a mentor to countless aspiring artists from our city. In his various roles he's provided them life-altering experiences."

11 ♪

Jazz Vespers
Honoring the Lord in Song

A name doesn't make the music. It's just called that to differentiate it from other types of music. —Art Blakey

Presenting secular music in a sacred setting was a foreign concept throughout most of the United States when the Rev. Jan van Arsdale, the energetic new pastor at Memorial West Presbyterian Church in Newark, introduced Jazz Vespers to his congregation in 1972. Aside from St. Peter's Lutheran Church in Manhattan, nothing like it was going on nationwide. Van Arsdale, in fact, patterned his jazz ministry after one created a decade before by his friend, the Rev. John Garcia Gensel, at St. Peter's. Like Gensel, he wanted his church to be a welcoming place where music brought people together whether or not they were religious.

However, getting church officials' approval to play America's only indigenous music in a church sanctuary could be tricky, especially for a new minister. As a by-product of New Orleans brothels and honky-tonks, the mere mention of jazz could evoke controversy. Some critics went so far as to call it "the Devil's music." According to Hugh Wyatt of *The Spiritual Herald*, an online faith-based publication, objections to jazz among churchgoers stem primarily from its bawdy reputation as a "rebellious, often volatile and mesmerizing music style" that has made it "something of a social outcast for more than a century." According to Wyatt, its association with speakeasies and gangsters and ties to "far-out artists and intellectuals who are too elite for the average person" didn't help much either.

Surprisingly perhaps, van Arsdale faced no opposition whatsoever when he suggested creating a jazz ministry at Memorial West. Not only were the members of his inner-city congregation "very accepting and supportive," he says, they, too, saw jazz as an honor to God. Van Arsdale's interest in jazz dates to his high school days in Homeland, Pennsylvania, a dot on the map 120 miles northeast of Philadelphia. As a teenager, his stomping ground was the nearby Lakewood Ballroom, where concerts were presented by Duke Ellington and other big-band leaders.

By the time van Arsdale entered nearby Waynesburg College, his collection of LPs, which grew to more than 2,000 over time, was his prized possession. Ellington, Dizzy Gillespie and saxophonist Lucky Thompson, an early proponent of bebop, were among his favorite musicians. "Even when we downsized, Jan's records went with us," his wife Mary Anne says. "Every time we moved we had to consider whether the floorboards would hold the weight."

After graduating from Brunswick Seminary in New Brunswick, New Jersey, in the early 1970s, van Arsdale served briefly at Trinity Reformed Church in Newark's Ironbound area, then accepted an invitation to become pastor at Memorial West in the West Ward, where he spent the next several years. Like many newly ordained ministers, he was brimming with ideas for making the church more relevant to the broader community at a time when Newark was in a shambles. Jazz Vespers, he believed, was a sign of hope for a new beginning in a city struggling to reverse the calamitous effects of the 1967 civil rebellions.

With the approval of church officials and his friend Gensel's guidance, van Arsdale brought Jazz Vespers to Memorial West, a stately Federal-style edifice at South Orange Avenue and South Seventh Street, just west of Bergen Street, on September 17, 1972. Financial support for the program came from the Newark Presbytery and the Synod of New Jersey, along with the National Endowment for the Arts, which provided a small start-up grant.

By bringing jazz into the church, van Arsdale found himself working harder than ever, attending to what he called "two congregations"—those who attended Sunday morning services and a more diverse audience of jazz fans who came on Sunday nights at five o'clock for Jazz Vespers. "We were not trying to promote any particular school of jazz," he explains. "Instead, our focus is on different styles of music, performed by good musicians, known and unknown." The inaugural program that September featured Borah Bergman, a brilliant but relatively unknown pianist from New York, recommended by Gensel.

"We didn't pay the musicians one cent," van Arsdale says. "Our total budget, which included money for food and incidentals, was only $1,000 annually." Paid or not, no one turned down an offer to play. Almost every musician, on the bill or not, was attracted by the camaraderie. "Jazz Vespers at Memorial West was a big part of the (jazz) scene," says saxophonist Bob Ackerman. "It's where I met all the guys in the jazz community. (Drummer) Eddie Gladden, (bassist) Andy McCloud, (trumpeter) Charlie Mason and (drummer) Eddie Crawford all played there. On Saturdays, the church was open to us all day long. Jan used to let all the avant-garde musicians practice there. So, to me, it was everything. There was never anything like it before or after." When Ackerman and singer Pam Purvis married in the fall of 1975, van Arsdale presided over the nuptials. By then, Purvis, too, was a Jazz Vespers veteran.

When Vespers got underway, van Arsdale and Herbert Johnson, a drummer known as Geronimo, spent many a night scouring Newark-area bars and clubs for talent. "I felt that was the only way I could build my ministry," van Arsdale explains. "I wanted to get to hear and meet the musicians." Wherever he and Johnson went there was no mistaking the fact that van Arsdale was a clergyman. He always wore his collar. As Geronimo knew and van Arsdale soon discovered, a wealth of top-notch musical talent was at their disposal. The days when bars in every Newark neighborhood offered music seven nights a week were long gone, but some spots were still going strong despite the advent of television and changing musical tastes. The Key Club, Cadillac Club (later Sparky J's), Front Room and Playbill Lounge were still hanging on.

Geronimo was a worthy partner. He knew everyone in the business and just about everyone knew him. In short order, almost every musician, singer and club owner in Newark also knew van Arsdale and was eager to become part of Jazz Vespers. Before long, the list of musicians who appeared at the church included some of the area's top names, such as saxophonist Gene Phipps Sr., who came from a musical family and played with Billie Holiday; bassist Vinnie Burke, whose associations included Bobby Hackett and Marian McPartland; saxophonist Buddy Terry, a Dizzy Gillespie alumnus; drummer Chink Wing, who recorded with James Moody and Sonny Stitt; and Grachan Moncur III, *DownBeat*'s No. 1 trombonist in the 1964 readers' poll.

Van Arsdale and Moncur shared a unique kinship. Not only did they both love jazz, they were born on the same day, August 8, 1937. Moncur, who grew up in Newark, where he still makes his home, was at the top of his game, given his associations with Sonny Rollins, Jackie McLean, Ray Charles, Art Farmer and Benny Golson. At Memorial West, Moncur and his friends freely donated their time to Jazz Vespers and benefits to support it. One of the most successful affairs was downtown at Dwyer's Elbow Room. "The benefits were successful because people like Eddie Dwyer, (the affable owner of Dwyer's), also loved jazz and donated their rooms," van Arsdale says.

Jesse Morrison, a tenor sax and flute player who was born and raised in Newark and played at area clubs, became the first Newark musician to perform at Memorial West in October 1972. By Christmas, Morrison was a Sunday night regular, along with Ackerman, Crawford, Mason, Harry Leahy, Ronnie Naspo, Jimmy Anderson, Calvin Ridley and Mickey Tucker. On Christmas Eve, all of them participated in Memorial West's first Candlelight Jazz Vespers, organized by Lou Grassi. Bergman, Lee Pezet and three Newark musicians—bassists Vinnie Burke and Andy McCloud and pianist George Gordon—also were on the bill. But attendance was generally poor, prompting van Arsdale to issue an appeal for better publicity.

"Attendance has been pitifully low, considering the artistry of the musicians," he wrote in the weekly program. "We feel that we are offering something that is needed and not provided elsewhere in the area. If people will give us a try, they'll return. We could hardly be considered a private club," he added, noting that half the audience, until that point, was composed of people who had no church affiliation. Of those who did, eleven denominations were represented. All told, they came not only from Newark, but twenty-eight towns outside the city.

In January 1973, Miss Bu Pleasant, who began her career playing piano for Arnett Cobb's big band, became the first woman to headline a Sunday night concert at Memorial West. A few months later, Honi Gordon, a longtime member of the church, became the first singer, male or female to appear at Jazz Vespers, accompanied by her father, George Gordon, a well-known jazz composer and arranger. Other Newark singers who performed regularly at Jazz Vespers included Carol Mitchell, formerly with Andy Kirk and Erskine Hawkins; Duke Ellington alumna Lu Elliott, and Swing Era veteran Miss Rhapsody, then in her seventies. Another concert featured Sheila Jordan, who won the 1963 Jazz Critics Poll as a Jazz Singer Deserving Greater Recognition. Mitchell made her debut on September 2, 1973. Also an actress, she later appeared in a recurring role on the TV hit *Miami Vice*. Elliott was a Key Club regular.

On September 23, 1973, Memorial West celebrated the first anniversary of Jazz Vespers with a daylong all-star show, starting with a set by Ackerman's group. The party concluded hours later with a performance by the Herman Bradley Quartet. Others on the program were the Al Giglio Trio, featuring Bob DeVos on guitar; Transformation, featuring Andy Martin on electric bass, and the Vinnie Burke Trio.

When Miss Rhapsody appeared at the church for the first time in June 1974, Lu Elliott gave her a glowing introduction. "This is not her first time with us," Elliott told the audience. "She recently appeared with us for our benefit at Dwyer's. She really is the last of the great female blues singers." Miss Rhapsody's voice was characterized by one critic as "a marriage between Ella (Fitzgerald) and Billie (Holiday), but with more voice than Billie and more soul than Ella." By the time she sang at Jazz Vespers, more than 100 musicians from Newark and beyond had donated their time and talent to the concerts, attracting more than 2,000 jazz fans to more than sixty programs.

On September 14, 1975, Memorial West hosted its most fantastic event ever—a third anniversary celebration that doubled as an eightieth birthday tribute to J. C. Johnson, a jazz composer whose many tunes included Bessie Smith's *Empty Bed Blues*. Johnson was there to take it all in. Tapes of his early recordings played throughout the day and an evening concert starred oldtime blues singer Edith Wilson. Among the many well-wishers were singer Maxine Sullivan and Maurice Waller, Fats Waller's son. The all-star birthday bash included performances by Elliott, Ackerman, Leahy, Naspo, Miss Rhapsody, Herman Bradley, Harold Ousley, the Richie Nesbitt Quartet, the Don Carter Trio, Teddy Clancy and Gerry Cappuccio.

When van Arsdale left Newark in 1980 to pastor a church in Hacksensack, Jazz Vespers at Memorial West came to an end. But what a wonderful gift to the greater Newark community it was, one he went on to share with churches he subsequently served. In 1996, when his health began to fail, he retired from the ministry at age fifty-nine. "Just about everywhere we went, Jan took Jazz Vespers with him," his wife notes. "But, as he often tells me, he was happiest in Newark. He always felt that people have a calling to become a pastor. For Jan, that calling was specific to the inner city." Now in his seventies, van Arsdale lives in Duncannon, Pennsylvania, just west of Harrisburg.

Episcopal House of Prayer

Following van Arsdale's departure from Memorial West, more than a decade passed before Jazz Vespers found its way back to Newark at the Episcopal House of Prayer at the northern end of Broad Street.

"Forrest Drennen, a jazz pianist who was our organist at the time, was the inspiration," according to Doug Eldridge, a church elder. "There were no objections because we had a priest prior to that who composed folk Masses and a children's choir that sang rock 'n' roll."

The inaugural Jazz Vespers concert at the House of Prayer occurred in April 1994 with Drennen accompanying trombonist Grachan Moncur III on keyboards. Other artists who appeared over the next year or so included pianist Tomoko Ohno, the husband-and-wife team of Pam Purvis and Bob Ackerman, and Ernie Edwards, who plays for Masses at St. Rocco's Roman Catholic Church in Newark. While Edwards often appears at cocktail lounges and restaurants, jazz is his forte. A few years back he was the lunchtime piano player at the Priory. Being part of Jazz Vespers, he says, "was good for me because it let people know I was out there."

But keeping the Sunday night concerts going at the House of Prayer proved problematic: The church had only forty members and attendance was spotty. "When we had a big name, we had a big audience," Drennen says. "If we didn't, nobody came." And so, the Sunday night concerts shut down in mid-1995. Once again, Newark was without a Jazz Vespers program.

Bethany Baptist Church

Just days into the 21st century, Newark's longest-running Jazz Vespers ministry began at Bethany Baptist Church in the Central Ward on January 6, 2000, at the urging of the pastor, the Rev. M. William Howard Jr. Howard's penchant for jazz dates to his youth in Americus, Georgia, a working-class town about 130 miles outside of Atlanta. Like Jan van Arsdale, he loves nothing more than listening to jazz or talking about it—even from the pulpit. Hardly a Sunday goes by at Bethany that jazz greats like John Coltrane or Dizzy Gillespie fail to get a mention in his morning messages.

Howard's interest in jazz as a teenager was cultivated by his aunt, Nell Howard Due, who lived in Chicago and sent him his first LP, *Coltrane Sound*. That, he says, was the start of a burgeoning collection of jazz records. By the time he entered Morehouse College in Atlanta, he was familiar with a wide range of jazz artists, from Dakota Staton to Cozy Cole.

As a Morehouse man whose interests were becoming more eclectic, Howard came under the influence of Willis Laurence James, a professor at nearby Spelman College who taught music appreciation at Morehouse. "He taught us about all kinds of music, from baroque to modern jazz," Howard says, "but most importantly Willis Laurence James taught us the connections between jazz and other musical forms." By then, he adds, he and his friends had begun sneaking into one of the most popular jazz clubs in Atlanta.

By the time Howard began his studies at Princeton Seminary, he was leading a jazz life, to the point where he urged investors to turn the old St. Andrew's Presbyterian Church, which had merged with another congregation, into a jazz center. That didn't occur, but the idea kept simmering. After spending most of his career in church administration, Howard became pastor of Bethany, providing him his first opportunity to incorporate his love of jazz into a church setting. His interest in the music led him to invite a skeptical deacon to accompany him to St. Peter's Lutheran Church in Manhattan, where Jazz Vespers got its start. "Members like Bill Lee, who helped in the beginning, were excited about bringing Jazz Vespers to Bethany," he notes, but other members were hardly enthusiastic about a jazz ministry. Whatever opposition exists today, he explains, has been mostly silenced by the program's success.

Howard credits the late Russel Brown, a Bethany deacon, with helping to turn things around. "After his wife Martha told me that Russel once played saxophone in jazz clubs in and around Newark, I asked him to get his friends together and play at Jazz Vespers," Howard recalls. Brown complied, gathering a group that included his cousin, the guitarist Eddie Blackwell. From then on, Howard says, "a lot of the fence sitters became more accepting of the music."

The first jazz program at Bethany on October 28, 2000, was part of a weeklong series of events tied to Howard's installation as the new pastor. The full-scale concert in the sanctuary featured performances by Jason "Malletman" Taylor, Bradford Hayes, Greg Searvance, Steve Colson, Carrie Jackson and the Earl May Quintet. Since then, Jazz Vespers has become a first-Saturday-night-of-the-month staple on the church calendar from October through June. Each Sunday in August, while the church musicians are on vacation, Bethany also celebrates jazz during morning worship services, inviting artists like Ruth Naomi Floyd, a well-known Christian jazz singer, and composer and multi-instrumentalist Wycliffe Gordon to participate.

"Overall, I believe the spiritual content of jazz has been ignored by the church," Howard says. "This is a way of reaching out and having people bring their whole selves into the black church." Accordingly, the theme for Jazz Vespers is "Worshiping the Lord to the Sounds of Jazz." He also points to the spiritual content and religious importance of works of jazz created by such world-renowned artists as Mary Lou Williams, Duke Ellington, John Coltrane and Geri Allen. "If it were not for the church, Ellington's *Come Sunday*, Williams' *Mary Lou's Mass*, Coltrane's *A Love Supreme* and Allen's *A Child Is Born* would have no audience," he says. Gary Walker, a popular on-air host at WBGO who served as the emcee for Bethany's inaugural Jazz Vespers program in early 2001, also touched on the spiritual content of the music. "This music is sacred, and it's here at Bethany where it belongs," Walker told the audience.

Unlike more staid Sunday morning church services, Jazz Vespers at Bethany takes place in a "come-as-you-are" setting on Saturday nights. "It's OK to wear jeans or a sweater. We want people to feel relaxed. We don't want them to feel afraid to come," says Howard, crediting Dorthaan Kirk, the widow of jazz innovator Rahsaan Roland Kirk, with providing the impetus for the series' success.

As the longtime special events coordinator at WBGO and chairwoman of Bethany's Jazz Committee, Kirk has encouraged some of the world's greatest talent to perform in Newark. The roster of performers who have appeared at the church includes Cedar Walton, Jimmy Heath, Randy Westin, Junior Mance, Cyrus Chestnut, Hilton Ruiz, David "Fathead" Newman, Sonny Fortune, Rhoda Scott, Cecil Brooks III and Houston Person. Add to that a number of well-known vocalists, including local favorites Yvette Glover, Carrie Jackson, Antoinette Montague and Cynthia Holiday.

In December 2011, avant-garde jazz pianist Geri Allen, a Bethany member, launched her first Christmas CD, *A Child Is Born*, at the church. As Allen noted that night, her appearance in the sanctuary two years before provided the foundation for music she subsequently recorded. Another favorite, organist Rhoda Scott, performed in February 2013. Scott's appearance was a special treat for her legions of fans from the Key Club.

From the start, interest in Jazz Vespers at Bethany has never waned. Jazz fans from Newark and the suburbs—black and white, rich and poor, young and old—have continued to pack the pews for more than a decade. Such diversity, Howard says, proves that jazz is a universal language, a medium that transcends class, race and nationality. Not only does it broaden people's sense of what is sacred and what is secular, he believes it also is a vehicle for mutual understanding and respect because of the camaraderie it creates.

On average, Jazz Vespers at Bethany attracts 300 to 400 jazz fans, a number that hit an all-time high on January 5, 2013, when Bill Cosby appeared at the church with the Cecil Brooks Quintet. That night, more than 650 people packed the sanctuary and adjacent chapel to worship the Lord through jazz. When Rhoda Scott performed the following month, many of the same people turned out. While Brooks and his musicians had an energized audience on its feet tune after tune, Cosby brought the house down with a forty-five-minute monologue on the devastating effects of black-on-black crime and the threat it poses to the future of the race. "This music belongs here," Cosby told the crowd. "You should applaud it. It's why we don't allow the devil to have all the good music."

Flatted Fifth Jazz Vespers Series

On Saturday, September 29, 2010, after an absence of nearly forty years, the ruling elders of Memorial West Presbyterian Church revived Jazz Vespers, calling it the Flatted Fifth Jazz Vespers Series.

The name comes from a chromatic blues chord made famous by stride pianist Art Tatum and early bebop proponents. Talk of building on the foundation laid long ago by Jan van Arsdale had gone on for years, according to Elder Josephine Jackson. "Finally, we decided to give it a try. We wanted to reach people's hearts—to make them feel good about being here and help them see that there is a Power above. By presenting secular music and poetry (a new element) in a spiritual setting, we are speaking to all of humanity." That, she says, includes a number of Muslims who live in the neighborhood and come to join in fellowship and enjoy the music.

The new series was launched by Antoinette Montague and the Bill Easley Quartet. The second program, on February 26, 2011, featured Carrie Jackson and her Jazzin' All Stars: Norman Simmons on piano; Cornell McGhee, trombone; Earl Grice, drums; and Thaddeus Expose, bass. Jazz photographer and bassist Bill May was the emcee. The program also marked the debut of twelve-year-old Hasadiyah Wheeler, then a member of Jackson's Jazz Vocal Collective.

In July 2012, Stephen Fuller, another member of the collective, and singer Kym Lawrence presented the third Jazz Vespers concert at the church, followed by another appearance by Montague in September. The biggest turnout was in December 2012, when Freddy Cole followed up a show at Birdland with a visit to Memorial West. While his relaxed style resembles that of his brother, Nat King Cole, Freddy Cole, a Juilliard graduate, is more a jazz artist. At Memorial West, his effortless, laid-back songbook included *Pennies From Heaven* and *Blue Moon*. After presenting a medley of tunes made famous by his brother, including *Straighten Up and Fly Right* and *Love*, Cole capped his show with a comedic rendition of *I'm Not My Brother*. Josephine Jackson and her committee could not have been more pleased with the turnout or the performance. "It was a wonderful night for our community," she said afterward.

A 1958 gig at Broadway Open House. *From left:* unidentified bass player; Roland Andrews, piano; Jimmy Anderson, saxophone; Chink Wing, drums. *(Courtesy of John Hamilton).*

A 1950s jam session at Club 83. *From left:* Jimmy Anderson, saxophone; unidentified drummer; Grachan "Brother" Moncur, bass; Freddie Roach, organ. *(Courtesy of Grachan Moncur III.)*

BROADWAY OPEN HOUSE

879 Broadway   *Newark, N. J.*

JAM SESSION NITE

MONDAY MAY 4, 1959

9 p. m until

FEATURING

JOHN COLTRANE

of the MILES DAVIS QUINTET

BOBBY "STIX" DARDEN

and HIS ALL STARS

EVERY   FRI.   SAT.   SUN.

All Star Attraction

A flyer for a 1950 appearance by John Coltrane at Broadway Open House. *(Courtesy of Bob "Stix" Darden.)*

The Nat Phipps Orchestra, late 1950s. *From left: Front row,* Jimmy Pinkman, Billy Phipps and Wayne Shorter, saxophones; Harold Phipps, congas; Nat Phipps, vibraphone. *Back row,* Grachan Moncur III, trombone; Eddie Station, Owen Francis and Charlie Mason, trumpets; Bobby Thomas, drums, Ed Lightsey, bass. *(Courtesy of Nat Phipps.)*

The Megatones, 1950s. *From left:* Billy Phipps, Nat Phipps, Bob "Stix" Darden, Ed Lightsey, Charlie Mason. *(Courtesy of Nat Phipps.)*

Andy Bey and the Bey Sisters, late 1950s. *(Photograph by Maurice Seymour. From the personal collection of Darius de Haas.)*

Ronnell Bey during a
performance at the Priory, 2013.
(Courtesy of Herb Glenn.)

Singer Andy Bey.
(Author's collection.)

The Gordons, 1950s. *From left:* George Jr., Richard, Honi and George Sr.
(Courtesy of Honi Gordon.)

The original Key Club on West Street in the old Third
Ward, 1957. *(Courtesy of Maxine Harvard.)*

NEWARK...
and all that jazz!*

honoring
the 20th Anniversary
of Newark's own
KEY CLUB

the second oldest jazz club in the New York/New Jersey metropolitan area

---

FEATURING Jazz Greats
Who Call the KEY CLUB Home

Ray Bryant	Irene Reid	Joe Thomas
Lu Elliot	Jack Mc Duff	Sam Williams

Houston Person and Etta Jones with Sonny Phillips

Plus TWO surprise very special guests

TIME: 7:30 p.m
PLACE: Essex County College Auditorium
DATE: Wednesday evening
January 26

FREE   **FREE**

ESSEX COUNTY COLLEGE
303 University Avenue
Newark (the home of the jazz greats)

The second of ECC's special series spotlighting nationally-known jazz artists
whose roots are ... NEWARK!
*Jazz series made possible by a grant from the National Endowment for the Arts

LEFT: A flyer from the Key Club's twentieth anniversary celebration at Essex County College, 1977. *(Courtesy of Maxine Harvard.)*

BELOW: Lu Elliott singing at the Key Club, 1960s. *(Courtesy of John Hamilton.)*

The Key Club's twentieth anniversary celebration at Essex County College. *From left:* Eddie Young, bartender; Jeanne Dawkins, owner; Maxine Harvard, organizer; Aaron Bell, music department chairman. *(Courtesy of Maxine Harvard.)*

Lu Elliott and her husband Horace Sims rehearsing for a show at the Key Club, 1970s. *(Author's collection.)*

Leo Johnson (*left*) with Larry Smith (*hidden*) and Connie Lester at Pitt's Place on Hartford Street, 1962. (*Courtesy of Leo Johnson.*)

Singer Carrie Smith with Big Tiny Little's band, 1970s. Little is on piano. (*Author's collection.*)

ABOVE: Carrie Smith singing the blues.
(Photograph by Bill May. Author's collection.)

LEFT: Organist Jimmy McGriff's Christmas card. *(Author's collection.)*

ABOVE: Jimmy McGriff on a gig with drummer Don Williams and guitarist Herb Boyd, 2002. *(Courtesy of Don Williams.)*

BELOW: Charlie Gattuso, guitar; Buddy Terry, tenor sax; Dan Kostelnik, keyboards; and Eddie Gladden, drums, at Jasmine's on Lock Street, 1993. *(Courtesy of Buddy Terry.)*

Dorthaan Kirk, James Moody and Maxine Harvard at the Playbill Lounge, 1970s.
(Courtesy of Maxine Harvard.)

LEFT: The Al Patterson Quintet. *From left:* Greg Maker, string bass; Tomas Olrich, cello; Warren Smith, drums; Alfred Patterson, leader, trombone, and synthesizer; and Billy Phipps, reeds. *(Courtesy of Alfred Patterson.)*

BELOW: Etta Jones and Houston Person at the Taste in Chicago, with Billy James on drums and Dave Braham on organ, mid-1980s. *(Courtesy of Dave Braham.)*

Honi Gordon singing at Jazz Vespers at Memorial West Presbyterian Church, early 1970s. *(Courtesy of Honi Gordon.)*

The Rev. Jan van Arsdale, pastor of Memorial West Presbyterian Church, talking with a neighborhood child, 1970s. *(Courtesy of Jan van Arsdale.)*

Blues singer Edith Wilson at a Jazz Vespers program at Memorial West Presbyterian Church, mid-1970s. *(Courtesy of Jan van Arsdale.)*

FREE!   FREE!   FREE!

NEWARK JAZZ WEEK · 7 BIG DAYS!

JUNE 6th THRU JUNE 12th

MONDAY, JUNE 6th at 11:30 A.M.

Jazz Week Opens on the Steps of City Hall with Mayor Gibson

■CONCERT IN CITY HALL PARK!■

JUNE 6
7:30 P.M.
Essex County College
Featuring:
GRACHAN MONCUR
ALAN SHORTEN · LARRY YOUNG

JUNE 8 — 10:00 P.M.
1940's Jazz Ball at
EBONY MANOR

JUNE 9 — 7:30 P.M.
New Faces in Jazz
MEMORIAL WEST CHURCH

JUNE 10
7:30 P.M.
Rutgers-Newark
Robeson Student Center
THE JAZZ PROFESSORS

NEWARK
salutes
JAZZ

JUNE 7
10:00 P.M.
All Star Jam Sessions at
SPARKY J's & THE KEY CLUB

JUNE 11
3:30 P.M.
Concert in Branch Brook Park

JUNE 12 ● 5:00 P.M.
Memorial West Church ● JAZZ VESPERS
7 P.M. ● Jazz Block Party, William & Halsey Sts.

PLUS... Daily Jazz at Penn Station ● Newark Airport 8 A.M.   9 A.M.
Lunchtime Jazz in Downtown Parks
Jazz in Various Neighborhoods 5:30 ● 6:30 P.M.

ALL EVENTS ARE FREE and are presented with the co-operation
of the City of Newark • Essex County College • Rutgers Institute of
Jazz Studies • Local No. 16, A.F.M.

RIGHT:
An advertisement for the City of Newark's first Jazz Week, 1977. *(Courtesy of Maxine Harvard.)*

BELOW:
Forrest Drennen, keyboards, and Grachan Moncur III, trombone, at Jazz Vespers at the House of Prayer, 1994. *(Courtesy of Forrest Drennen.)*

Joe Thomas and Buddy Terry at the 1997 Organ Jam at the Robert Treat Hotel. *(Photograph by Liz King. Courtesy of Buddy Terry.)*

Flyer for a Newark Museum benefit featuring Houston Person and Etta Jones. No date. *(Courtesy of the Newark Museum.)*

JAZZ UP YOUR THURSDAY

The Newark Museum Council's second annual outdoor
Jazz Reception
featuring **HOUSTON PERSON & ETTA JONES**
Co-sponsored by Renaissance Newark, Inc.

A great opportunity to meet new friends at this special evening performance in the Museum's Alice Ransom Dreyfuss Memorial Garden

**Thursday, June 25
5 to 7 p.m.**
$7 members • $10 non-members
Cash Bar • Appetizers

Proceeds will benefit the Museum's Thursday summer garden jazz concerts

To reserve tickets, call 201 596 6550
or purchase at The Newark Museum Garden Information Desk beginning June 1
(Wednesday - Sunday, noon - 5:00 p.m.)

12 ♪

Beyond the Clubs

Other Venues

The Adams was my real university when it came to playing big-band drums. —Charli Persip

From the late 1930s through the mid-1950s, the Adams Theater—a block off Broad Street in downtown Newark—was a paradise for truancy officers on the prowl for teenagers cutting classes to see shows starring their favorite jazz artists. In retrospect, the list of wayward students reads like an almanac of Newark's most noted entertainers: Sarah Vaughan, Wayne Shorter, James Moody, Charli Persip, Joe Thomas and Walter Davis Jr., to name a few.

Amiri Baraka, New Jersey's former poet laureate, was one of the teenagers who found ingenious ways to sneak into the Adams during his days at Barringer High School. Shorter went so far as to forge his parents' signatures on excuses from school to hang out at the Adams. Moody, meanwhile, was dreaming of the day he would follow stars like Buddy Tate, Earl Warren and Georgie Auld on stage at the Adams. "I first heard Georgie Auld in Artie Shaw's band," he told a *DownBeat* interviewer. "George would play *Body and Soul* and I thought it was so beautiful with the strings behind it . . . really liked the tenor, so as soon as she could, my mother got me a tenor." While other kids haunted the Adams during school hours, Kenneth Gibson, who served four terms (1970–86) as Newark's first African-American mayor, was legit. By the time the curtain went up on late-afternoon matinees he attended, school was out.

As one of the largest music halls in the city, the Adams Theater at 28 Branford Place was in a league of its own, offering nonstop live music and a double feature every day of the week for fifty cents. Other venues, like the Newark Armory, Krueger's Auditorium and the Mosque Theater, presented jazz events from time to time. Over time, the Adams became such a treasure that it got a mention in Philip Roth's 1998 Pulitzer Prize-winning novel *American Pastoral*.

Opened in 1912 as the Shubert Theatre, the Adams initially presented Broadway plays and tryouts. After a couple of name changes early on, vaudeville shows and movies became the standard fare. Show business history reveals that the 2,000-seat theater was renamed in 1931 by Greek immigrant brothers who bought it, shortened their name to Adams and changed the theater's name, too. Inside, architect William E. Lehman's design had a royal air about it, replete with opera boxes, brass railings, a domed ceiling and a heavy red velvet curtain that opened and closed the acts and signaled intermissions. Although tickets were a bit pricey in the aftermath of the Great Depression and World War II, the Adams had no shortage of customers. When name acts came to town, lines to get in often stretched a block away to Broad Street.

Fans also got a chance to hear music at the Adams on ABC radio broadcasts like "Your Saturday Night With Duke," featuring the Duke Ellington Orchestra. Ellington reportedly got $3,092.04 for a 1945 show. With the exception of Johnny Hodges, who was paid $300, the band members received $120 to $200 each. Three years earlier Cab Calloway's orchestra received a whopping $19,000 for a date at the Adams.

The Adams also was a great place for a date. According to Ron Pasquale, whose father managed the theater for more than forty years, its huge, dark balconies "sparked many a romance through the years." The upper tier, Pasquale says, was a favorite hiding place for young people like Shorter, who sometimes sneaked in through the fire escape doors. "I know this," he notes, "because my brothers and I ushered for some years and had to give chase a few times."

Bebop pianist Walter Davis Jr. began hanging out at the Adams in the 1950s while attending East Orange High School. Until then, he was considering a career in classical music, but that changed after he heard Billy Eckstine perform at the Adams. From then on, bebop was his thing. Drummer Charli Persip, later a mainstay in Dizzy Gillespie's orchestra, was at Arts High when he saw his first show at the Adams. "The Adams was my real university when it came to playing big-band drums," he told a critic. "That and listening to a lot of records my older sister had."

Almost all the big bands of the Swing Era played the Adams: Calloway, Gillespie, Ellington, Hampton, Stan Kenton, Benny Carter, Erskine Hawkins, Charlie Spivak and Count Basie. The roster of singers is just as heady: Eckstine, Dinah Washington, the Nat King Cole Trio, Jimmy Scott and the Mills Brothers, to name a few. For Sarah Vaughan, performing at the Adams in December 1947 was a triumphant homecoming. A few years earlier she was a kid worshipping her idols in the darkened theater. Now, she was the attraction other young people came to see. She was *their* idol.

Since the Adams shut down in 1986, large-scale jazz events have taken place at the Terrace Ballroom at Symphony Hall as well as at the Alice Ransome Memorial Garden and Billy Johnson Auditorium at the Newark Museum and, more recently, NJPAC. The studio at WBGO and the Institute of Jazz Studies at Rutgers-Newark sponsor smaller events.

Terrace Ballroom—Newark Symphony Hall

When older Newark residents recall the days when going out at night meant dressing to the nines—women wearing elegant ball gowns and men attired in dark suits or black tie—the Terrace Ballroom comes foremost to mind. From big-band concerts and dances of the 1940s to a recent spate of organ jams reuniting Key Club and Cadillac Club patrons, the ballroom has been a favorite gathering place for more than eighty years. During that span, the downstairs hall at the former Mosque Theater, with its spacious dance floor, large bars and viewing areas from terraces abutting the area below, has been headquarters to hundreds of dances, fashion shows, jazz concerts, after-theater parties and other events, attracting people from all walks of life.

"When I was young, the Terrace Ballroom was the hub of black social life in Newark," says retired educator Franotie Washington. "The dances at the Terrace Room were straight out of Hollywood. Seeing the women in their gowns and men wearing tuxedos made it seem as if they had just stepped off the screen. In those days, people didn't buy tickets to the dances. When one of my mother's organizations had an affair, she'd buy a table and invite friends to come. That's what bids were. I remember people calling our house to see if they were going to be invited."

Gas rationing during World War II made the ballroom more of an attraction since it was impractical for people who lived near Newark to drive to outlying venues like the Meadowbrook in Cedar Grove to socialize and hear big-band music. It was *the* spot for dances sponsored by organizations such as the Captivators, Swanksmen, Cosmetologists and Old Timers. The Bartenders Ball was another hugely popular event.

In those days, some events were catered. Many party-goers, however, brought their own food, often packed in coolers or on trays. Some even sneaked in their own hootch. The dance music was supplied by contingents led by Nat Phipps, Duke and Billy Anderson, Brady Hodge, Bobby Jarrett and Mandy Ross. Johnny Jackson, another popular bandleader, called his group Johnny Jackson's High Society Orchestra, a fitting title given the formality of the times.

As life in America grew more casual, formal affairs at the Terrace Ballroom fell off. By the 1960s, jazz concerts filled the void as the dance band era ran its course. Bassist Bill May, who played there occasionally with Herb Morgan and Buddy Terry, recalls a night in the spring of 1964 when some of the biggest names in jazz were the attraction. "Dizzy Gillespie was there with Chris White on bass, along with Art Blakey and the Jazz Messengers and Lambert, Hendricks and Ross," May recounts. "It was a weeknight, but the place was filled."

In the 1970s and 1980s, WBGO began sponsoring events like "Jazz Fridays" in the ballroom. A band led by Swing Era trumpeter Hal Mitchell, who left Newark in the 1940s to travel with Tiny Bradshaw's big band, was one of the first groups to perform, backed by Miss Rhapsody on vocals. On April 21, 1989, WBGO marked its tenth anniversary with "A Newark Affair to Remember," a buffet dinner in the ballroom featuring music by Etta James, the Stanley Turrentine Quintet and the Chris White Quartet. Lionel Hampton was a special guest.

Subsequent concerts hosted by the radio station at the Terrace Ballroom were part of the Newark Jazz Festival. After the Key Club and Sparky J's closed, a series of hugely popular organ jams that continue to this day, was initiated. In 1997, the New Friends of Symphony Hall presented a series of "Jammin' Jazz Organ" concerts. The opener that June was an all-female event featuring Shirley Scott, Gloria Coleman and Trudy Pitts, backed by Geary Moore on guitar; Gene Ghee, saxophone; Mondre Moffett, trumpet, and Don Williams, drums. That September, Jimmy McGriff, Amina Claudine Meyers and Seleno Clarke were the headliners, followed by Captain Jack McDuff, Radam Schwartz and Sarah McLawler in October and Dr. Lonnie Smith, Gene Ludwig, Mel Davis and Dave Braham in November.

One of the most popular events during that period was an annual Memorial Day reunion sponsored by the Third Ward Elites, a group of women who graduated in the 1950s from Central High School. For years their dances attracted more than 1,500 people annually. Though many of the faces in the crowd are the same today, events at the Terrace Ballroom are far less formal. Sports jackets for men and dresses or pant suits for ladies are now acceptable attire. No one brings food, although there may be a bottle or two hidden away somewhere. Liquor is still served from the two giant bars opposite each other just past the entranceway. Old friends still move from table to table to greet former neighbors and schoolmates.

In recent years, the Terrace Ballroom has hosted a series of jazz events, including organ jams that reunite those who patronized the Key Club and Cadillac Club years ago. Rhoda Scott, forever a Newark favorite, made it a point to synchronize her visits back home from France to coincide with these events. One of those occasions was a Jazz Jam honoring Philip Thomas upon his retirement as executive director of Newark Symphony Hall in April 2013.

During Thomas's tenure (2007–11), the 3,000-seat Sarah Vaughan Concert Hall was refurbished by the city of Newark, which owns the building. As part of the initial $1.5 million provided by the city, the ballroom was modernized, the roof replaced and other critical upgrades made. To supplement funding for the project, Thomas staged a "Jazz Marathon" honoring WBGO'S Dorthaan Kirk. "Singer Yvette Glover originated the idea for this event," Thomas says. "She suggested we contact some of the area jazz musicians, singers and tap dancers who care passionately about Newark Symphony Hall and its future." The event was co-sponsored by the Lincoln Park Coast Cultural District and WBGO.

"Newark Symphony Hall has a significant role to play as we move our city forward," Mayor Cory Booker said at the time. "We intend to make sure it continues to be a resource for the arts, entertainment and cultural activities for the residents of Newark and the citizens of New Jersey."

Newark Museum

The sound of jazz emanating from the Newark Museum garden at lunchtime during the summer months has been a ritual for nearly a half-century. Through the years, the audiences have been as diverse as the music—hand-holding toddlers and senior citizens who arrive by bus, workers from nearby office towers toting lunch bags, and fans from as far as Central and South Jersey who come for the camaraderie. A few even take the PATH train from New York.

Nearing its fiftieth season, Jazz in the Garden in the museum's Alice Ransome Memorial Garden has taken place on consecutive

Thursdays each July and August, offering those who attend a reprieve from the humdrum of daily living by relaxing outdoors in a beautiful setting. Some spectators sit on blankets on the lush lawn or under a huge shade tree, others on white folding chairs nearer the bandstand.

Even when rain threatens—as it did for the season opener featuring Nat Adderly Jr. and his band in 2013—the faithful show up, generally filling all 300 seats in the museum's Billy Johnson Auditorium. For the 2013 occasion, the son of cornetist Nat Adderly and nephew of hard-bop saxophonist Cannonball Adderly brought along a stellar cast: Don Braden on saxophone and flute; Kenny Davis, bass, and Greg Bufford, drums.

"I enjoyed playing at the museum just as much as the audience enjoyed us," Bufford recapped after the performance. If the audience's response was the measuring stick, his assessment was spot on. From what Adderly Jr. called "a little bit of Herbie (Hancock)" to the melancholic strains of *Good Morning Heartache*, the quartet was in a groove. And the audience was most appreciative, cheering and shouting when the band broke into a funky version of *Music Makes the World Go Round*. Eyes closed, hands moving to the beat as if she were conducting the group, Sharon Mingo-Clark admittedly was in a world of her own as she mouthed the words to one of her favorite tunes. Like many concert-goers, Mingo-Clark returns to the museum each year to get her fill of jazz Newark-style. "I'm just sorry it had to be indoors this time," she noted, explaining how she loves being outdoors when weather permits. "To my mind I'm at my own private estate enjoying wonderful music."

The roster of nationally known musicians who have appeared on the summer stage over the course of nearly five decades has grown to the point where it reads like a mini-Who's Who of modern jazz, including Cedar Walton, Wycliffe Gordon, Frank Morgan, Dr. Lonnie Smith, David Murray and Art Blakey, Jr. In 1993, Houston Person and singer Etta Jones headlined a benefit to supplement funding for the summer series. Singer Andy Bey, an Arts High graduate, and saxophonist Jimmy Heath played for other fundraisers. Local favorites who have participated in the concerts include musicians Billy Ford, Duke Anderson, Buddy Terry, Joe Thomas, Al Patterson, Vinnie Burke, Billy Phipps, Andy McCloud, Bradford Hayes and Leo Johnson, and singers Carrie Smith, Carrie Jackson, Pam Purvis, Antoinette Montague, Pat Tandy, Doris Spears, Marlene Ver Planck and Jeanie Bryson.

"Jazz in the Garden is an important part of our summer," says Walter Chambers, who has attended the concerts for years. "We're all retirees, so it's a half-day outing that we enjoy each week. After the concerts, we have lunch and spend another hour-and-a-half together." Chambers and his friends—Ted and Joan Pinckney, Charlie Cann, Rose Spears, Jessie Martin, Stan Myers, Dolores Johnson and a few others—even have a nickname—"The Jazz Posse."

Elissa and Aaron Hairston, who live thirty miles from Newark in East Brunswick, also are among the regulars. "The concerts are something my husband and I look forward to," she says. "We're jazz fans, so we find listening to great music outdoors a wonderful way to relax."

For the past decade the series has been produced by Sheila Anderson, WBGO's overnight host. "It's been important for us to have someone like Sheila in charge," says Mary Sue Sweeney Price, who retired as the museum's director in 2013 after more than twenty years at the helm. "Sheila's the right person for the job."

"When I took over, everyone on the staff went blank when I mentioned someone like (bassist) Ron Carter," Anderson says. "Now, everyone who works here looks forward to the series." Anderson's aim is to create an eclectic mix of music, ranging from down-home blues to funk and bebop. In shaping the agenda, she looks for diversity as well as a cross section of generational talent, from master musicians to up-and-coming artists. "While many Newark residents attend our summer concerts, I don't see them as Newark events," Anderson says. "We're trying to draw people from everywhere."

Bringing in name artists, Anderson says, lets museum-goers avoid trekking to New York and paying exorbitant prices to hear them perform. Instead, their fans enjoy first-rate performances close to home for a mere $3 admission fee. One of the most well-received acts recently was Rene Marie, a sultry scat singer few people in the audience had heard before. By concert's end, the quality of her voice and exuberance of her performance had won her a new legion of fans. Every song, from a sexy version of *Black Lace* to two Abbey Lincoln tunes, *Throw It Away* and *I Know Why the Caged Bird Sings*, featuring Steve Wilson on soprano sax, was a showstopper.

"My goal is to make each program exciting," says Anderson. "That's why the lineup crosses the jazz spectrum from Latin jazz to post-bop." The 2009 schedule, launched by singer Antoinette Montague, is a perfectly balanced example. Also on the bill that season were Brazilian bass player Nilson Mattas and his group, drummer T.S. Monk, trumpeter Cecil Bridgewater, and Adam Niewood and his Rabble Rousers, an experimental music group. "Appearing at Jazz in the Garden was a thrill because I come from Newark," says Montague. "It was, in a sense, a stamp of approval, a way of getting myself out there in the jazz world at that point in my career."

As coordinator of Jazz in the Garden Anderson has made it a point to liven up the programming each season. To mark the opening of the fortieth anniversary of the series in 2005, for example, the museum paid tribute to Dan Morgenstern, the longtime director of the Newark-based Institute of Jazz Studies, and WBGO jazz luminary Dorthaan Kirk. In June 2009, a Jazz BBQ event featuring singer Carmen Lundy benefited the education and public programs.

In June 2012, pianist and composer Geri Allen presented a concert inspired by the life and work of artist Romare Bearden in conjunction with an exhibition of Bearden's work: *Romare Bearden: Southern Recollections*. In recent years, After Hours, a Thursday night jazz series, fell victim to budget cuts, a problem that's forced museum officials to trim Jazz in the Garden programming and institute an admission charge.

From Anderson's perspective the concerts are a wonderful educational experience as well as a bargain. "The people in our audiences get to learn more about jazz, and the musicians get an idea of what it's like to play outdoors, rather than in some stuffy club," she says. "Through the years, visitors who otherwise might not have come to Newark or stopped by if it weren't for *Jazz in the Garden* keep coming. In doing so, they have the chance to see the museum's world-class exhibits and hear great music." Just as importantly, Price says, each new face represents a building block for the future.

13 ♪

Festivals
Celebrating Jazz Citywide

*I've done what I've done, but it's not
enough. I'm a student of jazz and there's so
much more to learn. —James Moody*

When Brother Moncur, the Savoy Sultans' bassist, paid tribute to his wife, Ella, on their fiftieth anniversary in the mid-1980s, he did so in song, offering up a charming rendition of *Moody's Mood for Love*, the catchy tune made famous by saxophonist James Moody years before. Moody wasn't there that night at the Marriott Hotel at Newark International Airport. The likelihood was that he was playing a gig far away from Newark, but he was foremost in the minds of his friends.

Although Moody left East Side High School in Newark to join the Air Force in the early 1940s and spent most of his life traveling the world, he never forgot his roots. Every so often he'd return home to perform, early on at Lloyd's Manor or Cleo's in the Meadowlands, and later in life at the Lincoln Park Music Festival.

Moody's persona was anything but moody, according to anyone who knew him. He loved having fun and enjoying life, according to his wife Linda, a San Diego realtor. After they met in early 1989 at a Los Angeles jazz club, he was so smitten he ran up a $1,500 phone bill calling her from Africa while on a State Department tour. From the start, Linda Moody knew too that he was "the one" for her. Three months after their first date they married, with Moody's old friend Dizzy Gillespie as best man. It truly was a marriage made in heaven, she says, to the point where he never called her anything other than "Honey."

"When we met, I had never heard of James Moody," she notes. "I knew nothing about him or his music." *Moody's Mood*, the fast-paced tune he recorded in Stockholm in one take in 1949, was only vaguely familiar.

"The funny thing about it (*Moody's Mood*)," James Moody related years later, was that "I was trying to find the notes during the entire recording. It was a fluke," he maintained, crediting the song's success to Eddie Jefferson's lyrics. After his return to Newark and the record's release, Moody spent hours listening to his mother's Victrola trying to replicate the original version. While many singers have recorded the tune, one of Moody's favorites was by Queen Latifah. "She has a beautiful voice, and did a wonderful job," he said.

Born in Savannah, Georgia, on March 26, 1925, Moody moved with his family first to Reading, Pennsylvania, then to Newark, where he got his musical start. "We came to Newark because I was hard of hearing and they didn't know it," he said. "They thought I was out of it." Unfortunately, he was assigned to the Bruce Street School for the Deaf, a traumatic experience because the other children were deaf and he was not.

Before taking up tenor, Moody played piano. Duke Anderson, who saw him perform at a church in Newark's Ironbound section when he was six or seven, described the performance as "very remarkable." Raised in Pennington Court, one of the city's first public housing projects, Moody attended Arts High School, then East Side, before entering the Air Force in early 1943. By then he had taken up saxophone, inspired by legends such as Lester Young, Charlie Barnett and Jimmy Dorsey whom he heard at Newark's Adams Theater, as well as local saxophonists Pancho Diggs, Gene Phipps Sr. and Ike Quebec.

As a member of the Air Force band, Moody found himself in the company of stellar musicians: Thelonious Monk on piano; Ray Brown, bass; Milt Jackson, vibraphone; Connie Cockrell, drums; and Walter "Gil" Fuller, music director. But the band wasn't "authorized," he explained in an interview with Camille Cosby. "Authorized" meant white.

After completing military service, Moody played his first professional gig at Lloyd's Manor in the Central Ward. His $7 pay was what he described as "good money" at the time. "We played in the bar, but sometimes we'd go in the back for dances," he recalled. "Everything was bebop." Moody's first big break came when Babs Gonzalez told him about an opening in Dizzy Gillespie's band and encouraged him to go after it. He did and wound up playing with Gillespie for the next two years.

"I first met Dizzy while in the Air Force in Greensboro, North Carolina, where his band played for dances under a big tent," Moody said. Although he auditioned for a spot in Gillespie's big band after his discharge, he didn't make it because Fuller, the music director, didn't think he played loud enough. A couple of months later he got a telegram, inviting him to join the band. It was one hot group with Monk on piano; Ray Brown on bass; Cecil Payne on baritone sax; and Milt "Bags" Jackson on vibraphone.

In 1948, Moody made his first recording with Blue Note, then moved to Europe, where he spent the next three years because he believed America was scarred by racism. By the time he returned home in 1952, *Moody's Mood for Love* was on every jukebox in black America. Over the course of the next twenty years he made nearly forty LPs, mostly on Prestige, Argo, Milestone, Perception and Muse, playing flute, tenor and alto.

Moody rejoined Gillespie in 1964, laying the foundation for collaborations with pianist Kenny Barron and guitarist Les Spann. At the time, Gillespie's group included Chris White on bass and Lalo Schifrin on piano. Later in his career, he played with the Dizzy Gillespie Alumni All-Stars and the Dizzy Gillespie Alumni All-Stars Big Band, which led to travels in Australia, the Philippines, Japan and Canada.

By then a four-time Grammy nominee, Moody received one of the most prestigious honors in his field in 2007, the Kennedy Center Living Jazz Legend Award. Other honors include an honorary doctorate of music degree from the Berklee College of Music, the President's Medal from Juilliard and the Jazz Master Award from the National Endowment of the Arts. He also was named to the National Academy of Recording Artists and Sciences Hall of Fame and the New Jersey Hall of Fame. Newark Mayor Sharpe James and his successor, Cory Booker, sponsored James Moody Day celebrations at City Hall in his honor. Chief executives of several other cities followed suit.

Over the years, Moody enjoyed nothing more than getting together with old friends from Newark. "We came to Newark many times because my husband's mother (Ruby Watters) still lived in the city," says Linda Moody. "We'd have lunch and drive around to places like the Colonnade Apartments, where Moody once lived."

The last time Moody played in Newark was at the third annual Lincoln Park Music Festival in 2008. During ceremonies at City Hall, Mayor Cory Booker designated July 25th James Moody Day and Essex County Executive Joe DiVincenzo presented the jazz icon with a proclamation hailing his musical achievements. Elisabeth Withers, who was starring on Broadway in *The Color Purple*, sang *Moody's Mood for Love*. From there, the tribute moved to the park, where Moody's quartet, featuring Cyrus Chestnut, John Lee and Dennis Mackrel, performed. Moody's longtime friend and kindred soul, Amiri Baraka, was the emcee.

Soon after came the sad announcement by Linda Moody that her husband was suffering from pancreatic cancer, a devastating illness that claimed his life on December 9, 2010. The following summer Baraka rounded up Moody's friends again for a three-hour concert in his honor. The all-star presentation in Lincoln Park, sponsored by Friends of Moody and co-hosted by Sheila Anderson of WBGO, featured Bill Charlap, Todd Coolman, Jon Faddis, Antonio Hart, John Lee, Lewis Nash, Jimmy Owens and Renee Rosnes. Playing with Baraka's NewArkestra were Steve Colson, Al Patterson, Gene Ghee, Gene Goldston, Carlos Francis, Rene McLean, Takashi Otsuka, Billy Phipps and Charlie Rouse.

Many of the musicians had gathered the night before at a reception at the nearby Russell Aldo Murray Gallery for a "Celebration of the Life of James Moody," an exhibit by photographers Stephanie Myers and Tony Graves that traced Moody's life and career. The program also included performances by James Gibbs III and Ghee.

During the event, the mayor and other elected officials joined Moody's friends for a ribbon-cutting ceremony marking the opening of the James Moody Apartments, an affordable-housing community in the city's Central Ward. The multimillion-dollar project, which consists of sixty-eight apartments in four buildings, was the brainchild of the Lincoln Park Coast Cultural District, which sponsors the annual music festival. "This was the result of a multi-year neighborhood participatory planning process, which incorporated a vision of a green arts and cultural district that includes live work spaces, community programs and additional open space," according to Baye Adofo-Wilson, the district's executive director.

The most expansive salute to Moody's memory was yet to come—the James Moody Democracy of Jazz Festival—a star-studded series of events over a seven-day period in October 2012 at the New Jersey Performing Arts Center. "His spirit embodies the spirit of jazz," John Schreiber, NJPAC's president, told the *Star-Ledger*. "If we do our job right, this festival will resonate with that."

Presented in collaboration with WBGO, the festival featured two all-star concerts, the first starring musicians who worked closely with Moody over the years, including George Benson, David Sanborn, Paquito D'Rivera, Jimmy Heath and Kenny Barron. The second event, led by Terence Blanchard, Sean Jones and a jazz orchestra, re-created Gil Evans's arrangements of songs Moody made famous with Miles Davis.

Events got under way October 15 with a concert by Rufus Reid's Out Front Trio at Bethany Baptist Church. Other programs included a concert by the James Moody All-Stars at the Newark Museum, children's events and a panel discussion on Moody's life and career moderated by former *Star-Ledger* jazz critic George Kanzler at the Institute of Jazz Studies at Rutgers-Newark.

At each event, Linda Moody welled up as she spoke of her husband's unabiding love of Newark, his music, his fans and his zest for life. "You would never forget it if you were hit by one of Moody's love bullets," she told the crowd at the opening of Dorthaan's Place at NJPAC, a new venue that offers Sunday afternoon jazz performances. Pianist Geri Allen was the featured performer.

The festival's closing event was the first Sarah Vaughan International Vocal Competition in NJPAC's Victoria Theater. Amid a wealth of talent, Cyrille Aimee, a French-Canadian jazz/pop singer, emerged the winner. For Schreiber, the success of the weeklong festival was a portent of things to come—part of his quest to restore Newark's standing as a place to go for jazz in New Jersey.

In addition to concerts featuring such artists as Jimmy Heath, Sergio Mendes and Dianne Reeves, the second annual festival in 2013 celebrated the fiftieth anniversary of Amiri Baraka's *Blues People*, a seminal work on African-American music. It also marked the return of the Sarah Vaughan vocal competition and the second season of Dorthaan's Place. In addition, Newark-born Lorraine Gordon and the Village Vanguard, the jazz haunt she and her late husband Max Gordon ran in Greenwich Village for a half-century, were honored. Lorraine Gordon's roots in Newark date to the 1940s, when she was a student at Weequahic High School and president of the Newark Hot Club, a group of teenagers dedicated to promoting jazz. Her first husband, Alfred Lion, co-founded and served as president of Blue Note Records.

Newark's first citywide jazz celebration dates to 1977 when the Committee to Save Jazz in Newark staged A Salute to Jazz. With the cooperation of Mayor Kenneth A. Gibson, who issued a proclamation declaring June 8–12, 1977, Newark Jazz Week, the promoters presented a seven-day series of free concerts in city parks and malls, on street corners and in clubs. In some ways, the committee's attempt to revive the city's once-vibrant jazz scene was a throwback to the 1940s, when the *New Jersey Afro-American*, a black weekly, conducted annual polls to determine jazz fans' favorite singers and musicians. The broader aim was to increase patronage at Newark nightclubs by encouraging customers to go from club to club to secure their ballots. The 1977 events had a similar mission. "We hope to bring jazz to the people as well as bring people to jazz," said Herbert "Geronimo" Johnson, co-chairman of A Salute to Jazz with Maxine Harvard, the public relations director at Essex County College.

After the mayor launched the celebration on the steps of City Hall, Newark came alive with the sounds of jazz from morning to night. Wake Up jazz concerts got things rolling each morning at Newark International Airport. That Wednesday night, veterans of the Savoy Dictators, one of the city's most popular Swing Era bands, hosted a 1940s Jazz Ball at Ebony Manor on Clinton Avenue. Jam sessions and concerts throughout the city featured a wealth of local talent, including Buddy Terry, Chico Mendoza, Duke Anderson, Joe Thomas, Vinnie Burke, Chink Wing, Gene Phipps, Grachan Moncur III, Leo Johnson, Andy Bey, Miss Rhapsody, Hal Mitchell and Leon Eason.

After a lull the following year, Newark Jazz Week resumed in April 1979. By then, Newark had begun broadcasting jazz around the clock on WBGO. Designating Newark as home to National Public Radio's first New Jersey affiliate was a boon for jazz lovers. Hundreds of listeners came to Newark for the festival.

At a kickoff party in the mayor's office, Gibson surprised everyone by bringing out the horn his mother bought him as a child and playing bluesy alto sax. His supporting cast included musicians Leo Johnson, Dave Eubanks, Buddy Terry and Aaron Bell, and blues and jazz singer Miss Rhapsody. Again the schedule was packed with special events, including lunchtime and rush-hour concerts and nighttime performances at Essex County College, Rutgers-Newark and Memorial West Presbyterian Church, where awards were presented during Sunday Jazz Vespers. Despite the boost from WBGO, crowds never materialized, prompting *Star-Ledger* jazz critic Kanzler to blame the committee for not promoting the events properly.

Unfazed, Harvard and her committee decided to give it a go again the following year. This time the festival was an outgrowth of the Newark Jazz Society founded by Harvard, Dorthaan Kirk and organist Jimmy McGriff. "By 1980, Jazz Week was an idea that finally needed reality," Harvard says By then, too, the committee had much stronger support from the community. The Newark Chamber of Commerce also pitched in, publishing an extensive article Harvard had written on the history of jazz in Newark in its magazine, *Metro Newark!* Posters went up all over town and the concerts were better advertised.

Once again, Newark was alive with the sounds of jazz, from June 8–12, 1980, as morning concerts at Newark International Airport and other events continued into the wee hours. There also was a photo exhibit by Bob Parent in the Prudential lobby, a lunchtime concert in Military Park featuring Sam Jones and the New Jersey All-Stars, and an organ jam led by Jimmy McGriff and Jack McDuff at Sparky's. Again, the Savoy Dictators held sway at Ebony Manor. The celebration wound up with a block party outside Sparky's and the Key Club.

Eventually, the festival ran its course, leaving Newark without a citywide jazz celebration until 1991, when the Sarah Vaughan Jazz Festival sparked new interest in the city's rich jazz history. "It's difficult to piece together just what or who was the impetus for what became the Newark Jazz Festival," says Celeste Bateman, the festival's secretary, but there was no question that it was spurred in part by Vaughan's death the year before. Ada Vaughan, Sarah's mother, came from California for the series of events, but legal problems forced a name change the following year, when it became the Newark Jazz Festival.

With financial support from the city's Community Development Block Fund, the New Jersey State Council on the Arts and the Newark business community, the initial celebration took place in November 1991. Those in the forefront of the venture included Bateman, Alex Boyd, director of the Newark Public Library, and Catherine Lenix-Hooker, director of the Krueger Mansion Restoration Project.

The opening event at the Gateway Center featured flutist Haven Claiborne and singer Jackie Jones, friends from Arts High School. Top billing went to Abbey Lincoln, Tito Puente, the Count Basie Orchestra with Joe Williams, Roy Hargrove, Jimmy Heath and Hilton Ruiz. Other events included a three-day series of stride piano concerts, an on-air concert at WBGO, a premiere of *Listen to the Sun*, a film about Sarah Vaughan produced by Tom Guy, and a talk on black music in Newark by Amiri Baraka. Among the local favorites who performed were Jimmy Scott, Duke Anderson, Leo Johnson, Herb Morgan, Buddy Terry, Grachan Moncur III, Joe Thomas, James (Chops) Jones, and George Benson. Singer Rachelle Ferrelle was a new discovery.

The festival the following year included two all-star events. First came A Gala Night of Singing and Swinging starring Nancy Wilson and Tony Bennett in the newly named Sarah Vaughan Concert Hall at Newark Symphony Hall, followed by a Sunday afternoon Reunion Jazz Organ Jam in the Tri-state Ballroom at the Robert Treat Hotel. "The organ jam was just like the old days," says Stan Myers. Masters of the Hammond B3 organ, including McGriff, Captain Jack McDuff, Charles Earland, Gloria Coleman, Trudy Pitts and Jeff Brown, were on the bill.

In 1993, events kicked off with a symposium on Women in Jazz at the Newark Museum with WBGO's Rhonda Hamilton as host. The panelists were composer/arranger Sharon Freeman, singer Carrie Smith, author Sally Placksin and saxophonist-composer Jane Ira Bloom. A reception and concert featuring singer Ronnell Bey, pianist Bertha Hope, drummer Sylvia Cuenca and bassist Melissa Slocum followed. Rhoda Scott, just in from Paris, joined Bill Doggett, Trudy Pitts, Jack McDuff and a host of area musicians for the Hammond B3 organ jam at the Robert Treat.

By 1994 the organ reunion jam, celebrating the heyday of the Key Club and Sparky's J's was an institution. It also had a new twist—a digitalized, Japanese-made version of the Hammond B3. It proved, however, to be more gimmick than innovation. The concert at the

Robert Treat Hotel featuring Hank Marrs, Dr. Lonnie Smith, Papa John DeFrancesco, Gene Ludwig and Shirley Scott was well into its fifth hour before anyone touched it. That someone was Jimmy McGriff, who received the festival's Lifetime Achievement Award.

Another big show at Newark Symphony Hall featured Ramsey Lewis, who played everything from his pop-soul hit *The In Crowd* to *Sometimes I Feel Like a Motherless Child*. The blockbuster event came on Saturday night, when Freddie Hubbard and thirteen-year-old pianist Sergio Salvatore opened for Jimmy Scott and Gil Scott-Heron. Jay Lustig of the *Star-Ledger* called the sold-out concert at the Robert Treat "absolutely electrifying."

In 1995, the perennial organ jam featured performances by Big John Patton, Charles Earland, Seleno Clarke and Amina Claudine Myers. An unscheduled appearance by Rhoda Scott made it all the more a night to remember. Radam Schwartz, Dave Braham and two younger organists—Joey DeFrancesco and Larry Goldings— also were on the bill. The night before the jam, saxophonist Stanley Turrentine and singer Gloria Lynne tore the place up—Turrentine with his gritty tenor and Lynne with her endearing renditions of *My Funny Valentine* and *I'm Glad There is You*, her theme song.

The 1996 festival marked the return of George Benson, who spent two hours on stage romping through tunes with McDuff before inviting Rhoda Scott up to take McDuff's place for a fast-paced tribute to Ray Charles. Kanzler called it "churning waves of thunderous sound," embellished by "riff-laden solos." Saxophonist Lonnie Youngblood, he wrote, "had the crowd roaring even louder with his classic honking, screaming tenor solo."

Despite an outward appearance of success, the festival was nearing its end, plagued by financial problems that included an initial $50,000 operating deficit that kept mounting. "It was an ambitious undertaking from the start," Bateman says, "but, as I remember, we ran a deficit every year. Our spirits were high and our intentions were good, but our expenses far exceeded our revenues, which caused us to fold in 1997."

For a fifteen-year period Newark had no citywide jazz celebration. That changed when Schreiber created the James Moody
Democracy of Jazz Festival in 2012. Given Newark's vibrant jazz
history, NJPAC's president says the festival's success merits expan-
sion year-round. With bassist Christian McBride as NJPAC's artistic
director, that plan is taking shape.

14 ♪

Small Groups,
Big Sounds

*The spirit of jazz is the spirit of
openness. —Herbie Hancock*

During the Swing Era, internationally acclaimed trumpeter
Louis Armstrong was the quintessential small-band leader,
offering up some of the hottest sounds of that period with his Hot
Five. Generally, however, big bands were the rage, led by innovative
musicians like Duke Ellington, Count Basie, Cab Calloway and Lionel Hampton. With the advent of World War II, many large contingents disbanded when their members joined the military and went
off to war.

For a decade or so after the war ended, bebop was the more popular form of music at clubs throughout the city. Nat Phipps led a
swinging group called the Megatones, while hipsters Hank Mobley and James Moody reigned, respectively, over weekly jam sessions at the Picadilly and Lloyd's Manor. A decade later, organ jazz
was the new interest with Rhoda Scott, Captain Jack McDuff and
Jimmy McGriff at the helm at the Key Club and Cadillac Club,
which became Sparky J's. Today, horn players like Leo Johnson,
David Robinson and James Gibbs III are producing big sounds with
small units in and around Newark. Here's the lowdown on groups
led by Rudy Walker, Bradford Hayes and Ike Brown.

Rudy Walker

Considering the many challenges he's faced during his sixty-something years, it's a wonder Rudy Walker didn't choose another way to make a living than music. Hauling around a set of drums when you're in pain, as Walker has done most of his life, might have been prohibitive. But Walker, who's battled rheumatoid arthritis since childhood, considers the energy involved light stuff compared to other problems. "I'm so accustomed to it, I can do it in my sleep," he says, "although it can be a bit frustrating when everybody else is pulling out and you're still there with your drums."

Although he wasn't diagnosed until he was twelve, his medical woes date to being hit by a car that was backing out of a neighbor's driveway when he was nine. "I wasn't knocked down, so I didn't think anything of it at the time," he says. "I just kept playing." Thirty-five years later Walker found medical help through the Jazz Foundation of America at Englewood Hospital in Bergen County, where Dizzy Gillespie was treated for cancer during the latter stage of his life. By then, Walker's pain was so excruciating he could barely stand.

"Because so few musicians had medical insurance, Diz urged his doctor to start a program to help uninsured and underinsured musicians," Walker explains. "As the first one treated when the Jazz Foundation came aboard in 1994, I was sent to an orthopedist and had my left hip replaced." Since the start of the program, Dr. Frank Forte, the hospital's former medical director, has developed a team of fifty doctors that has provided more than 1,000 musicians more than $5 million in free medical care.

Walker was forty-seven when he had his operation, suffering by then from constant flare-ups "ten times more painful than a toothache." At times, he says, he could barely bear the weight of a bed sheet. But he kept playing, masking his problems from everyone but close friends such as bassist Andy McCloud. "I had good days and bad days, but I didn't want to use my pain as an excuse or crutch," he says. "I was determined I was going to be a jazz musician, so I just dealt with it. If I couldn't make a gig, I'd never tell the guys. I'd just get a sub. You play music because you love it, even if that means existing on peanut butter and jelly sandwiches. It's not work, especially when you have a good rapport with the musicians you're playing with. That's when the love kicks in."

Born in Orange, New Jersey, in 1947, Walker began taking lessons with Ed Dorflinger when he was eight. By the time he entered Orange High School, where he was a member of the orchestra and band, he was a devotee of Lionel Hampton and Philly Joe Jones. On the home front, his idol was Billy Brooks (singer Yvette Glover's brother), who later made a name for himself in Europe. "From the moment I saw Billy play at a high school concert, I wanted to play like him," says Walker, who got his first paid job performing with other teenagers at the YWCA in Orange when he was a junior in high school.

After entering St. Augustine's College in Raleigh, North Carolina, Walker got away from music. "I was a math major, but I didn't like it so I left after my freshman year," he says. "For a while I worked at a check printing company, then I got a job with Singer-Kearfott in West Paterson, not far from Gulliver's," a well-known jazz club.

By then he was sharing a third-floor apartment of a house on Springdale Avenue in East Orange with McCloud, his childhood friend from day camp at the Oakwood YMCA. "After I bought a drum kit, Andy taught me a little and I began playing music to pay the rent," he says. "Andy and I lived together for two or three years in the early 1970s until he got married. During that time, Andy began working with all the top players, and I got my first professional gig. I was paying my dues and immersing myself in the music."

In the mid-1970s Walker began playing with Bill Harris, who had taken over for Nat Phipps at jam sessions at the Peppermint Lounge. He also played with Harris at Mr. Wes's on Hill Street in Newark. Other encouragement came from drummers Eddie Gladden, Bobby "Stix" Darden, Charlie Mason and Eddie Crawford.

Walker's big break came one night in 1977 when he met Sir Roland Hanna at Gulliver's. "When I told Roland I played drums, he asked me to bring them the next night," he says. "I made the gig that Saturday night and wound up playing with him for the next three years. Roland Hanna was a big man in jazz. He helped me kick the New York door down. I love playing Newark, but when you play in New York you get a lot of opportunities. People from all over the world get to hear you play."

Walker's first trip to Europe was with Sonny Fortune in the summer of 1979. "That spring, Andy called me and invited me to a jam session at Sonny's house in New York. I didn't know it, but it was an audition. Three months later I was in Europe for the first time, touring with Sonny's band. Andy was the catalyst." In the late 1970s, Walker began studying West African drumming with Obara Wali Rahman and Chuck Davis, which led to a twice-a-week gig as accompanist for African dance classes at a Montclair studio.

Through the years Walker also has been a favorite at the Key Club, Playbill Lounge and Cadillac Club, as well as at the Cadillac's successor, Sparky J's. He also appears frequently at schools and senior citizens centers on programs sponsored by the Jazz Foundation of America. When the money's right, he's back on the road as a sideman.

Walker also leads his own group, mostly at the Priory. But getting work as a leader can be tough, he says. "It's a sad commentary, but sometimes you're more appreciated in Chicago than at home." Still, he's resilient enough to continue playing no matter what the circumstances. That's made him the subject of a documentary, *Rhythm in Pain*.

A few years ago a fire at Walker's apartment complex claimed everything he owned except the clothes he was wearing and his drums, which were waterlogged but still playable. "It wasn't just me who suffered a loss," he says. "Eight families lost their homes. Thankfully, no one was seriously injured."

Bradford Hayes

Whenever there's a major music event in Newark, saxophonist Brad-ford Hayes is in the house, most often as the leader. Within the last year or so that's meant appearing at Sounds of the City concerts at NJPAC and at the Newark YMCA's Living Legends dinner as well as receiving the Priory's first Unsung Heroes Award. He also was part of a Terrace Ballroom tribute to Philip Thomas, retired executive di-rector of Newark Symphony Hall.

Hayes seems to be everywhere, uncanny perhaps because he only performs on weekends and during the summer. Otherwise, he's tending to his music students at First Avenue School in Newark, his latest assignment during more than thirty years with the New-ark public schools.

Raised on a farm in Dinwiddie County, Virginia, Hayes came north to Newark after graduating from North Carolina Agricul-tural and Technical State College. He's been a force on the North-east jazz scene ever since. "In Newark, the schools provide musical instruments for students, but where I'm from, parents have to buy or rent them," he explains. "The first time I heard a man from the local music store do a demonstration at my school, I was floored. I wanted a horn. My great-aunt Katherine, who raised me, told me she'd think about it, but I had to wait a year and improve my be-havior. I was from a broken home, so I guess I was rebelling at the time."

Because of his keen interest in music, he adjusted his behavior to the point where he almost became a model child. A year later, Katherine and her sister Dorothy, who worked as a domestic for a wealthy family on Upper Mountain Avenue in Montclair, bought him his first horn. "I think it cost $500," he says, still appreciative of the sacrifice his aunts made.

At the time, Hayes was in the sixth grade, studying music in class and as a member of the school band under "Mr. Crumpett." Robert Harrey, the band director at Dinwiddie High School, was his next music teacher. But Hayes had little time to practice. "I was playing football, so I couldn't be in the band and play, too," he explains. Until he received a football scholarship to attend A&T, he hadn't given college much thought. His focus was on working alongside his uncle Thomas, Katherine's husband, on the railroad.

"At that point, I didn't know anything about jazz," he says. "I didn't even know what it was. In fact, I had never heard any black music growing up because Dinwiddie was so rural. I was in the church choir, but that was it." That changed at A&T. At seventeen, he began playing in rhythm and blues bands in the area around the college and was inspired by Ted McDaniels, the music department chairman, who took him and some friends to a jazz club in Winston-Salem to hear Woody Shaw. That experience, he says, changed his life. "It blew me away," he explains. "Mr. McDaniels was a friend of Woody's so we got to meet all the musicians—Mulgrew Miller, Tony Reedus, Carter Jefferson, Steve Turre and Stafford James. That's what pulled me into music even more."

Another life-altering experience occurred during his sophomore year, when the Duke Ellington Orchestra, under Mercer Ellington, visited the A&T campus. After the show, Hayes got autographs from Dave Eubanks, Mulgrew Miller, Kenny Garrett and Dave Young, a remembrance he still treasures.

After graduating from college more than thirty years ago, Hayes began teaching in Newark, spending half that time at the Luis Munoz Marin School in the city's North Ward. He also began participating in weekly jam sessions emceed by Tex Womble at the Peppermint Lounge. "Those were the good old days," he says. "There's never been anything like it since then."

Hayes also went to work for Teddy Powell, the East Coast's most prominent promoter. "When bands came to town, they only brought the rhythm section, so Teddy hired me to provide the trombone and trumpet players," he explains. "I'd get $1,000 or so and split it up, so it was a nice little hustle. We played for groups like the Dells and for Jerry Butler."

While Hayes has opened for everyone from Chico Freeman, Betty Carter and Joe Henderson to Max Roach, Marlena Shaw and

Hilton Ruiz, he's best known in the Newark area for leading his own groups, generally a quartet or quintet. Early in his career he spent fifteen years with Babatunde Olatunji's Drums of Passion Band, three of them as music director. The concert Hayes remembers most was at Yankee Stadium, marking Nelson Mandela's historic trip to the United States following his release from prison.

Being chosen as one of five musicians for the first photograph taken since 1948 by legendary photographer William Gottlieb after Gottlieb emerged from retirement, is another career highlight. Also in the photo are John Lee, Javon Jackson, Bill Saxton and Hilton Ruiz. "That was quite an honor," says Hayes, who is looking forward to its inclusion in a PBS jazz documentary on the late Gottlieb's work.

Hayes has longtime ties to the Priory, where he booked the acts for Jazz Fridays and Sunday Jazz Brunches in the early 1990s after the New Community Corporation began presenting jazz programs. That's also where he celebrated his fifty-fourth birthday in September 2013. Friends from the music world, the schools where he's taught, and the community at large turned out to pay tribute to him.

Ike Brown and the Jazz Prophets

When the Priory began offering jazz on Friday nights in the early 1990s, Ike Brown and the Jazz Prophets were one of the most popular draws. Like the Priory, Brown's group was just getting off the ground. After spending twenty-six years working for the Montclair Police Department, Brown was looking for a new gig to liven up his retirement. The Prophets were it. Until then, Brown's career in music was limited to hanging around jazz joints in Newark in his youth and playing after work in Montclair, where he was born and raised.

Brown took up trumpet as a student at Glenfield School in Montclair when he was twelve, accelerating his knowledge of the instrument by taking private lessons on Saturdays at the George Innes

School. "I wanted to play sax," he says, "but my teacher told me that would require six months of playing flute. I didn't want to do that, so I chose the trumpet, which led to a spot in the school's drum and bugle corps."

As a teenager he began haunting Pitt's Place on Hartford Street in Newark, where Leon Eason, whose blistering trumpet was reminiscent of Louis Armstrong, led the jam sessions, supported by Specks Williams on piano and Gus Young on drums. "Although I'd taken lessons for three years, I could hardly play anything," Brown says. "I can still hear Leon yelling at me to get off the stage—to go back to the woodshed." Brown followed Eason's advice, practicing until he became adept enough to play at the Sterington House in Montclair while he was still in high school. "Lloyd Wheeler had the house band," he recalls.

"I only played one or two gigs at the Sterington House before being sent to Fort Dix as an Army reservist," he adds. "If you played an instrument you could audition for the First Training Regimental Band. I was one of the recruits who made it and wound up playing for parades and other events on the base and in Wrightstown," where the base was located. Brown's yearlong tour of duty was divided between Fort Dix in New Jersey and Camp Drum in upstate New York, where he gained further musical experience. After he returned home, he opened a fish market on Bloomfield Avenue in Montclair, where he had worked part time while in school. "The storeowner was moving and the man who owned the building let me rent it. I was only twenty, but he trusted me because I knew all aspects of the business."

"That's where I knew Ike from as a kid," says drummer Bruce Tyler, who spent twenty years as the Jazz Prophets' drummer. "Ike was always a nice guy, always willing to help younger musicians. I've always been grateful to him for taking me to my first jam session at the Peppermint Lounge. Until then, I'd heard of musicians like Radam Schwartz, but I'd never seen any of them perform."

"I would have loved to have played music full time," Brown says, "but once I married and had a daughter, I had to work. It was rough out there, and you can't be out at night when you have a family to support." Fortunately, he was able to play part time at clubs in Newark and for weddings and dances throughout Essex County.

By the early 1980s, Brown began working for promoter Teddy Powell, playing back-up for rhythm and blues artists like the Dells, Jerry Butler and the Persuasions. A few years later he began playing jam sessions at Montclair's DLV Lounge with Henry Brown on bass, Richie Pierson on drums and Big John Patton on organ. "It was a really hip place because everyone knew John Patton," Brown says. "People like Grachan Moncur III and David Murray used to sit in."

The experience at the DLV became the genesis for creating the Jazz Prophets in 1991 with Henry Brown on bass; Cornell McGhee on trombone; Richard Banks, keyboards; Buddy Shelton, congas, and Jackie Johnson and Denise Hamilton sharing the vocals. Their first major gig was at the Priory. "The Priory kept us very busy," Brown says. "Sometimes, we played there two weeks in a row."

"Ike knew a lot of people, so we always had a great crowd," McGhee says. "The band had a lot of energy."

During their time together, the Prophets also were popular at the Renaissance Café in Newark, where singer Carrie Jackson did the booking; at Jasmine's on Lock Street in Newark, where the owner, a Vietnamese woman, was an ardent jazz fan; and at Trumpets in Montclair, where the band played every other Wednesday night. In the mid-1990s, the Prophets recorded *A Tribute to the Masters*, a CD that features the music of Dizzy Gillespie, Art Blakey and Tito Puente, live at the Priory.

Brown was also a regular at jazz sessions hosted by Rick Gee in the ballroom-like basement of Gee's South Orange apartment, events that attracted scores of area musicians. "Ike was the one who encouraged me to keep going," says Gee, now a promoter and jazz radio host in St. Petersburg, Florida. "He came to the first jam and enjoyed it so much he kept after me to do it again."

"Everybody who played jazz in the Newark area came to Rick's parties," says Brown, who remembers hearing Denise Hamilton, Carrie Jackson, Radam Schwartz and Jimmy Scott play there.

"There was always plenty of music and plenty of food and drinks. Rick was a great host."

After nearly two decades on the Newark music scene, Ike Brown and the Jazz Prophets folded in 2010. "My vision was failing because of glaucoma, so I was forced to call it quits," Brown says. Nevertheless, he treasures the years he spent as a working musician. "It was a great run, great fun while it lasted."

Newark Songbirds

Jazz Through the Years

*The hardest place to play is your
hometown. —Miss Rhapsody*

When $2.4 million was cut from the Newark Public Library budget in 2010, a group of city-based jazz singers known as the Newark Songbirds came together to present a benefit concert to help lessen the impact. "The money we raised went a long way to fund our Titles for Teens Initiative," says Carol Jenkins, president of the Friends of the Newark Public Library, the sponsoring organization. "There was no money in the budget for new books, so we pledged $10,000 to buy new titles of interest to young adults." Wilma Grey, the library director, called the benefit "a wonderful community event."

In addition to emcee Yvette Glover, the singers responsible for making the show a success were Carrie Jackson, Lady CiCi, Cynthia Holiday, Denise Hamilton, Pat Tandy, Pam Purvis, Antoinette Montague and Jackie Jones. The Songbirds' name comes from a 2011 calendar in which they were featured with Sarah Vaughan, Miss Rhapsody and Carrie Smith. Here's a look at the careers of the singers not highlighted elsewhere in this book.

Miss Rhapsody

Born Viola Wells in Newark on December 14, 1902, Miss Rhapsody spent more than sixty years singing jazz and blues throughout the United States and Europe. Like many roots-of-jazz singers, she started singing in church. Thirteenth Avenue Presbyterian in Newark's Third Ward, where her father was the sexton, was her training ground. At twelve, she began traveling with the Selika Johnson Singers, led by Ruth Reid, the choir director.

As a teenager, Miss Rhapsody, a name bestowed by a jazz critic years later, often sang at parties but didn't tell her family. "I wanted to sing, but I didn't want to defy my father who was opposed to it," she later said. "I was four when my mother died, so my father was my world. I didn't want to disappoint him." Her first paid job was in a traveling show at Miner's Theater in downtown Newark, starring blues singer Mamie Smith and Cora La Redd, a star at New York's world-famous Cotton Club. The troupe got only as far as Baltimore before the producers ran out of money. "I was only twenty-one so I was glad to get back home," Rhap said. Despite her inexperience, her deep, rich voice, enunciation and perfect intonation made her audiences feel she was going places.

A few years later she began traveling the East Coast with Banjo Bernie Robinson's Orchestra, singing and tending to the payroll. Excited to be singing for a living, she had no problem cooking for the musicians or ironing their clothes. For the first time, too, she got a taste of what it was like to be black in white America. "Almost everywhere we went, we had trouble finding a place to stay," she said. "We generally wound up in boarding houses owned by other blacks. When we performed for white audiences, we had to use the back door."

In the mid-1930s, Rhap joined blues singer Ida Cox on the road, but got only as far as Oklahoma when Cox fired her for getting better reviews. "There is only one star of this show, and that's me," Cox told her. With just a few dollars in her pocket, Rhap hitched a ride to Kansas City, a jazz hot spot even before Count Basie's arrival. For the next fourteen months she worked at the Sunset Crystal Palace, where she sang, emceed the shows and brought in new talent. One of her finds was Walter Page, whose recording of *Confessin' The Blues* was a minor hit.

In those days, every big name in jazz passed through Kansas City, including bandleader Jimmie Lunceford. His manager invited Rhap to join his orchestra, but it didn't pan out. Back home in Newark in 1938, she began singing at the Apollo Theater with Bunny Berigan, Erskine Hawkins and Claude Hopkins. In the 1940s, she also was a favorite at clubs all over Newark, mainly Fisher's Tavern and Dodger's Bar & Grill.

Rhap retired in 1950 after her father was murdered by their minister. As the story goes, Earl Wells, who was seventy at the time, confronted their pastor about fraudulently second-mortgaging their church. Mr. Wells died after having an ice pick plunged through his chest. Distraught over her father's murder, Rhap quit singing and opened a restaurant at South Orange Avenue and Bergen Street in Newark. She later became the cook at Pitt's Place on Hartford Street, where she occasionally emerged from the kitchen to sing a song or two.

In the early 1960s her career took off again after Derrick Stewart-Baxter, a British jazz journalist, and Sheldon Harris, a blues historian, came looking for her. With their help, she recorded her first LP in a New York studio. Harris also got her a gig at the International House in Harlem, which led to a *New York Times* article by John S. Wilson detailing her comeback.

In 1972, she became the vocalist for the Harlem Blues and Jazz Band, a group of oldtime sidemen from well-known big bands. The seven-member unit was brought together by Albert Vollmer, a Larchmont, New York, orthodontist who wanted to keep traditional jazz alive by providing work for some of America's greatest musicians in their golden years. As the vocalist for the original group, Miss Rhapsody was in stellar company, joining co-leaders trombonist Clyde Bernhardt, who played in King Oliver's band in the 1930s, and pianist Jay "June" Cole, brother of legendary drummer Cozy Cole. Other members were George James, who played with Louis Armstrong, on sax; Francis Williams, a Duke Ellington alumnus, trumpet; Tommy Benford, who spent much of his career in Europe, drums, and Barbara Dreiwitz, the band's youngest and only female musician, tuba. Early on, bassist Johnny Williams, who recorded with Billie Holiday, replaced Dreiwitz. After Bernhardt's death, longtime Count Basie trombonist Eddie Durham came aboard. So did Al Casey, Fats Waller's guitarist.

In 1975, Miss Rhapsody's life and career was the subject of a six-part series on French TV produced by Jean Christophe Averty. "Having a great time," she wrote from Denmark the following year during the Harlem Blues and Jazz Band's first tour of Europe. In 1980, Vollmer booked her into the Ginger Man, a New York supper club near Lincoln Center, for a yearlong engagement on Sunday nights. Roger (Ram) Ramirez, who wrote the Ellington standard *Lover Man*, was on piano; Al Hall, an Erroll Garner alumnus, on bass; and Shelton Gary on drums. During the quartet's engagement, celebrities like singer Linda Hopkins, the Broadway star of *Me and Bessie*, and actress Claudette Colbert, a New Year's Eve patron, came to hear Rhap sing. Lionel Hampton, who lived in an apartment complex across the way, occasionally sat in on drums. "Gimme *Crazy Rhythm*," he'd shout to the musicians. In a *New York Post* review, critic Curt Davis called Miss Rhapsody "the uptown Alberta Hunter," comparing her to the famous blues singer who was appearing downtown at the Cookery.

Rhap was the center of attention again in November 1982, when friends celebrated her eightieth birthday with a show in her honor at Essex County College. Singers Carrie Smith and Carol Mitchell, pianist Clem Moorman, bassist Vinnie Burke and guitarist Horace Sims were among those who performed. More than 500 friends and fans turned out for the free community event, titled The Lady, The Legend and Her Music. Husband-and-wife team Jimmy Butts and Edye Byrd and Rhap's accompanists, Ram Ramirez and Al Hall, also shared the stage. Saving the best for last, Miss Rhapsody brought down the house at the end, singing *Brown Gal*, her theme song for more than a half-century.

Days after her eighty-second birthday in December 1984, Rhap played her final gig at Sweet Basil's in Greenwich Village. At the request of saxophonist Eddie Chamblee, a Harlem Blues and Jazz

Band alumnus, she sang two of her favorite tunes, *All of Me* and *You're Nobody 'Til Somebody Loves You.* Two days later she was hospitalized with the flu. She died on December 22, 1984, in Clara Maass Medical Center in Belleville, New Jersey, and is buried in Heavenly Rest Cemetery in East Hanover. Her grave marker sums up the story of her life and career: *Newark's No. 1 Brown Gal.*

Denise Hamilton

Denise Hamilton didn't give much thought to singing professionally until her college roommate suggested she join a friend's band that was performing at Army bases and social functions near the Virginia State College campus in the mid-1970s. "I loved singing but had no experience to speak of except performing in school glee clubs," says Hamilton, who thought her friend's idea preposterous at first. Eventually, she accepted the invitation to join the band, considering it much-needed therapy following back-to-back tragedies that had rocked her life—the deaths of her mother and boyfriend—during her first two years of college.

At the time, Hamilton was studying special education at Virginia State on a full scholarship from the John Sawtell Foundation. College life was everything she expected until her mother, her key source of strength, died suddenly during her sophomore year. A year later her boyfriend was shot to death.

Hamilton's childhood was just as tragic. After being severely burned in a house fire when she was six months old, she spent her early years undergoing a series of seemingly endless surgeries. "The intense heat cooked me," she says. "They thought I was going to die. My mother was the one who was always looking out for me. She always told me that life is what you make it, that I should try harder to appreciate who I am. That's why losing her was so devastating. After my mother died, my boyfriend's family adopted me, so I was a basket case when he died. I didn't know where to turn." After spending two months at home in New Jersey, she regrouped and returned to school. "That's what my mother would have wanted," she says.

Having sung in middle school and high school with glee clubs and with an all-girl group, Hamilton found solace performing with the band at Virginia State. "We were mostly singing R&B and funk, but I always loved jazz, too," she says. "One of our songs became a hit on the radio, which shocked my whole family, especially my father." After receiving her bachelor's degree in special education in 1976, she spent thirty years teaching special needs children at Franklin School in East Orange, which became the Whitney Houston School for the Performing Arts.

Soon after she started teaching, Hamilton began hanging out at the Peppermint Lounge, famous for its Tuesday night jazz jams and Wednesday night talent shows. Singer Larry O'Neal, emcee Tex Womble and keyboardist Sam Manigault ran the weekly sessions. "I wasn't singing then, but I would go to the Peppermint on both nights," Hamilton says. "I also spent a lot of time at Mr. Wes's lounge on Hill Street in Newark." As a regular, she got to know many of the musicians.

Her first gig was a fundraiser for her brother John when he was running for a seat on the Montclair Municipal Council. Soon after, she began filling in for jazz singer Ann Bailey in drummer Chink Wing's band, sometimes with her brother on congas. Wing, a veteran of contingents led by James Moody and Erroll Garner, was in charge of jazz concerts for the Newark Department of Recreation and Parks, "so we did a lot of community work," Hamilton says. "The pay was minimal, but I got great experience. I'd also go from place to place, singing at spots like Mr. Wes's, where Goldie (Gene Goldston) ran a Melody Workshop, and hang out with oldtimers like Chink Wing, Chops Jones, Gene Phipps Jr., Leo Johnson and Buddy Terry. That was my training.

"At that time, all of the people on the circuit took newcomers like me under their wing," she says. "I didn't know a lot of songs or much about timing, but I knew you had to learn the melody first. If I nailed a song, I'd fine tune it the next time. Basically, I do smooth jazz and old standards mixed with R&B flavors. I particularly love doing tunes like *God Bless the Child* and *Good Morning Heartache*."

Highlights of Hamilton's career include singing at New York Mayor David Dinkins' campaign kickoff at Sweetwater's in New York and at a Clinton for President rally in New York. For a year or so, she and organist Gil Lewis played in the lounge at Trump Plaza in Atlantic City.

Hamilton also is well-known for the jam sessions she hosts at her home in Montclair, a tradition started by her grandfather Clarence Hamilton, the first African-American taxicab owner in Montclair. "We didn't have live music then," she says. "I started doing parties at my father's house on Lexington Avenue in Montclair in the 1980s. All kinds of musicians and well-known people like (actor) John Amos used to come, and we had all kinds of music, from funk and gospel to R&B and jazz."

Hamilton continued hosting parties after she bought a thirteen-room house on Custer Avenue in Newark. "I had four or five lounge areas in the basement, where the music was played," she says. "It was like a little club, where all the musicians came to jam." After returning to Montclair in the early 1990s, she moved the gatherings outdoors, adding a new décor or theme each time. One time the guests were invited to wear wild hats for a Mad Hatters Ball. Another time the theme was Hawaiian. Just about every musician and singer in the Newark area attended these events. "We don't have the Peppermint anymore, so the parties are the only time we get to know who's sick or who's alive or dead," Hamilton says. "People look forward to them. Generally, we go through the night until the police shut me down."

Before Skipper's closed in 2012, Hamilton spent several years hosting Friday night karaoke sessions at the club. Hamilton also has her own company, Music and More Enterprises, which has presented benefits including Show of Love honoring boxer-turned-slide-trombonist Jimmy Walker. Because so many uninvited guests turn up at her parties, she is looking forward to the day when she can cut expenses by charging a nominal fee to cover costs. "It's another way of keeping the music alive," she says.

Cynthia Holiday

Cynthia Holiday's got the whole package—the voice, the looks and the stage presence—to make it big in the very competitive world of jazz singing. When she sings a sexy blues tune, she has the entire audience at her command, especially the men. "When Cynthia sings, just a smile in their direction has the men drooling," her friends say. "They're practically falling off their seats."

Thankfully, Holiday has an understanding husband. "Not only do I have the approval of my husband," she says, "Bob (Moore) is the one who started me singing. I was singing in the shower when he heard me and told me I needed to pursue it." At the time, Holiday was working for Anheuser-Busch in Newark, from which she retired in 2010 after twenty years in administration. At the urging of her husband, a retired sales executive, she began doing "little gigs" here and there.

As a girl growing up in Newark, dance was Holiday's passion. From elementary school on, she studied at the Garden State School of Ballet downtown and at the Thompson Dance Studio on Bergen Street. While in college, she performed with the Morse Donaldson Modern Dance Company, earning her tuition by teaching younger students.

Holiday's exposure to jazz is hardly surprising. Her stepfather, Calvin Hughes, played trumpet with bandleaders Frank Foster, Clark Terry and Eddie "Lockjaw" Davis and toured with singer Big Maybelle. Holiday's mother, Betty Hughes, a Sarah Vaughan fan, and aunt, Alberta Hill, sang at weddings and other events at Metropolitan Baptist Church in Newark.

Even after her mother remarried, Holiday's father, Johnny Holiday, was very much a part of her life. "My stepsisters Valerie and Erica and I were known as 'The Holiday Girls,'" she says. "My older sister Valerie is the lead singer with Three Degrees. On Sundays we'd get together at my (paternal) grandmother's house and she would cook up a ton of fried chicken."

Holiday learned the ins and outs of show business first-hand by accompanying her stepfather on gigs. "I was always surrounded by musicians, so I was able to learn what life was like on the road and was coached on how to succeed in the business," she says. Initially, she kept secret her desire to sing. "When I became brave enough to let Calvin know I wanted to pursue singing, I handed him a cassette tape I'd made," she explains. "He took me to his friend Duke Anderson's house in Belleville, where I began taking lessons. I loved going to class with Duke. He was great fun and very knowledgeable about music. I felt I was improving because he believed in me."

Eventually, Holiday began working with her stepfather's band, Calvin Hughes and the Swinging Gents, at spots including the Bridge Club in downtown Newark. Although Hughes has been gone many years, Holiday has followed the advice he gave her early in her career: "Calvin always told me to follow the melody. That was his big lesson."

In 1990, Bob Harris, one of Anderson's friends, hired Holiday to sing with his big band, one of her first professional jobs. Shaking off a bout of nerves, she also began sitting in at Shanghai Jazz in Madison, a top New Jersey jazz club, with bassist Earl May and his group. "I was thrilled when Earl let me sing a blues tune at the end of his show, because that's what I like to sing most," she says.

Holiday credits the late Rita Da Costa Turrentine, the former wife of saxophonist Stanley Turrentine, with helping her perfect her style and stage presence. "Miss Rita was very much responsible for the way I present myself," she says. More recently, she's studied voice with Kevin Mahogany, Marion Cowings and Myrna Lake.

After playing her first paid gig at a place called Chopin's Holiday Inn, she began working with organist Radam Schwartz at the Peppermint Lounge in Orange. She also sang at local clubs with flutist Haven Claiborne in an R&B group called Kiss & Tell. "Radam taught me the difference between singing and being a jazz singer," she says, "things like singing after the beat, as Billie Holiday did. He's still teaching me. Each time we rehearse we have a good exchange."

Holiday points to the night in 2007 when she opened for Roy Ayers at Newark Symphony Hall for a jazz concert marking the venue's seventy-fifth anniversary and participating in the 2004 Harlem Jazz Tour with Gloria Lynne as career highlights. She's also been the featured vocalist at Birdland on a bill headlined by John Hicks and Javon Jackson and shared the stage with Cassandra Wilson and Jon Lucien at the Jersey Jazz by the Lake concert.

In 2010 she traveled to Russia for a six-city tour that included a performance in Siberia. "The Russian fans were wonderful," she says. "After each performance they presented me with a beautiful bouquet of flowers. It was wonderful to see the audiences smiling and singing along with each song." During her visit, she was invited to teach the "Art of Performance" to a group of Russian university students. "They all had master's degrees in music, and here I was teaching them," she says. Since then, she's visited Russia again.

So far she's released one CD, with Cedar Walton. Now she's looking to produce another in conjunction with a top jazz producer. What songs will she sing? "That's a secret," she says.

Jackie Jones

When jazz saxophonist Don Braden invited singer Jackie Jones to take over the Sarah Vaughan Vocal Residency at Arts High School in Newark in early 2013, it was a no-brainer. Not only was Jones a graduate of the school Vaughan once attended, she also was a long-time devotee of the Divine One's jazz pyrotechnics. "That may sound funny because I had no idea who Sarah Vaughan was when she came to our school for an assembly in the mid-1980s," Jones says. "All I remember is that attendance was mandatory and that Sarah did a little scatting on top of the melody as the jazz band played *Lil Darlin'*. I was in the company of royalty, but I didn't know it."

During Vaughan's visit to Arts, Tisha Campbell, who became a Hollywood star soon after, sang in her honor with the school band and she was feted at a luncheon in the library. "We had always told our kids about our alumni, so we were very proud to have Sarah Vaughan back home," says Hilton Otero, the principal at the time.

More than twenty-five years later, Jones became the singer in charge of the school's six-week Sarah Vaughan Jazz Vocal Residency, sponsored by NJPAC's Jazz for Teens program. To fulfill her duties, she met with vocal students twice weekly. At the end, the group presented a concert for the student body at a downtown venue, backed by the school band. "Being at Arts High again was wonderful because my high school years are the favorite part of my life," Jones says. "As my first experience teaching vocal music, the residency was great, because it gave me a chance to share what I know about singing with the students."

Like many of the young people she's worked with, Jones never thought of becoming a singer while in high school. Her entry into the world of vocal music was pretty much a fluke. She wanted to be a doctor, which led her to enroll at Rutgers University in New Brunswick as a pre-med student. But she also loved playing flute, so she signed up for the music program at the university's Mason Gross School of the Arts, where jazz greats Kenny Barron, Dion Parson, Ralph Bowen and Fred Lacy became her teachers.

Jones's first paid job as a singer came out of the blue. "I was standing on a porch in New Brunswick when Robert Brice, a friend from Newark, heard me humming and asked me to join his band," she explains. "I hadn't sung one word." Jones took Brice up on his offer and began playing with his group on campus. At one point, she replaced Regina Belle in a show starring Peabo Bryson called *A Whole New World*. "I think I got $50," she says. "I sang some jazz, but I also was doing contemporary music like *Just the Two of Us*."

She had not contemplated singing professionally, but after graduating from Rutgers in 1991 she decided to give it a try. Twenty-plus years later she's still at it, singing on average twice a week throughout North and Central Jersey and abroad. "I'm really grateful I don't have to seek out many of these gigs," she notes. "At least eighty percent of the work I do comes by word of mouth, often from people who see me at other venues."

Jones's "first real gig" was at Jones's Chateau in Plainfield (a co-incidence since the name has nothing to do with her family), where vocalist Dena Allen invited her do a tune. "I sang *My Funny Valentine* (her signature song) and got invited back on a regular basis." One of her greatest experiences was opening for Lou Rawls at the Pepper-mint Lounge in 1993. During that period she also appeared at the Blue Note in New York.

Jones's first trip abroad came in 1990, when she performed in Ger-many. Since then she has appeared at a reception at the American Embassy in Kingston, Jamaica, and at a jazz festival in the Madeira Islands in Portugal on a bill that included the Brecker Brothers, Rus-sell Malone and Billy Joel. "I was overwhelmed when I was selected to sing in Jamaica," she says. "Every year they pick an American jazz artist to perform, and that year they picked me. I got to ride in a motorcade, as if I were a big star." In Portugal, she was on a bill that included Phil Woods and bassist Ray Brown. "It was a lot of fun because it was a celebration of Ray Brown's seventy-fifth birthday."

In 2012, Jones spent a week in Russia, playing the Club Compos-itora in Moscow before moving on to Perm, a two-hour plane ride from the Russian capital. "The fans in Russia were fantastic," she says. "It was great, too, because they pay a lot more than we do and everything was first class."

On the home front, Jones has performed at the Asbury Park Jazz Festival and at clubs in the Newark area, often accompanied by Nat Adderly Jr., Cannonball Adderly's nephew. In Newark, she's a favor-ite at the Priory, where she's appeared more than twenty times. She also was a regular at Skipper's. "I don't sing because I want to become famous," she says. "I do it because it's my favorite thing to do on the planet. No matter how far I get, I'll always sing."

Antoinette Montague

Looking back on her childhood, Antoinette Montague remembers how exciting it was seeing some of the top names in jazz arrive by limousine at Lloyd's Manor on Beacon Street, one of Newark's most popular jazz clubs. These were exciting times, too, for Montague's aunt and her neighbors who lived on the otherwise lackluster block in the Newark's old Third Ward. "I can still see my aunt leaning out her window yelling, 'The Queen, the Queen,' when a limo pulled up one night," Montague says. "Everyone thought it was Dinah Washington," but that was impossible.

Washington, known as Queen of the Blues, had died a year or so before, but that was of no consequence to Montague and her friends, who spent the summers of their youth riding their bikes up and down Beacon Street "to get a glimpse of all the beautifully dressed women" arriving at Lloyd's in grand style. "There wasn't much else happening," she says, "so it was like the Academy Awards."

This was in the early 1960s, when Montague was about five years old. Even then, music seemed to be everywhere in her life, especially at home on South 13th Street in Newark, where she and her six siblings were exposed to all forms of song. "I heard everything from hymns like *In the Garden* and *God Will Take Care of You* that my mother sang in church to my oldest brother's records of Swing Era artists like Ella Fitzgerald and Sarah Vaughan," she recalls. "My younger brother's favorites were Jimmy Hendrix and The Who. We were always singing. After supper, we all sang in the kitchen while we washed the dishes. People said my mother sounded like Ella Fitzgerald."

Both Montague's parents, Percola and James Montague Sr., nurtured her musical interests. "On his way to work on Saturdays, my dad would drop me off at the Newark Public Library, where I would listen to Louis Armstrong and Duke Ellington," she says. "The pictures of Duke from the 1920s and 1930s, especially the one with his top hat, blew my mind. He was gorgeous!"

Montague's first on-stage appearance was a salute to Walt Disney at the Essex County Girls Vocational School. "I sang *When You Wish Upon a Star*, but my knees were knocking the whole time," she remembers. At graduation, she sang *Send in the Clowns*, the Sarah Vaughan standard. As a full scholarship student at Seton Hall University she was a member of the gospel choir that backed jazz pianist Mary Lou Williams for a presentation of *Mary Lou's Mass*, quite a thrill for an aspiring young singer. By then she was hanging out at jam sessions at the Peppermint Lounge, where friends encouraged her to sit in. "That was my introduction," she says. "I began to listen, learn, practice and figure it all out." Before long, she was part of a rhythm and blues band.

Montague's interest in performing full time gathered momentum after she saw blues and jazz singer Carrie Smith on Broadway in *Black and Blue*. "I was feeling pretty blue because my mother had just died of breast cancer. Hearing this amazing woman (Smith) was like an electrical shock," she says. "She was so inspiring, I saw the show four times." After hearing Smith sing at a jazz concert at East Orange City Hall, she became her constant companion, a friendship that proved mutually beneficial. While Smith taught her various aspects of the business, she began assisting Smith in her later years. Along the way Montague met many of the musicians and vocalists in Smith's circle, including Norman Simmons, Carline Ray, Bernard Purdie and Etta Jones.

"Carrie was singing on a cruise on the QE II when she introduced me to Etta," she notes. "While Carrie could be very critical of my singing, Etta was extremely encouraging when I sat in at jam sessions. We had an instant connection, as if we had adopted each other. To have the two of them in my corner was amazing." Jones also introduced her to Della Griffin and Myrna Lake, who provided further support. "I'm especially indebted to Inez McClendon, who taught Lauryn Hill," she adds. "Whenever I perform, Inez is there."

Montague credits Norman Simmons, with whom she frequently works, and saxophonist Bill Easley, who fronted her band for several years, with helping her hone her musical talent. "You've got to surround yourself with good musicians and embrace an entrepreneurial spirit to get anywhere in music," she says. "It's a business, so who's to tell anyone not to live up to their highest expectations? That's why I don't read my reviews, good or bad. I just keep learning from my mistakes and doing what I do. God really does take care of you, if you follow your heart."

That sense of positivity has carried her far. She's played most of New York's major clubs—including Dizzy's Club Coca Cola at Lincoln Center, the Blue Note and Lenox Lounge—performed with the forty-six member Ashdod Orchestra in Israel and was the first African-American artist to appear with the Belgrade Philharmonic Orchestra in Russia. More recently, she headlined a jazz festival in Eleuthera and performed in Korea.

Montague is currently working on a musical tribute to Florence Mills, the uniquely talented, but long-forgotten 1920s Broadway star who was in her twenties when she died. She's also planning a public access television project, *Peace in the Key of Jazz*. "Like Louis Armstrong, I want to help restore peace in the world," she says.

Not that she's forgotten her roots. Since the 1990s, she has appeared all over Newark—at the Newark Public Library, as the opening act for the Newark Museum Jazz in the Garden series, at Sounds of the City, an outdoor concert series at NJPAC, and at a 2011 March Madness concert sponsored by WBGO as part of the Final Four Eastern Regional Men's Collegiate Basketball Tournament. "Playing in Newark is always like a homecoming," she says. "When I look around, I see friends from grammar school and my neighborhood. I can't tell you how awesome that is. During March Madness, I felt like I was part of a *This Is Your Life* episode."

Madame Pat Tandy

When Pat Tandy's fans request *Big Fat Daddy*, everyone gets into the act. "I want a big fat daddy," she sings, swaying her ample hips. "Big fat daddy," her audience responds. And so it goes. Except for the sexually suggestive lyrics, the call and response pattern is straight out of the black church, even though Tandy is singing secular music. She sings and her fans respond.

Those who come to hear Tandy perform call her a blues singer, which she is, but she didn't always sing jazz and blues. That's a fairly recent thing, she says, explaining how in her youth she sang in the gospel choir at a Baptist church in Jacksonville, Florida, where her grandmother was the minister. Her interest in music continued in Newark at Miller Street School and South Side High School, where she sang in the choirs.

In her teens, Tandy sang lead with Miss Tea & Sugar, a rhythm and blues duo she and her sister Linda formed. "We competed in talent shows all over Newark," she says, recalling how they won a trophy their first time out. Guided by producer Jerry Hankins, they cut their first 45 rpm, *I Don't Want to Be Second Choice,* as teenagers. "When our friend Edith Lewis, who lived in the same house on Camden Street, began singing with us, we became the Mellowettes," Tandy recalls. "We used to sit on the front porch singing doowop and harmonies. We were into all the popular groups, especially Diana Ross and the Supremes."

Not that she had forsaken gospel music. She and her sister continued to sing at Greater Harvest Baptist Church, where their mother belonged. After enrolling at Essex County College as a music major in the early 1970s, Tandy became the lead soloist with the gospel choir directed by Jo Sandra Flint. Her introduction to jazz came via former Duke Ellington bassist Aaron Bell, the music department chairman. Before long, she began singing with Bell's group at New York clubs and at shows at the college. "One of the biggest things we did was a show with the Mercer Ellington Orchestra in upstate New York," she notes. "Al Hibbler was on the show, so it was quite a thrill. Al and I also sang together on a commercial for the college."

After earning an associate's degree in music education, Tandy worked as a secretary for several Newark-area companies, including Merck and Warner-Lambert. Singing was reserved for nights and weekends. Her first break came in the early 1970s after she and her sister appeared at the Terrace Ballroom on a show featuring the Pretenders and Black Ivory. "When the Pretenders lost their lead singer, I was approached to do leads," Tandy recounts. "We spent the next seven years recording on Carnival Records and had a few hits, including *I'm the One Love Forgot* and *I Call It Love.*" Joe Evans, who also managed the Manhattans, was their producer and manager. On weekends, the group performed at clubs along the East Coast as far south as Virginia, a tiring schedule for a young woman with a day job. "Sometimes I was so tired, I'd fall asleep at my desk, hoping that no one would notice," Tandy says.

Billed as Madame Pat Tandy, she began singing jazz in the early 1980s with a group led by Newark saxophonist Jimmy Anderson. Charlie Slade was on drums and Big John Patton was on organ. "Our first job was at Jackson's Manor in Jersey City," she says. "I think I got about $50 per show. At that time I wasn't much into blues. I was singing all the standards, like *All of Me, Here's That Rainy Day* and *My One and Only Love.*"

Tandy's penchant for singing the blues surfaced after she heard Irene Reid perform at the Showman in New York. Since then, she's taken a page out of Reid's repertoire, singing tunes like *Big Fat Daddy* and *One-Eyed Man.* "Irene was singing *One-Eyed Man* one night when a friend and I went to hear her," she says. "'She's singing your song,' my friend blurted, loud enough for Irene to hear. 'No,' Irene shot back. 'It's our song, Pat's and mine.' For me, that was quite a compliment." From then on, whenever Tandy sang, Reid was in the audience and vice versa. In later years, she sang at a benefit in Reid's behalf and at her funeral. As a tribute to Reid she recorded *Madame Pat Tandy Remembers Irene Reid* on BlueArk in 2009.

Over the years Tandy has performed at clubs throughout New York and New Jersey, especially at the Priory. She became a favorite at Midas Gold, Mr. Wes's and Skipper's in Newark and still sings at Private Place in Orange. More often than not, she's backed by organist Radam Schwartz with whom she's teamed for more than twenty years, playing club dates and recording, and tenor saxophonist Tommy Grice and drummer Gordon Lane. Tandy began performing on cruise ships in 2000. Since then she's been booked on Southern Caribbean twice a year and toured Japan and Russia with the Harlem Blues and Jazz Band.

Tandy also leads the Nu Taste Female Jazz Ensemble with Carol Sudhalter on sax; Simona Premazzi, keyboards; Luciana Padmore, drums; and Rene Carlson, harmonica. With Sudhalter, she traveled all over Italy with a big band led by Fabio Lepore.

"It's really rough out there now," she says. "Finding work has become more difficult, because there are many singers and musicians but far fewer opportunities. You just have to work a lot harder to keep going."

16 ♪

A New Vision

The Jazz Vocal Collective

I never sing a song the same
way twice. —Billie Holiday

Jazz has always been a marginalized form of music, always there, but never nearly as popular as pop, rhythm and blues, or even doo wop. Maybe that's because the style is far more complex than others, or perhaps it's too eclectic for popular tastes. Whatever the reason, it's had its ups and downs, yet survived.

In an article about the history of jazz, Jacob Teichroew argues against measuring the strength of jazz, whatever the time frame, and takes issue with the constant debate of whether jazz is on its way out. "Jazz is not off track," he writes. "So let's not search for ways to get it back. Any attempt to do this would threaten its authenticity and hinder its authentication."

Certainly there's little likelihood of returning to the days when Swing Era jazz was one of Newark's major businesses or when jean-wearing hipsters introduced a more modern form of the music called bebop. But that doesn't mean that the future of jazz is simply a matter of popularity or commercial success. Those who create it believe it cannot be contained, that it keeps re-creating itself no matter what its present state. For jazz lovers everywhere, it remains an uplifting force when life seems otherwise unbearable.

While critics often link the demise of Newark's musical heyday to the flight of the city's middle class following the 1967 civil rebellions, it took another decade or two for the city's skyrocketing crime rate and the deadly grip of the American drug culture to affect the jazz scene. The 1970s and early 1980s, in fact, were quite productive years for many Newark musicians, especially proponents of bebop.

Whatever ups and downs jazz has seen, there's always someone out there who provides new oomph when necessary. In Newark, singer Carrie Jackson, who created the Newark-based Jazz Vocal Collective a few years ago, is one such advocate. "We welcome anyone who wants to learn more about jazz and improve their skills," she says, "so this is not a group just for young singers. It's for everyone." Members meet each Saturday to perfect their vocal skills, learn the ins and outs of the business and interact with each other. They are singers supporting singers, providing each other a boost when they perform publicly at showcases Jackson arranges. During a recent show at Trumpets, for example, two newcomers, Tarryk Rainford and Patricia Walton, were featured while other members cheered them on from the sidelines.

Jackson's goal is to breathe new life into Newark's fading jazz scene. Like Duke Anderson, the Swing Era pianist who was her mentor, she wants to share what she knows about the music, including the business end, with those who want to be part of the jazz world. That's why she started C-Jay Records in 1995 and why she became the collective's founder. "When I was starting out, Duke taught me everything I needed to know—how to sing, play piano, present myself to an audience and market my skills," she says. "I want to honor him by passing that on."

Anderson, an alumnus of Dizzy Gillespie's 1943 orchestra, was teaching at the Newark Community School of the Arts when he and Jackson met in the early 1980s. Through the years, he taught and inspired hundreds of young singers and musicians from the Newark area, taking Jackson, for one, on many gigs. Since Anderson's death in 1999, Jackson's assumed a similar role, helping often-overlooked vocalists record, find work and otherwise showcase their abilities.

"I never wanted to be just a singer," she explains. "I always wanted to own my own entertainment business. I wanted to employ other singers and give them a chance to record they would not have had otherwise."

Jackson still sings full-time, a rarity when finding work can be a twenty-four-hour-a-day proposition in itself. It's not just sheer determination and hard work that keeps her going, she explains. It's her belief that "you've got to know everything about the business—how to create business cards and flyers, put together press releases and promotional packages, and negotiate with club owners—then make it all work for you."

Finding places to perform regularly in the Newark area, however, has become increasingly difficult as people who visit the city look to other forms of entertainment, such as New Jersey Devils hockey games and rock concerts at the new Prudential Center. Apart from the Priory, where Jackson headlines the New Year's Eve show and celebrates her birthday every August, she and her peers have been forced to look for work elsewhere. She's now traveling farther to sing, but that, she says, is what any singer must do these days to work steadily.

Born in Trenton, New Jersey, Jackson moved to Newark as an infant. She began singing in the children's choir at Mt. Calvary Missionary Baptist Church as a kindergarten pupil at Peshine Avenue School. In the seventh or eighth grade, she's not quite certain, Melba Moore, who won a Tony on Broadway for her role in *Purlie*, was her music teacher. As a teenager, Jackson traveled in Mt. Calvary's gospel choir and sang with the group on WRRL radio. She also was a background singer for her brother Frank's doo wop group. After graduating from Weequahic High School, she spent twenty-five years working for the Newark and Essex County court systems before devoting herself completely to music.

One of Jackson's first public performances was at a Tuesday night jam session at the Peppermint Lounge with Corky Caldwell on piano. Soon after, she started taking piano lessons with Anderson. "I was a little nervous when Duke started taking me on gigs," she says, "but I knew that appearing before live audiences was the only way I could improve."

She also had strong family support. "My mother (Loretta Jackson) was my biggest fan," she says. "Maybe that's because she was musical, too. She played the piano. I've always loved jazz because that's all we listened to at home—Sarah Vaughan (her favorite), Billie Holiday, Ella Fitzgerald, Billy Eckstine, Arthur Prysock, Gloria Lynne—all the greats."

Anderson taught her well, insisting that she study the music she sang, respect the lyrics, enunciate and create her own concept for each song. "Starting out, I felt I had an advantage because I met so many of the older musicians through Duke," she says. "As the featured singer with his group I didn't get paid much, but I got to meet and work with a lot of great guys, especially Calvin Hughes, Eddie Wright and Chops Jones. After Duke took me under his wing, he taught me how to interact with my fans and musicians and how to dress to impress. To this day, if I'm wearing gold, black or whatever, my guys wear the same color bow ties."

In addition to playing clubs in North and Central Jersey, Jackson ventures into New York for gigs at places like Birdland, where she introduced her latest CD, *Carrie Jackson: A Tribute to Sarah Vaughan*. Her wide-ranging experience also includes a featured role in the musical *Ain't Misbehavin'* at the Village Theater in New Brunswick and a principal role in the 49th Street musical tribute to Eubie Blake, Duke Ellington, Billie Holiday and Alberta Hunter. She also was a principal performer in *Nunsense*.

Jackson believes in constantly building her repertoire, adding tunes her listeners have not heard before. "To me, singing the same songs over and over is disrespectful to my audience," she says. "When people come to hear me over and over, they deserve something new."

The Jazz Vocal Collective is her latest project. After starting out at Skipper's, Jackson and pianist Bill de Benedette, a onetime big-band musician, moved the group's weekly meetings to Memorial West Presbyterian Church. "Most of the singers have some experience," she explains. "We have jazz veterans like Honi Gordon, who's been singing since she was a girl, and newer members like Ann Kirk, a retired dentist who always wanted to sing."

Phyllis Blanford Colleran, a mezzo-soprano who lived in Rome for twenty years and sang all over Europe, began singing years ago on the Lower East Side of Manhattan, where she was cast in *O Jerusalem* at the LaMama Theater. From there, she was off to Rome, where she learned to speak fluent Italian and sang in jazz clubs and musicals all over the Continent. She even got to perform for the pope. But that was long ago, Colleran says. By the time she returned to Newark and met Jackson, she hadn't sung in nearly a decade. "I had stopped for so long, I'd lost the courage to perform," she explains. But Jackson kept after her. "After Carrie heard me singing to myself downstairs at Trumpets one night, she invited me to sing at an open mic session." Apprehensive at first, she took the challenge, joined the collective and restored her confidence.

Stephen Fuller also credits Jackson with helping him revive his career. Fuller, a product of Arts High School, where he studied German lieder and opera before turning to jazz and pop, began singing professionally at Colgate University, where he led a band that opened for acts like Bill Withers and Stevie Wonder.

After graduating from Colgate, Fuller worked in Kansas City, where he frequently sang the National Anthem for the National Basketball Association's Kansas City Kings. His group, the Steve Fuller Quartet, also played at area hotels. Fuller's introduction to the collective came via his friend Brenda Mitchell, a Newark resident who appeared on Broadway in the early 1960s in Alex Bradford's *Black Nativity*. "I liked what I saw, so I joined," he explains. "After not having sung for a while, Carrie helped me with my voice techniques, delivery and stage presence."

Since joining the collective Fuller has performed twice at Memorial West's Flatted Fifth Jazz Vespers Series, first with singer Kym Lawrence and then on a program featuring Freddy Cole, Nat King Cole's brother. He's also appeared at the Priory, Skipper's, Trumpets in Montclair and Hibiscus in Morristown.

Hadren Simmons, who also sang during the program featuring Cole, began singing in his youth in the choir at Humanity Baptist Church in Newark, where his father was pastor. At South Side High School, Simmons sang in several groups, including the Madrigals, under the direction of Dorothy Schneider, a well-known Newark music teacher.

After returning home from a two-year hitch in the Army in the early 1970s, Simmons began writing songs. Two of his compositions were incorporated into *Cry of the People*, an urban opera written by Robert Banks, the music director at Simmons's father's church. "Every Thursday I'd go into New York to try to peddle my songs," Simmons says. "I'd hang out at the American Guild of Authors and Composers, where we'd listen to each other's songs and trade advice."

Until he joined the Jazz Vocal Collective, Simmons considered himself "more a songwriter than singer." "I'd always been part of a choir or chorus, so it was pretty scary being up there by myself singing," he says. Learning stage presence, he adds, has been a big help. As someone who loves singing Nat King Cole tunes such as *Mona Lisa* and *Love*, Simmons reveled in sharing the bill with Freddy Cole. "I also feel more comfortable now singing alone," he says. "Being part of the group has been a great help. We criticize each other and complement each other. We're like a little family."

Ann Kirk agrees. "We all learn from each other," says Kirk, who had not sung in years before meeting Jackson one night at the Priory. "In high school, I sang with a group that performed at places like the Port Authority at Christmas time. I had always wanted to sing and was intrigued by undertaking a new set of problem-solving skills, so I joined the collective. By finding a personal hook in a song, I get a real charge when I'm performing. It's fun singing with a band, but when I first started I was terrified out of my mind." With Jackson's help and encouragement, she kept on. "Carrie helps you build your confidence," she says. "She's incredibly generous with her time and advice."

Kirk's most important gig so far was at Birdland. "Carrie sang first, followed by Stephen and Hadren," she notes. "I suffered for

three hours, waiting until midnight to get on, but I finally did."
Thankfully, she adds, her version of *Someone to Watch Over Me*
was well-received, another confidence builder in her life as a new
jazz singer.

Meanwhile, Kirk and her new-found friends also are learning at
the hands of a jazz master—Norman Simmons, who spent thirty
years as music director for Joe Williams and Carmen McRae. In the
spring of 2013, Simmons conducted a master class for the collective
that was open to the community. "It gave the audience a chance
to see a great artist in person and better understand what goes on
behind the scenes before a show," Jackson says. "For our singers, it
was a wonderful opportunity to perform for the public at the hands
of a master."

Bassist Earl May solos during a Jazz
Vespers program at Bethany Baptist
Church, early 2000. *(Photograph by
Barry Gray. Courtesy of the Bethany Baptist
Church Jazz Vespers Committee.)*

Steve Colson at Jazz Vespers at Bethany Baptist Church, c. 2007. *(Photograph by Barry Gray.
Courtesy of the Bethany Baptist Church Jazz Vespers Committee.)*

LEFT: Saxophonist David Robinson listens to a soloist during Jazz Vespers at Bethany Baptist Church. *(Photograph by Barry Gray. Courtesy of the Bethany Baptist Church Jazz Vespers Committee.)*

BELOW: Yvette Glover singing at Jazz Vespers at Bethany Baptist Church, 2006. *(Photograph by Barry Gray Courtesy of the Bethany Baptist Church Jazz Vespers Committee.)*

Amina Baraka, then Sylvia Robinson, second row, fifth from left, as a member of the Poetry Club at Robert Treat Junior High School, 1957–1958. *(Courtesy of Amina Baraka.)*

Singer Abbey Lincoln *(center)*, with Amina and Amiri Baraka at Kimako's Blues People, 1988. The bassist is Brian Smith. *(Courtesy of Amina Baraka.)*

Saxophonist Wayne Shorter, flanked by Philip Thomas, founder of the Carter G. Woodson Foundation, and poet Amiri Baraka, 1988. *(Photograph by Bill May. Courtesy of Philip Thomas.)*

Legendary drummer Max Roach, flanked by poet Amiri Baraka and drummer Rudy Walker. *(Courtesy of Rudy Walker.)*

RIGHT: A flyer from the 2002 Jazz
Series at the Priory. *(Author's collection.)*

BELOW: Ike Brown and the Jazz
Prophets at the Priory, 1997. *From left:*
Yusef Ali, congas; Don Hunt, timbals;
Bruce Tyler, drums; Ray Johnston,
tenor saxophone; Ike Brown, trumpet;
Ken Watts, keyboards; Matt Jordan,
fender bass; Cornell McGhee,
trombone. *(Courtesy of Ike Brown.)*

Saxophonist Bradford Hayes. *(Courtesy of Bradford Hayes.)*

Robert Banks performing at the Priory, 2004. *(Author's collection.)*

WBGO's Dorthaan Kirk. *(Courtesy of Dorthaan Kirk.)*

Carrie Jackson at the Priory with, *from left,* Charlie Cann, Walter Chambers and Stan Myers. *(Courtesy of Carrie Jackson.)*

LEFT: Lady CiCi and Don Williams. *(Courtesy of Cheryl Williams.)*

BELOW: Bob Ackerman and Pam Purvis at Cecil's in West Orange. *(Courtesy of Pam Purvis.)*

Pianist Wallace "Corky" Caldwell. *(Photograph by Al Henderson. Courtesy of Cheryl Williams.)*

Organist Radam Schwartz at a parade. *(Courtesy of Radam Schwartz.)*

Newark Songbirds at the Newark Public Library, 2011. *From left:* Antoinette Montague, Carrie Jackson, Yvette Glover, Pam Purvis, Jackie Jones, Madame Pat Tandy, Denise Hamilton (*front*), Lady CiCi, and Cynthia Holiday. *(Courtesy of Carol Jenkins.)*

Singer Denise Hamilton. *(Courtesy of Denise Hamilton.)*

Singer Cynthia Holiday. *(Courtesy of Cynthia Holiday.)*

Antoinette Montague singing at the Newark Museum during a show sponsored by WBGO as part of the March Madness Men's Eastern Regional College Basketball Finals, 2011. *(Photograph by Tony Graves. Courtesy of Antoinette Montague.)*

Jackie Jones singing at a Newark event. *(Courtesy of Jackie Jones.)*

LEFT: Balladeer Eugene "Goldie" Goldston. *(Courtesy of Eugene Goldston.)*

BELOW: Madame Pat Tandy performing at Skipper's, 2011. *(Courtesy of Pat Tandy.)*

Russell Malone on guitar; unidentified conga player; Greg Bufford, drums; and Dave Braham, keyboard, at SuzyQue's in West Orange, 2013. *(Courtesy of Ernest Williams.)*

Savion and Yvette Glover outside Bethany Baptist Church, 2012. *(Author's collection.)*

The Newark Public Schools Super Band with leader Bill May, front right, early 2000s. The "trombone player" is Newark Executive School Superintendent Marion A. Bolden. *(Photograph by Howard Best. Courtesy of Bill May.)*

A Tribute to Newark Jazz Clubs, a mural created in 2013 by Gladys Barker Grauer and a team of Newark artists, including students, on a wall of the former South Ward Boys Club in Newark's South Ward. *(Courtesy of the Newark Public Art Program.)*

17 ♪

The Barakas

The Arts Personified

*A man is either free, or he is not. There is no
apprenticeship for freedom.* —Amiri Baraka

Amiri and Amina Baraka's home on South 10th Street in Newark's South Ward has been a symbol of artistic creativity for
more than forty years: the place where he produced books, essays
and poetry that made him one of America's most noted writers,
where she created a one-woman show as an ode to oppressed people, and where they've collaborated on an array of other projects. It
also has been arts central for renowned artists such as Sonia San-
chez, Abbey Lincoln, David Murray, Reggie Workman and Grachan
Moncur III.

In the late 1960s, the Barakas lived on Sterling Street near the
Essex County Courthouse in Newark in a sprawling building
known as Spirit House. Painted green, black and red to signify the
African motherland and the blood shed by black people brought to
America against their will, it was where the Committee for a Uni-
fied Newark and Black and Latino Coalition laid the groundwork
for Kenneth Gibson's 1970 election as the Northeast's first African-
American mayor. After moving to South 10th Street, where they
raised their five children, their new home became the focal point of
their creativity and political involvement.

Born LeRoi Jones in Newark in 1934, Baraka was one of two children of Anna Lois Russ, a social worker, and Coyt Jones, a postal supervisor. His entry into the world of music came early. "My people were into big bands," he explains. "My parents belonged to a lot of organizations that sponsored dances at the Terrace Ballroom, so I was listening to Count Basie and Duke Ellington when I was a kid. The first live shows I remember seeing were at the Adams Theater—Nat King Cole and Louis Jordan. I was about fourteen, just entering Barringer High."

Like many black teenagers, Baraka, then LeRoi Jones, was heavily into doo wop in his youth, hanging out at the Masonic Temple on Belmont Avenue to hear singers Ruth Brown and Little Esther, one of his favorites, and groups like the Orioles and Ravens perform. "It was one hot little place, and I was there all the time," he says. By then, he had inherited a large collection of jazz records from his cousin George Harvest. "That's when I first got in touch with bebop," he remarks, noting that the temple was home to rival teenage jazz bands led by Jackie Bland and Nat Phipps, his Barringer High School classmate. "These young bands were really popular," Baraka says. "They were making bebop history, so the place was always crowded when they played. Wayne and Alan Shorter and Grachan Moncur were in Jackie's band. I sort of idolized Wayne because he was the epitome of a hipster. In our world, bebop sort of had a mass appeal."

After graduating from Barringer and attending Howard University, Baraka served in the Air Force before establishing himself as a revolutionary poet and playwright in Greenwich Village, where he and his first wife edited a counter-culture magazine. After they split, he moved to Harlem and founded the Black Arts Literary Movement.

In 1965, weary of the New York scene, Baraka returned to Newark, where he was born and grew up. Soon after his arrival, he was introduced to Amina Baraka, then Sylvia Robinson Wilson, at an arts space called the Loft on Shipman Street. At the time, he was one of the most controversial writers in America, celebrated by black artists who likened him to James Baldwin after he won an Obie for his play *Dutchman*, yet reviled by fearful whites and more moderate blacks for his "take no prisoners" stance.

After attending Arts High School as an arts major, Amina Baraka was bent on a career as a dancer and actress. She and Amiri were firebrands, she says, but in different ways. "Roi was angry with white people, while I was angry at black people, the Negroes who treated me and others like we weren't good enough for them. For a time, the Loft (which staged theatrical productions, poetry readings and Sunday afternoon jazz jams) was the center for jazz and the arts in Newark," she says. The sponsoring organization was the Newark Arts Society, which she co-founded with bassist Art Williams and Tom White, a Halsey Street merchant who sold goods imported from Africa and Latin America.

"The Loft was just down the street from the house I was renting on Sterling Street, so it was at the center of my universe," Amiri Baraka adds.

Playwright Ben Caldwell, who introduced the Barakas, was among the regulars. So were poets Gaston Neal and John Sinclair. Williams, Bill Harris, a pianist, and drummer Eddie Gladden had the house band, augmented by musicians including Jimmy Anderson, Leo Johnson, Charlie Mason, Freddie Roach, Harold Van Pelt and Herb Morgan, along with an up-and-coming younger crew that included Woody Shaw and Tyrone Washington. Albert Ayler and Sun Ra often dropped by. Historian Stan Myers emceed the jam sessions.

"At that stage of my life, all I could think of was dancing and acting," Amina Baraka says. Tall and lanky with long dark hair, she personified that image. She also was married and the mother of two young girls, but that changed when Amiri Baraka began hanging out at the Loft, where his friends Gene Campbell and Wilbur McNeil began staging rehearsals for a new version of *Dutchman*.

About the same time, Baraka began using the Loft for auditions and rehearsals for *Black Mask* and *Jello*, plays he presented downtown at RKO Proctor's. "As vice chair of the Newark Arts Society, I had the keys to the building, so I had to open up," says Amina

Baraka, who successfully auditioned for both productions and won a starring role in one. Before long, she and Baraka, who married in 1967, were an item, "not because Roi had a modicum of fame, but because I was so much into the arts," she says. "I also was impressed by what Roi had to say about working-class people after I heard him speak at the longshoremen's hall." That led her to divorce her first husband "to be with Roi."

After the Barakas got together, Amina moved to Sterling Street, where Amiri ran Spirit House and she founded the African Free School, just as civil rebellions were flaring in Newark and around the nation. Amina's so-called militancy, like his, was shaped by her interest in the arts as a means of acting on the inequities affecting working-class people. "Before I met Roi, my political and religious convictions were influenced by Malcolm X," she says. "I met Malcolm after I heard him speak on the oppression of women. I was taken with the ideology and bought into it."

While Amiri Baraka's family was considered middle class in terms of the black social hierarchy, Amina's was working class. Born in New York City in 1942, Amina Baraka came to Newark as a child to be raised by her grandparents, Leona and Patrick Bacote, while her mother, Ruth Robinson, was at work. "Everyone in our family played music," she says. "In their younger years my grandparents played piano by ear in juke joints. My grandmother also played guitar and my grandfather played harmonica and guitar."

For as long as she can remember, she was intrigued by all forms of the arts—music as well as acting, dance and poetry—an interest she developed as a member of the Poetry Club at Robert Treat Junior High School. In tribute to Edgar Allan Poe, her oldest daughter's middle name is Lenora—straight out of his often-quoted poem *The Raven*.

When a schism developed among members at the Loft, some members stayed upstairs, while the others moved downstairs to an area called the Cellar. According to Stan Myers, the controversy centered on whether or not whites should be allowed to participate in the artistic presentations, either as performers or audience members—an issue that boiled over after a group of white students from Rutgers started hanging at the hall. "One group was into music and the other was political," says Amina Baraka. "I stayed with my friend Art Williams and the arts group." Years later, in his autobiography, her husband wrote: "Art (Williams) had no such restraints (racial exclusion). He wanted to bring in the music, whoever was playing it and whoever wanted to listen to it, and groove."

In the intervening years Amina Baraka developed a song and poetry program based on themes of political and social oppression. She has presented it at schools, jazz clubs and theaters in the United States, South Africa, Europe and South America. It's called *I've Got a Right to Sing the Blues*. In 1983, she co-authored a book with her husband called *Confirmation*.

It's been fifty years since Amiri Baraka wrote *Blues People: Negro Music in White America*, his historic treatise on American music, yet he's remained musically and politically active in every imaginable way. In the interim, he's written a plethora of poems, plays and other books—including *The Autobiography: LeRoi Jones/Amiri Baraka* and *Digging: The Afro-American Soul of American Classical Music*— won a myriad of literary prizes and produced a musical about stride pianist Willie Smith.

According to Arnold Rampersad, the noted biographer and literary critic, "Baraka . . . stands with (Phyllis) Wheatley, (Paul Laurence) Dunbar, (Richard) Wright, (Frederick) Douglass, (Langston) Hughes, (Ralph) Ellison and (Zora Neale) Hurston as one of eight figures who have significantly affected the course of African-American literary culture. His change of heart and head is testimony to his energy, honesty and relentless search for meaning."

Sometimes it's hard to tell whether Baraka loves politics or music more because of his conviction that they are inextricably linked to the history and fate of his people. Rarely, if ever, do his writings stray from the inequalities he sees as inherent in American life, the source of his rage against racism and discrimination that took root as a young man. That's the central premise of *Blues People*—that the notion that all Americans were and are created equally is a subterfuge for people of color without the rights, privileges and respect that goes with it. It's also the theme of his recent poem about the murder of Florida teenager Trayvon Martin.

For Baraka, secular music like the blues—created by Africans brought here in bondage and their descendants—emanated from the field hollers and work songs that provided enslaved people the ability to communicate. Jazz, he explains, is an outgrowth of the darker blues that told the trials and tribulations of black life in America. The classic blues sung by Ma Rainey, Clara Smith and Bessie Smith, he says, "brought blues to a social and cultural significance that it never has had before or since. The jazz people took over from there."

In *Digging*, a collection of essays through the years, Baraka devotes two chapters to jazz in Newark: *Newark's Coast and the Hidden Legacy of Urban Culture* and *Newark's Influence on American Music*. The Coast, he explains, was one of four major Afro-American cultural centers in the United States during the 1920s and 1930s, along with Hell's Kitchen in New York, the French Quarter in New Orleans and the Levee in South Chicago.

As home to Savoy Records as well as to many bars and clubs, Newark was fertile ground for innovative jazz musicians, explains Baraka, whose fascination with jazz in Newark centers on the Coast because it was where most black musicians performed in the 1930s and 1940s. As a result, he staged a tribute to stride pianist Willie "The Lion" Smith at NJPAC in 1997. Pianist Robert Banks was featured in the title role. The backdrop was provided by the NewArkestra, directed by Steve Colson, and a chorus composed of Amina Baraka, Dwight West, Rasheema, James Orange and Halim Suliman.

As a founding member of Newark's Lincoln Park Cultural District, Baraka anticipates the area's eventual rebirth as a place where people of all backgrounds can come together to share their ideas, experiences, music, food and other aspects of their culture. In pursuing that mission, he has presented tributes to childhood friends James Moody and Wayne Shorter as part of the Lincoln Park Music Festival.

In June 2013, the Barakas re-opened Kimako's Blues People, an arts space they ran for more than a decade in their basement to foster black culture and expression. Eighty-three-year-old Robert Banks, who played Willie Smith at the arts center, was the featured attraction. Better known as a gospel musician, Banks' interest in jazz began in the late 1930s as a member of the jazz band at Newark's Eighteenth Avenue School. Over the course of the next seven decades he accompanied Ray Charles, Mahalia Jackson and Dinah Washington, performed at Newark jazz clubs and wrote more than 700 tunes, including *Shangra-La*, made famous in the 1950s by the Four Coins. In Newark music circles he's known as "The Genius."

When the Barakas created Kimako's they named it for his sister Kimako (Sandra Elaine Jones), a Broadway dancer and actress who was stabbed to death in her New York apartment by an acquaintance. Until it shut down nearly fifteen years later, it was the headquarters for like-minded artistic types, "an exciting place to be because you never knew who you'd find sitting in a corner somewhere," says Dwight West, Amina Baraka's younger brother. "Maybe Danny Glover or Maya Angelou." For a time, too, Nina Simone was part of the Baraka household, camping in for a year or so.

As the lead singer for BluArk, a group formed by his sister and brother-in-law, West isn't only a family member. He's had an impressive resume since his days at Weequahic High when he sang with the Decades, a rhythm and blues group that once opened for Barbra Streisand in New York with Bob Hope as emcee. West got into scat in the early 1990s, crafting new lyrics to standard tunes. "Being the professor that he is, Amiri would throw a song at me, tunes like *Come Sunday* or *Don't Get Around Much Anymore* because he was a big Ellington fan. I found myself rapping and rhyming." West and his wife Julie also founded BlueArk Records, which produces his music. Madame Pat Tandy's tribute to blues singer Irene Reid and Radam Schwartz's *Conspiracy for Positivity* also can be heard on the label.

When Kimako's originated, says poet Richard Cammerieri, it filled a huge gap that had existed in music, poetry and political awareness in Newark for most of the 1980s. "There was nothing like it in those days in Newark. Just to be part of it was a very uplifting feeling. For something like $5 you got to see people you'd pay goo gobs of money to see play anywhere else playing in this basement. Joe Lee Wilson and David Murray particularly come to mind."

"That's why it was an honor to be present when Kimako's opened again in June 2013," Cammerieri says. Other friends of the Barakas who paid a return visit included singer Ronnell Bey; Celeste Bateman, who runs a Newark-based booking agency for black artists, and Chris Funkhouser, a New Jersey Institute of Technology professor who manages Amiri Baraka's website.

Between tunes on opening night Banks interspersed tidbits of Newark's jazz history and presented his take on the interrelationships among jazz, blues, gospel, country and classical music. "Name any musician, club or event and Robert can tell you about it, not because he read about it, but because he's been part of it," his wife Cassandra says. "He's accompanied and written for everyone imaginable." During his days as a record producer, Banks guided the careers of Connie Pitts, a stellar singer from Newark, on Savoy and Nina Simone on Jubilee.

During the ten years Banks spent as a jazz musician, Bill Fredericks, who owned Fredericks' Lounge on Boston Street in Newark, was his manager. "Bill paid me $150 a week whether or not I had a gig," he says, but it was not enough to support his wife and large family. So, he got a day job and began devoting himself to recording and playing gospel music. Occasionally, Banks still presents jazz programs like the one at Kimako's. "I love jazz, but it's gotten too synthetic for me," he says. "I love the purity of it, not the artifices."

With jazz on the decline in Newark in recent years, the re-opening of Kimako's Blues People is seen by some as a sign of hope for the city's musical rebirth even though the turnout for the first show was sparse. Nevertheless, it was an historic evening, a re-creation of the artistic showcase the Barakas introduced nearly two decades ago. "The first time I was here was during my time as cultural affairs director for the city of Newark," Celeste Bateman recounts. "The mayor (Sharpe James) sent me to present a proclamation to the Barakas, but I came back several times on my own. It was an important place then. Hopefully it will be again."

18 ♪

New Audiences!
Or New Audiences?

*I don't know where jazz is going. Maybe it's going
to hell. You can't make anything go anywhere.
It just happens. —Thelonious Monk*

With music programs the first to go when school budget cuts occur, where will future generations of jazz musicians and singers come from? Maybe, as Thelonious Monk once said, it will just happen, but things are far different today than when he was growing up and most children learned to play a musical instrument at school. In today's world, that rarely happens. Most music programs are imports run by outside sources and cater to select groups of students. These days, few students enjoy music classes on a regular basis or have their own music teacher, drastically limiting the pool of potential professionals and their audiences.

Bill May, former director of performing and visual arts for Newark Public Schools, an outspoken critic of recent changes in music education, says: "We have an administration that is totally clueless about the importance of the arts and how it relates to Newark's history at all levels of government. The people who work at 2 Cedar Street (school board headquarters) and the people they've put in charge of reforming public education, including charter schools, do not seem to understand how valuable the arts are as a means of fully educating our students."

Anzella K. Nelms, former deputy superintendent of Newark's public schools, attributes increased reliance on outside programming to school-based budgeting, a process that allows principals to determine which programs to eliminate when a budget crisis occurs. As a consequence, she says, the arts and library science, which are not part of the core curriculum, generally suffer most. "Outside programs are much cheaper to produce," Nelms says. "They are wonderful but highly selective."

Consequently, many educators fear across-the-board in-school music education, once a staple of American public education, is nearing extinction, especially in densely populated areas like Newark. "Today's students hardly know what a musical instrument looks like," says jazz organist Dave Braham, who taught in Newark for seven years. "When I was in school, music was all over TV—on shows like *Ed Sullivan* and *Lawrence Welk*. Today's students are lucky if they get to see a musical instrument in the background on *American Idol*."

That's vastly different from when former Mayor Kenneth A. Gibson was growing up in Newark. "When I was in school, every student was required to study music at an early age," says Gibson, now in his eighties. "By the time I got to Central High School, we were putting on shows that rivaled Broadway, and I was playing saxophone in a band that performed in clubs all over town." Gibson's parents also paid for private saxophone lessons because they considered the sacrifice vital to his overall education.

James Scheeley, whose position as director of visual and performing arts for the school district was abolished during a recent round of cuts, also believes there's "far less of a push for music education in urban areas now." Overall, there's less and less music instruction, he says. Statistics he compiled show that the student-to-teacher ratio in Newark increased from 300–1 in the early 2000s to 700–1 for the 2012–13 school year.

Bradford Hayes, a Newark music teacher for three decades, sees the district's entire music education program at risk. "If you cut off the head, it doesn't take long for the body to die," he reasons. "I would not be surprised if we were phased out entirely. If that happens, I could retire, but younger teachers would have nowhere to go." Hayes also worries that Newark children will be denied the joy of having music in their lives at an early age. "Unfortunately, the people who make these decisions live in the suburbs, where music education is a priority," he says. "Their districts have teachers who don't have to cover other classes as we do. Their teachers have strong support from the people in charge."

Braham, who toured for several years with Houston Person and Etta Jones, could have chosen jazz as a full-time career but became a teacher because he wanted to work with children. "I wasn't only looking for benefits and a steady income stream when I stopped traveling," he says. "I wanted to pass our country's rich musical tradition on to new generations." Braham found that impossible while teaching in Newark as the hours he was assigned to teach instrumental music gradually diminished. After he was transferred to Arts High and relegated to covering classes for other teachers for most of the day, he'd had enough. He left Newark and took a job as an instrumental music teacher in nearby Union Township. "We've had budget cuts here, too," he says, "but they haven't seriously affected us because music education, originally part of a desegregation program, is such a strong tradition. Here, I teach all instruments and interact with every fifth-grader in the district. I'm teaching my kids to play all kinds of instruments and how to play together, and I still get to play gigs (often with Don Williams and Lady CiCi) on holidays and the weekends."

Hayes, who began teaching in Newark in 1983 and spent more than half his time at Luis Munoz Marin Middle School, says he's survived a variety of changes affecting his work because of the strong support he's received from his superiors. "When I got to Marin I thought I had died and gone to heaven," he says. "Whatever I needed and asked for I got, because the principal saw that I was producing. Before long, I had a hundred students in my bands."

Hayes says music education in Newark schools began unraveling midway through his tenure, when Fred Ransom, the department director, and Vernon Ross, who coordinated the instrumental music program, retired. Instead of replacing them, administrators combined the music and art departments. "I think music in the schools flourished the most under Bill May," he adds. "Bill was our advocate. He fought for us and stood up for us after the state (of New Jersey) took over the district in 1995 and tried to abolish our department." Braham concurs. "If I needed a tuba or any other instrument, I'd just call Bill, and before you knew it, there it was. His leadership made things much easier for all of us. He understood us because he's a musician, too."

May didn't just hold his ground. He also hired longtime professional musicians, some of them well-known nationally, to teach in the schools and introduced programs that gave Newark students more opportunities to learn and play jazz. With Braham on keyboards and Otis Brown, then a teacher at West Side, on drums, he organized the Newark Public Schools Super Band, a group of teachers that performed at district-wide events. May's other recruits included Santi Debriano, Thaddeus Expose and Hassan Williams, who played with Woody Shaw. "Eventually, we had so many music teachers in the band I wound up playing trombone," Braham says. "Our first gig was *Out of School and Oh So Cool* at the Priory," May recalls. "We also performed at convocations at NJPAC and Newark Symphony Hall, where we opened for the Dizzy Gillespie Alumni Band."

"Fortunately, NJPAC was going up in Newark at that time," says Braham. "How would it have looked to have a major music center in the city and have no music program in the schools?" Instead, center officials took the high road by hiring Philip S. Thomas, a Newark-based arts administrator, as vice president of arts education. "Our goal with our Jazz for Teens program was to train a new generation of jazz musicians by having them work with professionals as a means of deepening their understanding of jazz music and history, exploring new improvisational techniques and jamming alongside jazz musicians," Thomas says. "They also have the opportunity to write music and perform at various events."

Other outside, yet select, programs that benefit Newark public school students include Jazz House Kids, the Thelonious Monk

Institute, the WBGO Kids Jazz Series and various school-based residencies that allow professional singers and musicians to interact with students. The newest program for high school students is the Brick City Jazz Orchestra.

Tyshawn Sorey, who travels the world as a full-time jazz drummer and is completing his studies for a doctorate in jazz theory and composition at Columbia University in New York, is one of the most talented young musicians to come out of Jazz for Teens. "A lot of people didn't realize it then, but Tyshawn was a genius when he was at Arts High School," says Eleta Caldwell, the former principal. During that time he won the Connie Woodruff Music Prize, a jazz competition for Newark Public School students, then won a $10,000-per-year scholarship from the *Star-Ledger* to study jazz at William Paterson University.

"I can still remember the night when Ty got to play with James Moody at the Victoria Theater at the New Jersey Performing Arts Center," says Joanna Gibson Barowski, manager of Jazz for Teens when Sorey was in high school. "Watching him meet Moody backstage was a real moment, especially because Moody was so warm. For Ty, getting to play with Moody was even more powerful."

Jazz pianist and composer Steve Colson, the current listening coach for Jazz for Teens, began working with the program in the early 2000s. "My job is to introduce the students to musicians whose names or music they've never heard," Colson says. "My students are young, fourteen or fifteen, so it's not surprising that many of them don't know Duke Ellington or Count Basie. I also introduce them to different styles played by musicians. Working with young people is very cool because they are enthusiastic and optimistic."

Like many of his colleagues, Colson sees arts education in the United States as underappreciated, underrated and underfunded. "Those in charge fail to realize that the arts often keeps kids who don't want to come to school in school," he says. "It's a nationwide problem."

The Thelonious Monk Institute also offers young jazz musicians a chance to develop their talent and perform publicly. One of its

rising stars is Rahsaan Pickett, who was sixteen when he first performed on stage with the Arts High Jazz Ensemble at NJPAC in
late 2012. The program featured Wayne Shorter, Jimmy Heath and
Antonio Hart. "I play Wayne Shorter's music every day, so it meant
a lot to meet him, especially because he's a graduate of my high
school," says Pickett, who plays guitar and also belongs to Jazz for
Teens and Jazz House Kids.

As one of twenty-five young musicians from Arts, East Side,
Barringer and Science Park high schools participating in the Monk
institute, Pickett got to perform again at NJPAC in 2013, this time
on a program featuring trumpeter Jon Faddis and Tim Green, one
of today's top alto saxophonists. Pickett's desire for a career as a
jazz musician also has gotten a boost from double-bass player Curtis
Lundy, who brought him to Sante Fe, New Mexico, for a November
2012 gig, and WBGO's Dorthaan Kirk, who had him headline the
Jazz Vespers concert at Bethany Baptist Church in June 2013. He's
looking forward to becoming a full-time jazz musician, but plans to
finish college first.

Jazz House Kids, a Montclair-based initiative, serves students of
all ages, including those at the elementary school level. Younger children, including toddlers, learn the rudiments of jazz via the WBGO
Kids Jazz Series. "We offer a wide range of creative programming
that develops musical potential, enhances leadership skills and
strengthens academic performance," says singer Melissa Walker, executive director of Jazz House Kids. Students also get to perform at
community-based events like the 2012 Student Jazz Festival at Science Park High School.

"Our band has been swinging all over town," Oliver Street School
Principal Havier Nazario said in 2012, after his students shared the
stage at NJPAC with Shorter, an Oliver Street alumnus who went
on to Arts High School. Sharing the bill with the frequent Grammy
award-winner were Christian McBride, Maceo Parker and Angelique
Kidjo. "I can't tell you how thrilled our kids were," Nazario says.

Bobby Sanabria, a jazz drummer who teaches at the Manhattan
School of Music, also is concerned about the future of music edu-

cation in public schools. "Because jazz is highly intelligent, visceral and soulful, you could make a conspiracy theory out of the lack of it," says Sanabria, whose nine-piece Latin jazz band performed at the kickoff concert of WBGO's 2013 Kids Jazz Series at Newark Symphony Hall. "But I think it's more a matter of money, an unwillingness among the powers that be, whether in the schools or society at large, to invest in such a unique form of cultural expression. I can't tell you how important programs like the WBGO Kids Jazz Series are to our children," Sanabria says. "All children have a right as Americans to know about music in general and jazz as our country's original music, but they are being kept away from it. They are growing up in a vacuous state."

Nearly 300 parents and children turned out for Sanabria's spring concert in Newark, many of them toddlers accompanied by parents and other relatives. A third of the audience was from three Newark elementary schools—Chancellor Avenue, 13th Avenue and Camden. From the opening note, Sanabria implored the children and their parents to join in—stand up, wave, jump up and down, do whatever they felt like doing. Alice Lang's three-year-old granddaughter Aliyah was among the first to comply, dancing enthusiastically to Sanabria's complex rhythms. "Is that a trombone?" four-year-old Michael Pierce shouted at one point. It wasn't. But that was exactly what Sanabria and Dorthaan Kirk, who coordinates the program, wanted to see and hear—kids enjoying the music, joining in and having fun. Most of all, they wanted them to come back again, as most generally do, for that's what the program is all about.

Michael's mother was pleased, too. "I want to introduce him to America's original art form," Gaynor Pearce says, sounding as if she had memorized the promotional brochure for the concerts. "He's having a good time, so we'll be back for the rest of the series." "If jazz is to survive," Sanabria says, "we'll need a revolution, starting in our schools. We live in a very complacent society that needs to be re-educated about the importance of music in our lives."

But that's a tenuous goal, especially when music education in the schools is in a shambles. Carolyn Whitley, who spent two decades as president of the Parent Teacher Student Organization at Arts High School, traces the de-emphasis on the arts in Newark schools to the 1970s, when budget cuts known as "program modifications" were implemented. "We fought them (the administration), but the overall effect was devastating," Whitley says. "I don't think the music program ever fully recovered."

The greatest push for restoring services came during Marion A. Bolden's tenure (1999–2008) as state district schools superintendent. By then, a state law requiring every student to receive a "thorough and efficient education" was in effect. "Under the law, our children were entitled to art and music education, but we still had to fight to get it," Bolden says. "Since then, everything we tried to do to strengthen the arts has been undone."

Nevertheless, dedicated music teachers like Hayes, presently assigned to First Avenue School, press on. Despite his belief that "the powers that be are out to kill our morale," Hayes remains intent on seeing to it that all children have the opportunity to learn music at school. At First Avenue he interacts with 380 students at least once a week, starting in kindergarten, where he uses cartoons and other forms of animation to interest them. From there it's on to basic theory in first grade and learning how to read music and play the recorder as his students advance from grade to grade. Transferring that knowledge to other instruments comes next.

Hayes presently meets three times a week with twenty-six fifth-graders who play violin, twenty-seven seventh-graders in his band and thirty-eight students in his advanced band, nearly 100 of the 700 students enrolled at his school. He also makes the most of his time covering homeroom periods for other teachers. "If we just let the older kids sit around, we're doing them a disservice," he says. "We have to prepare them for high school. That's why I have my homerooms, from fifth grade up, listen to John Coltrane, Woody Shaw and Sarah Vaughan. This is my way of enhancing my program. If we don't teach children their history, we are denying them their culture."

WHO'S WHO OF NEWARK JAZZ

ACKERMAN, BOB   Multi-reed player (saxophone, flute and clarinet)/pianist. Born March 16, 1940, Irvington, New Jersey. Regular at Jazz Vespers, Memorial West Presbyterian Church (1970s); performs with wife Pam Purvis (since mid-1970s); played Midwestern, Southern venues (1977–86); appeared at Priory, Maize in Newark, Trumpets in Montclair, Headquarters Hotel in Morristown, Cecil's in West Orange; operates instrument repair business.

BANKS, ROBERT   Pianist/organist/arranger/composer. Born February 3, 1930, Newark. Began taking lessons from Dr. Wilbur Bell in elementary school; member, school jazz band; minister of music, Abyssinian Baptist Church at age fifteen; played dual pianos with Emerson Yearwood, Coleman Hotel (1950s); accompanist and record producer, Savoy label (1950s); accompanied Dinah Washington, Johnnie Ray (1960s); played Willie "The Lion" Smith, NJPAC (1997); left jazz to focus on gospel music; minister of music, Humanity Baptist Church.

BARAKA, AMINA   Dancer/actress/singer/poet/author/political activist. Born Sylvia Robinson December 5, 1942, Charlotte, North Carolina. Founding member, Newark Arts Society; founder, African Free School for community children; co-founder, BlukArk ensemble; co-founder, Kimako's Blues People (1980s); wrote *Songs for the Masses*; co-wrote *Confirmation: An Anthology of African-American Women Writers* with Amiri Baraka (1983); performs song/poetry program *I've Got a Right to Sing the Blues*; in Willie "The Lion" Smith tribute, NJPAC (1997).

BARAKA, AMIRI   Author/poet/playwright/essayist/retired college professor. Born LeRoi Jones October 7, 1934, Newark. Founder, Black Arts

Movement (1960s); product, Barringer High School, Howard University; Air Force veteran; books include *Blues People: Negro Music in White America*, *Digging: The African-American Soul of American Classical Music*; heads BluArk ensemble; co-founder, Kimako's Blues People; produced Willie Smith tribute, NJPAC (1997); produced Lincoln Park Music Festival tributes to James Moody (2005) and Wayne Shorter (2013); honors include fellowships from Guggenheim Foundation and National Endowment for the Arts, PEN/Faulkner Award, Rockefeller Foundation Award for Drama, American Academy of Arts and Letters Award, James Weldon Johnson Medal; Obie for *Dutchman* (1964).

BELL, AARON   Double-bassist/arranger. Born April 24, 1921, Muskogee, Oklahoma; died July 28, 2003. Played with Duke Ellington (1960–62); chairman, Performing Arts Department, Essex County College (late 1970s); retired (early 1990s).

BENSON, GEORGE   Guitarist/singer. Born March 22, 1943, Pittsburgh, Pennsylvania. Hung out at Newark clubs (1970s); Key Club favorite; hit charts with *This Masquerade* (1976); headlined Key Club's twentieth anniversary celebration at Essex County College (1977).

BENSON, GIL   Singer. From Paterson, New Jersey. Scat specialist; product of Howard University; appeared at Newark-area clubs, including Priory (1990s–2010).

BEY, ANDY   Singer/pianist. Born Andrew Wideman October 28, 1939, Newark. Piano prodigy; appeared with Connie Francis on TV's *Showtime* as child; recorded *I'm Not a Boy Anymore* on Jubilee, age twelve; honor student, Newton Street School; graduate, Arts High School; organized Andy Bey and the Bey Sisters as teenager (1956); worked with Horace Silver, Gary Bartz (1974); Jazz Journalists' Association's Jazz Vocalist of the Year (2003); Grammy nomination, Best Jazz Vocal Album, *American Song* (2005).

BEY, RONNELL   Singer/musical theater actress. Born in Newark. Niece of singer Andy Bey; graduate, Arts High School; toured nationally/internationally in *Ain't Misbehavin'*; starring role, *The Life and Life of Bumpy Johnson*; Priory favorite.

BOSTICK, RODMAN   Trumpeter. Born 1959, Newark. Began playing as teenager; with Jazz Vanguards (1998); with Stanley Turrentine, Shirley Scott, Big John Patton; leads own group.

BRAHAM, DAVE   Organist; also plays trumpet, guitar, piano. Born October 26, 1954, Uniontown, Pennsylvania. Studied with Richard "Groove"

Holmes, Captain Jack McDuff; traveled with Houston Person, Etta Jones (1980s), Lou Donaldson; music education degree, Pennsylvania State University; elementary music teacher, Newark, Orange, East Orange, Union (since 1993); thirty-year association with Jazz Just-Us quartet; led Latin jazz group; plays Tuesday night jam sessions at SuzyQue's, West Orange.

BRODIE, HUGH Tenor saxophonist/composer. Grew up in Newark; attended Arts High School; classmate, Wayne Shorter; influenced by teacher Eddie Babe; played chitlin' circuit, including Atlantic City, with blues organ trio; joined Illinois Jacquet's big band; played with George Benson, Sonny Stitt; leads Hugh Brodie and His Cosmic Ensemble.

BROOKS, CECIL, III Drummer/bandleader. Born 1961, Pittsburgh, Pennsylvania. Father was drummer; original band member, *Bill Cosby Show*; traveled with Houston Person, Etta Jones (early career); ran Cecil's jazz club (nine years); leader, CB3 band; records extensively.

BROWN, IKE Trumpeter/bandleader. Born September 11, 1938, Montclair, New Jersey. Led Ike Brown and Jazz Prophets; first paid gig at Sterington House, Montclair; Army reservist in First Training Regimental Band, Fort Dix; with Shad Royful's Orchestra, Just Friends band; backed the Dells, Jerry Butler, Persuasions (late 1970s); formed Prophets after playing at DLV Lounge jam sessions; retired Montclair police officer.

BROWN, RUSSEL P. Vocalist/trumpeter/producer/composer/arranger. Born in Newark. Studied music, Essex County College, Rutgers University; performs classical jazz selections on *The Kickoff* (CD); performs at New Brunswick–area clubs.

BUFFORD, GREG Drummer/composer/producer/educator. Born January 25, 1956, Germany. Studied, Berklee College of Music, Rutgers University, privately with Philly Joe Jones, Kenny Barron; regular on New York, international music scene (since 1979) with Madonna, Duke Ellington Orchestra; in pit bands on and off-Broadway; wrote for *Sesame Street*, *The Bernie Mac Show*; created Classic Gold recording *Bounce, Rock, Skate Roll* (1979); established Greg Bufford School of Music (2012); runs Tuesday night jam sessions at SuzyQue's, West Orange (2013).

BURKE, VINNIE Bassist. Born Vincenzo Bucci March 15, 1921; died February 1, 2001. Newark resident; with Marian McPartland, Bobby Hackett, Vic Dickenson, Bucky Pizzarelli; led small combos.

BUTTERFIELD, ERSKINE Pianist/singer. Born February 13, 1913, Syracuse, New York; died May 17, 1961, New York City. Moved to Newark, age five; demonstrated tunes for publisher Clarence Williams; with Russell Mann and his Royal Ambassadors (during Depression); worked with Noble Sissle; joined NBC studio staff (1938); recorded on Decca and other labels with small groups (early 1940s); featured twice weekly as "Singing Vagabond of the Keys," WOR Radio, New York (1941); served in Army; led own trio.

CARDEN, JAN   Born in Philadelphia. Singer. Retired Arts High School fine arts teacher; with Barry Herman Orchestra (several years); appearances include Priory, Skipper's, Trumpets; often appears with daughter, Stephanie Battles.

COLEMAN, GLORIA   Pianist/organist/composer/arranger; also played violin, bass. Born, New York City; died February 18, 2010. Began career (1952) as bassist with Sarah McLawler, Myrtle Young, Sonny Thompson; played organ with Sonny Stitt, Willis Jackson, Gene Ammons, Joe Lee Wilson, Little Jimmy Scott; recorded two albums with saxophonist husband George Coleman (of Miles Davis fame); composed tunes for Irene Reid, Hank Crawford, Ernestine Anderson; played Monterey Jazz Festival, Billie Holiday Jazz Festival, the latter with quartet led by son, George Coleman Jr.; member, Newark Jazz Elders.

COLLERAN, PHYLLIS BLANFORD   Singer. Born in Newark. Appeared in *O Jerusalem* at La Mama Theater New York (early on); appeared before pope in Rome; sang in jazz clubs, musicals throughout Europe (twenty years); appeared in world premiere of *Rosa—A Horse Drama*, contemporary opera in Amsterdam; with Dutch Orchestra, Lincoln Center; member, Jazz Vocal Collective.

CORRAO, VINNIE   Guitarist. Born February 15, 1941, Brooklyn, New York; also plays electric bass. Raised in Passaic and Clifton, New Jersey; father played mandolin and guitar; fixture on East Coast organ circuit with Charles Earland (early 1960s); joined Jack McDuff (1965) in Seattle; played Newark's Cadillac Club with McDuff, Willis "Gatortail" Jackson and Bu Pleasant; recorded with organists Don Patterson and Freddie Roach; made two LPs with Roach; backed Ella Fitzgerald (1969) at American Hotel, New York City; appeared with her orchestra on *Johnny Carson* and *Dick Cavett* shows (1969); part of duo with Aldo Cavalli (fifteen years).

CRAWFORD, EDDIE   Drummer. Died in automobile accident. Played with Horace Silver; worked regularly with Mickey Tucker; regular at Jazz Vespers, Memorial West Presbyterian Church (early 1970s); sideman at Newark-area clubs; played Catskills with Pam Purvis, Bob Ackerman (1970s);

with Jimmy Ford, Midas Gold (1977); remembered in *Digging Max*, Amiri Baraka's poem honoring drummer Max Roach on Roach's seventy-fifth birthday.

DARDEN, BOB (STIX)   Drummer. Born October 29, 1928, Newark. Retired Newark public schools Title I coordinator; began playing drums, West Side High School (early 1940s); played with Elks' Pride of Newark Drum and Bugle Corps; sat in at Baltimore clubs with Sonny Rollins, Thelonious Monk (1949–53); Army veteran; backed Monk, Billie Holiday, Lester Young, Cannonball Adderly, Charlie Rouse; played Newark-area clubs with Nat Phipps's Megatones, Ernie Scott Trio; his Getz cymbals, a gift from Max Roach.

DAVIS, WALTER, JR.   Pianist. Born September 2, 1932, Richmond, Virginia; died July 2, 1990. Nickname: "Humphrey"; raised in East Orange; recognized (early 1950s) for work at Picadilly Club with Hank Mobley Quintet; studied classical piano with Dolores and Albert Tillery; first gig, Harlem's Apollo Theater (1949); joined Charlie Parker shortly afterward; schooled at New York jazz clubs by Thelonious Monk, Bud Powell; first recorded with Max Roach (early 1950s) on Debut; toured on and off with Dizzy Gillespie (twenty-five years); with Art Blakey's Jazz Messengers (early 1970s); group's principal arranger-composer (1975); with Sonny Rollins, Jackie McLean, Archie Schepp, Etta Jones, Bobby Watson (1970s); turned to small-group sessions, solo concerts, piano-bass gigs at Bradley's in New York (1980s).

DEVOS, BOB   Guitarist. Born February 6, 1946, Paterson, New Jersey. Studied under Harry Leahy; leader, Bob DeVos Organ Trio; played and recorded with organ groups led by Trudy Pitts, "Groove" Holmes, Jimmy McGriff, Charles Earland; music director/organist, *An Organ Summit Supreme* at African American Education and Cultural Center, Newark (2005); former artist in residence, Arts High School; taught at William Paterson College, Lehigh University.

DURANT, HERN (HANK)   Tenor saxophonist. From Newark. Played with Dizzy Gillespie; recorded on Savoy with Bobby Banks Trio, featuring Nappy Brown on vocals (1955).

EARLAND, CHARLES (THE MIGHTY BURNER)   Organist/saxophonist. Born May 24, 1941, Philadelphia; died December 11, 1999. Sideman with Lou Donaldson; *I Love You More Than Yesterday*, signature song; played everything from pop tunes to funk jazz; Key Club fixture (1970s); recorded on Mercury, Muse; comeback LP *Inseparable* (1990s); traveled extensively (later years); hit at Berlin Jazz Festival (1994).

EDWARDS, ERNIE   Pianist. Born April 5, 1953, New York City. Performs at lounges in New York-New Jersey area; played during lunchtime in Atrium at St. Joseph's Plaza; played Jazz Vespers, House of Prayer (1980s); minister of music, St. Rocco's Catholic Church, Newark.

ELLIOTT, LU   Singer. Born in New York City; deceased. Sang, and recorded with Duke Ellington (1950s); recorded *Lu Elliott: Way Out from Down Under* (ABC) while touring Australia (1967); popular Key Club performer (1960s– late 1970s); took over for Alberta Hunter at Cookery, New York (1981); wife of guitarist Horace Sims.

EXPOSE, THADDEUS   Bassist. Born November 23, 1962, New Orleans. "Coolest name in jazz"; music teacher, Maple Avenue School, Newark; studied (early on) with bassist Walter Payton; toured with Marcus Roberts (1996–98); seasonal gig in Singapore with Red Holt (1998); house bassist, House Standard, New York (1999–2001); freelanced throughout North America, Europe, Africa, Asia (since early 2000s); author, *The Ultimate Jazz Method: A Comprehensive Performance-Based Curriculum for Individual or Group Instruction* (2013).

FORD, LESLIE   Trumpeter. Born May 24, 1947, Newark. Self-taught; influenced by Freddie Hubbard; played with Horace Silver, Frank Foster, James Spaulding, Steve Turre, Duke Anderson, Jack Onque, Harold Van Pelt, Yusef Ali, Carrie Jackson All-Stars; leads own band; founded New Brunswick-based Jazz Institute of New Jersey to train young musicians; member, Newark Jazz Elders.

FOSTER, JOY   Singer. Born August 17, 1960, Newark. Influenced by Sarah Vaughan, Ella Fitzgerald, Bessie Smith, Duke Ellington; has appeared at the Priory, Skipper's, Cecil's, Trumpets; regular at Crossroads and SuzyQue's.

FULLER, STEPHEN   Singer. Born September 11, 1951, Newark. Graduate, Arts High School, Colgate University; participated in Westminster School summer program; member, All-State Choir; led own bands in college and Kansas City; played North Jersey–New York clubs with Ted Klum, Vince Seneri; member, Jazz Vocal Collective.

GIBBS, JAMES, III   Trumpeter/composer/bandleader. Born October 28, 1977, Newark. Self-taught multi-instrumentalist; trained with Radam Schwartz at New Jersey Jazz Institute; first professional show at Five Spot in New York for WBGO membership gala (1994); performed with singer Betty Carter after auditioning for her Jazz Ahead program for young musicians; influenced by Freddie Hubbard; performed with Wynton Marsalis, Roy

Hargrove. T.S. Monk, Cecil Brooks III; tours with nine-time Grammy winner Joe Thomas; leads Urban Soul Collective band.

GIBSON, KENNETH A.   Alto saxophonist. Born May 15, 1931, Enterprise, Alabama. Four-term mayor of Newark (1970–86); first African-American Northeast mayor; graduate, Central High School, Newark (1950); member, school orchestra, All-State Orchestra; joined Jackie Bland's band as teenager, played canteens at Graham Auditorium, jam sessions at Newark clubs.

GILMER, STAN   Singer. Born March 2, 1948, Newark. Composed *Atlantic City: That Big Time Town* with Harvey Scales; recorded it with Frank Foster (late 1970s); developed songwriting skills, Essex County College (1980–83); male vocalist for band led by Chink Wing; founded Colonnade Music (2003).

GLADDEN, EDDIE   Drummer. Born December 6, 1937, Newark; died September 3, 2003, Newark. Music major, Arts High School; legendary work with Dizzy Gillespie, Dexter Gordon, James Moody, Woody Shaw, Chet Baker, Horace Silver, Kenny Durham, Larry Young Jr.; influenced by Max Roach, Art Blakey, Bobby Thomas, Buddy Mack; performed on fifty-plus albums, including *Live at Carnegie Hall*, *Nights at the Keystone* with Dexter Gordon; New York-New Jersey club appearances (1950s–80s).

GLOVER, YVETTE   Singer. Born November 13, 1940, Newark. Product of Newark schools; daughter of Newark Swing Era greats Anna Lundy and Billy Lewis; mother of tap dance phenomenon Savion Glover; favorite at Priory, Skipper's; promotes tap shows; command performance before King of Morocco (1980s).

GOLDSTON, GENE (GOLDIE)   Singer. Born January 22, 1933, Greensboro, North Carolina. Moved to Newark, age five; traveled at age nine with Bethany Baptist Church unit of Hall Johnson Choir; sang lead with school choir, Laurinburg Institute, North Carolina; served in Army (1952–55); led jam sessions, Mr. Wes's (early 1970s–early 1980s); played East Coast venues with Chink Wing and Tomoko Ohno; ran jam sessions, Skipper's (2008–12), Ideal Bar (2012–present).

GORDON, GEORGE   Pianist/composer/arranger. Born June 16, 1916, Newark; died 1980s. Product of Burnet Street, Barringer High schools; played Newark clubs solo or with George Gordon Trio (Eddie Wright, guitar, Hank Young, bass); accompanied daughter Honi and sons George Jr. and Richard (The Gordons) on recordings with Charles Mingus, Dizzy Gillespie,

Lionel Hampton; left music for ministry; staff member, United Community Corporation's Senior Citizen Project; revived Freddie Roach's play *Soul Pieces* (1970s).

GORDON, MEREDITH (HONI)   Singer. Born August 14, 1937, Newark. Lead singer with The Gordons, family group that recorded on Debut; also recorded with Charles Mingus, Dizzy Gillespie, Lionel Hampton; sang parts of *Mary Lou's Mass* with composer Mary Lou Williams and at memorial tribute to Williams; classic LP, *Honi Gordon Sings*; member, Jazz Vocal Collective.

GRANT, ROSALIND   Singer. Born Rosalind Jeanette Barboza May 7, 1949, Jersey City, New Jersey. Also plays piano; sang in choirs, St. Clair's United Methodist Church, Jersey City; studied with Inez McClendon, Newark Community School of Arts, Edith Phillips in Jersey City; began singing jazz (1990s); has appeared with Spirit of Life Ensemble.

GRICE, (SIR) G. EARL, JR.   Drummer/actor. Born in Newark. Currently with Crown Heights Affair; has shared stage with Sonny Rollins, Clark Terry, Rhoda Scott, Stevie Wonder, George Benson; performances abroad include Blue Note in Milan, Coronet Theater, London; associations include Mel Davis, Jeff Hacksworth, Roy Meriwether; fifty-plus movie/television credits include *Sleepers*, *Shaft*, *The Cosby Show*, *Law and Order*.

HAMILTON, DENISE   Singer. Born in the Bronx, New York. Began singing at jam sessions at Peppermint Lounge (1970s–80s); first paid job with band led by Chink Wing; yearlong gig with Gil Lewis's band in lounge at Trump Plaza, Atlantic City; ran karaoke sessions, Skipper's (2008–12); regular at Private Place, Orange.

HAYES, BRADFORD   Saxophonist/educator. Born September 25, 1959, Dinwiddie County, Virginia. Came to Newark (1983) after earning music education degree, North Carolina A&T State University; teaches music at First Avenue School, Newark; led Summer Jazz Workshops, Arts High School; toured with Babatunde Olatunji's Drums of Passion Band for fifteen years (beginning mid-1980s); leads Bradford Hayes Quartet.

HAYES, HUNTER   Singer/saxophonist/composer/arranger. Born Douglas Hayes Pinkney, 1951, Montclair, New Jersey. Self-taught; raised in church; recorded with Hotline, his band, on Del-Lite Records at age eighteen; went solo (mid-1980s); recorded *Are You Wid It*, *This Time*, Island Records (1986–87); signed by Columbia (1990); wrote theme song for TV show *Due Process* (1991).

HOLIDAY, CYNTHIA   Singer. Born in Newark. Stepdaughter of big-band trumpeter Calvin Hughes; studied with Duke Anderson, Newark Community School of Arts; performed with Bob Harris Orchestra; featured vocalist at Birdland with John Hicks; former director, New York Jazzmobile; toured Russia and Japan.

HOLMES, RICHARD (GROOVE)   Organist. Born May 2, 1931, Camden, New Jersey; died June 29, 1991, St. Louis. Key Club regular (1970s); best known for recording of *Misty* (1965); made first album with Ben Webster (1961); recorded prolifically with Houston Person.

HUGHES, CALVIN   Trumpeter. Born December 20, 1925, Perth Amboy, New Jersey; died August 7, 2007. Played first trumpet, elementary and high school bands; selected in teens to play with Don Linton's Counts of Rhythm; played alongside Clark Terry (then unknown) during four years in Navy's Special Services unit; two-time member, Duke Anderson Orchestra; backed Billie Holiday, Coleman Hawkins, Della Reese, Redd Foxx, Smokey Robinson, Gladys Knight and the Pips, Big Maybelle, the Temptations; toured with Teddy Ritchwood (1948); started Calvin Hughes and Sophisticated Gents (1981); later led Calvin Hughes Quartet; taught at Newark Community School of Arts.

HUTCHERSON, BRAD   Drummer. Born August 28, 1939, Oxford, North Carolina. Played with Jazz Correspondents, teenage musicians from South Side High School; appeared locally with Jive Five; traveled with the Intruders, a group that included Bobby Wooten.

HUTCHERSON, WILLIE   Pianist. Born August 17, 1940, Oxford, North Carolina. Led Jive Five jazz combo at South Side High School with brother Brad on drums, Buddy Terry on saxophone, Dennis Moorman on piano, singer Melba Moore; matinees at Len & Len's.

JACKSON, CARRIE   Singer. Born in Newark. Performs Great American Songbook; sang in Mt. Calvary Church Children's Choir; teenage talent contest winner; toured with WWRL Gospel Chorus; studied piano and vocal music with Duke Anderson; sang with Anderson's band (several years); studied at Newark Community School of Arts with Inez McClendon, Nadine Herman; president, C-Jay Records; founder, Jazz Vocal Collective.

JOHNSON, HERBERT (GERONIMO)   Drummer. From East Orange. Played at original Key Club; scouted talent with Rev. Jan van Arsdale for Jazz Vespers, Memorial West Presbyterian Church (early 1970s); organizer, first Newark Jazz Week (late 1970s).

JOHNSON, LEO   Saxophonist. Born October 19, 1939, Daytona Beach, Florida. Mainstay on Newark jazz scene and beyond; after military service in bands led by Specks Williams, Bobby "Blue" Bland, Bill Doggett, Jack McDuff, Jimmy McGriff, Chico Mendoza; Jimmy Scott's former music director; played Europe with Rhoda Scott; music director, Newark Jazz Elders; teaches music, Essex County College.

JONES, JACKIE   Singer. Born in Newark. Graduate, Arts High School, Mason Gross School of Arts at Rutgers University; sang on opening night (2008) at Skipper's; appears all over North and Central Jersey, frequently with Nat Adderly Jr.

JONES, JAMES (CHOPS)   Trumpeter/bassist/drummer. Born August 18, 1916, Newark; deceased. Original member, Barons of Rhythm; self-taught; influenced by Roy Eldridge, Dizzy Gillespie; played in Army bands in Virginia; joined Amy Garrison's band at Boston Plaza after Army discharge (1943); later with Mandy Ross's Walkin' Rhythm; booked jazz acts as city's assistant director of parks/recreation.

JONES, JIMMY   Saxophonist/clarinetist/flutist/arranger. Born April 21, 1926, Essex County, New Jersey. Began playing clarinet in grammar school; Army veteran; member, Shadful Royful's Big Band (thirty years plus); arranger, Diane Moser's Big Band; played or sat in all over Newark.

JONES, VICTOR   Drummer. Born 1954, Newark. Studied trumpet (ten years); took up drums after hearing Beatles on *Ed Sullivan Show*; played with Lou Donaldson (two years), followed by stint with Stan Getz; toured internationally with James Moody, Woody Shaw, Freddie Hubbard, Dizzy Gillespie, Stanley Turrentine, Phyllis Hyman, Chaka Kahn; performed throughout United States, Japan with Victor Jones's R&B Bop Band.

KETTRELL, DAILLE   Pianist/vocalist/songwriter/educator. Born in Camden, New Jersey. Performed in marching, concert, jazz bands, Camden High School; bachelor's degree in music, Clark University; joined Shad Royful's Renaissance Band (1990); studied jazz piano with Duke Anderson; founded Rites of Passage (1993); frequently performs at Priory, Private Place.

KIRK, RAHSAAN ROLAND   Hard-bop/soul multi-instrumentalist. Born Ronald Theodore Kirk August 7, 1935, Columbus, Ohio; died December 5, 1977. Played several instruments simultaneously; became blind (early age); preferred leading own bands; early work as leader includes *Triple Threat* on King, *Introducing Roland Kirk* on Prestige, *We Free Kings* on Mercury; recorded thirty-plus LPs on Argo, Verve, Atlantic, Warner Bros. (1956–77); husband of WBGO's Dorthaan Kirk.

KOSTELNIK, DAN   Organist. Frequently plays in Europe; recently released first CD; member, Bob DeVos Trio; appearances at Priory, Skipper's, Cecil's.

LADY CICI   See Williams, Cheryl.

LANE, GORDON   Drummer. Born June 6, 1963, Elizabeth City, North Carolina; grew up in Baton Rouge, Louisiana. Former member, Roy Meriweather Trio; recent appearances with Stanley Jordan at Iridium in New York, Carrie Jackson's Jazzin' All-Stars, Stephen Fuller Quintet at North Jersey clubs.

LESTER, CONRAD (CONNIE)   Saxophonist. Born June 12, 1931, Roselle, New Jersey. Mostly self-taught; played Newark and Jersey Shore clubs with own group (1950–early 1960s); played in bands led by Specks Williams, Jimmy McGriff, Vinnie Corrao, Bill Doggett, Fred Thomas, Dave Braham, Aaron Bell; member, Newark Jazz Elders.

LIGHTSEY, ED   Bassist. Born January 31, 1930; died August 22, 2009. Started playing with Nat Phipps Orchestra, Barringer High School; original member, Nat Phipps & Megatones; graduate, Manhattan School of Music; served in Korea with 82nd Airborne Division, black paratroopers' unit.

LOGAN, MICHAEL   Bassist/composer. Born July 31, 1953, Chicago. Began playing guitar after high school, switched to bass; gigged around Chicago with Association for Advancement of Creative Musicians; moved to New York (1983); toured Europe with Muhal Richard Abrams; performed with Clifford Jordan, Walter Bishop Jr., John Hicks; appears frequently at Priory, Trumpets; compositions include *Newark*, a post-1960s ode to his first New Jersey hometown.

MASON, CHARLIE   Trumpeter. Spent early part of career with Nat Phipps & the Megatones, including two-year stint at Glitter Club; also with Nat Phipps Orchestra, drummer Rudy Walker at Key Club, Sparky J's, other Newark venues.

MAY, WILLIAM M. (BILL)   Bassist. Born April 15, 1946, Headland, Alabama. Came to Newark, 1950; Freelance musician throughout New York, New Jersey; double bassist/principal bassist, New Jersey Pops Orchestra (twenty-six years); director, Newark Public Schools' Department of Visual and Performing Arts (1998–2008); music director, Neil's New Yorker dinner theater (1976–94); jazz photographer/historian; toured internationally, *Ain't*

Misbehavin' (2011); president/business agent, Northern Jersey Musicians' Guild (Local 16/248), American Federation of Music (2013–present).

McCLOUD, ANDY   Bassist/composer/leader. Born 1948, Newark; deceased. Led band during college; led Andy McCloud's Gentlemen of Jazz; wrote all tunes for *Blues for Mr. Bighead* album/CD; worked with Mary Lou Williams, Elvin Jones, Frank Foster (two years), Clifford Jordan, Arthur Blythe, Don Pullen, Jon Hendricks (three years), Hilton Ruiz (nine years); freelance bassist with Dizzy Gillespie, McCoy Tyner.

McCRAE, RICHIE   Pianist/organist. Born July 11, 1936, Newark. Arts High School graduate (1954); began playing professionally as teenager at 42nd Club, Orange; main influences: Larry Young Jr. Hank Durant, Jimmy Anderson; played at Lyric Bar, Newark (five years), Orbit Lounge (two years); on road with Paul Farano's R&B band; toured United States with Perry and Harmonics (of *Do the Monkey With James* fame); member, Newark Jazz Elders.

McDUFF, JACK (CAPTAIN OR BROTHER)   Organist. Born 1926; died 2001. Began playing bass; switched to piano before taking up organ; first big hit with Honeydrippers (1961); with Sonny Stitt, Gene Ammons (1962); with Joe Dukes (1960s–92); Key Club fixture (1970s) with George Benson.

McGHEE, CORNELL   Trombonist. Born February 28, 1955, Newark. B.A. degree, Fairleigh Dickinson University, Madison; roomed with future Count Basie trombonist Clarence Banks; on metropolitan jazz scene (thirty years); worked in Europe; studied with Grachan Moncur III, Steve Turre; early influences include Benny Green, Benny Powell, J. J. Johnson, Slide Hampton, Curtis Fuller; often works with Mel Davis, Radam Schwartz, Bradford Hayes, Carlos Francis; with Jazz Vanguards, Ike Brown's Jazz Prophets (1990s).

McGRIFF, JIMMY   Organist. Born April 3, 1936, Philadelphia; died May 24, 2008. Known for hard-bop, soul-jazz Hammond B3 initiatives; owner, Golden Slipper (early 1970s); breakthrough LP, *I've Got a Woman* (Sue, 1962); former military police officer and Philadelphia motorcycle cop.

MENDOZA, CHICO   Pianist/drummer. Born Ira Roberts Jr.; raised in Montclair, New Jersey. Began playing percussion instruments at four; professional career began with Cubaneers, local band that specialized in Calypso, mambo, straight-ahead jazz; became its regular pianist; influenced by Machito, Tito Rodriguez, Tito Puente; formed own band (1955).

MISS RHAPSODY   Born Viola Wells, December 14, 1902, 21 Scott Street, Newark; died December 22, 1984. Spent sixty years in show business; replaced Mamie Smith in traveling show at Miner's Theater, Newark (1920s); toured East Coast with Banjo Bernie's orchestra, Midwest with blues singer Ida Cox (1930s); top draw at Newark clubs, including Dodger's Bar & Grill, Fisher's Tavern (1940s); recorded on Savoy (1944–45); featured on French TV (1975); founding member, New Eden Baptist Church, Newark.

MOBLEY, HANK   Tenor saxophonist/composer. Born July 7, 1930, Eastman, Georgia; died, May 30, 1986. Raised in Elizabeth, New Jersey; ran jam sessions at Picadilly (late 1940s–early 1950s); with Jerry Bogar's Club Orchestra (early 1950s); joined Max Roach (early 1950s); subsequently with Dizzy Gillespie; founding member, Jazz Messengers; toured worldwide with group (thirty years); later led own groups; known for recording of *Little Girl Blue*.

MONCUR, GRACHAN, III   Jazz trombonist/composer/arranger. Born June 3, 1937, New York City. Son of Grachan "Brother" Moncur, bassist with Savoy Sultans; grew up in Newark; graduate, Laurinberg Institute, North Carolina; studied at Juilliard; in bands with Ray Charles, Art Farmer, Benny Golson; worked with Sonny Rollins, Jackie McLean, Archie Shepp; appeared in European tour of *Blues for Mr. Charlie*; *DownBeat*'s Trombonist Deserving Greater Recognition (1964); No. 1 trombonist, European Popular Jazz Poll (1970); *Echoes of Prayer* LP named *Melody Maker*'s Jazz Album of Year (1975).

MONTAGUE, ANTOINETTE   Singer. Born July 21, 1960, Newark. Sang in gospel choir on program featuring Mary Lou Williams, Seton Hall University; mentors include Carrie Smith, Myrna Lake, Della Griffin, Etta Jones; credits include Blue Note, Lenox Lounge, Newark Museum Jazz in Garden Series, Jazz Vespers at Bethany Baptist Church; kicked off Flatted Fifth Jazz Vespers Series, Memorial West Presbyterian Church (2010); performed in Russia, Israel, Korea.

MOODY, JAMES   Saxophonist. Born March 26, 1925, Savannah, Georgia; died December 9, 2010. Also played flute; led jam sessions, Lloyd's Manor (1940s); with Dizzy Gillespie (1946–48); rejoined Gillespie (1964); prolific recording artist; best known for *Moody's Mood for Love*; honored by City of Newark (2008) and appeared at Lincoln Park Music Festival (2008); NJPAC's James Moody Democracy of Jazz Festival honors his work.

MORGAN, HERB   Saxophonist. Born in Newark; died July 19, 2013; also known as Karim Abdul Rahman or Herbie Morgan. First recorded on Vanguard with Dave Burns as leader and eighteen-year-old Kenny Barron on piano; favorite recording, *Mother Ship* with Larry Young Jr. (Blue Note, 1969); longtime association with Amina and Amiri Baraka's BluArk ensemble.

ONQUE, JACK   Saxophonist. Born August 1, 1939, Irvington, New Jersey. Makes mouthpieces for other musicians; worked for Giardinelli Music Company, New York; started playing at age seventeen while at Barringer High School; paid $6 for first gig at T-Bar on West Market Street; led trio with Eddie Gladden on drums and John Lightfoot, organ; played for WBGO benefit at Town Hall, New York City.

PATTERSON, ALFRED (AL)   Trombonist/composer/arranger. Born May 28, 1937, Cleveland County, North Carolina; also plays piano, cello, soprano saxophone. Toured or performed with Muhal Richard Abrams, Slide Hampton, David Murray, Roscoe Mitchell, Oliver Lake; in bands led by Allen Jackson, Duke Anderson, Calvin Hughes, Nat Phipps, Freddie Roach, Hal Mitchell, Larry Young Jr.; in pit bands of Broadway musicals, including *Dream Girls*, *La Cage Aux Folles*; toured or played with New Jersey Symphony Orchestra, Alvin Ailey Dance Company, American Ballet Company, Bolshoi Ballet; member, Newark Jazz Elders.

PERSIP, CHARLI   Drummer. Born July 26, 1929, Morristown, New Jersey. First paid gigs in Newark with Billy Ford, Joe Holliday; with Tadd Dameron (1953), Dizzy Gillespie (September 1953–January 1958); led own groups, including SuperSound (thirty years); author, *How Not to Play Drums*.

PERSON, HOUSTON   Saxophonist/record producer. Born November 10, 1934, Florence, South Carolina. Plays everything from jazz to hard bop; best known for soul jazz; inducted, South Carolina State College Hall of Fame (1999); continued studies at Hartt College of Music after playing in United States Air Force band (two years); toured internationally with singer Etta Jones (many years); recorded more than 75 albums, CDs on labels including Muse, Prestige, Mercury; recipient, Eubie Blake Jazz Award (1982).

PHILLIPS, STEVE   Drummer. Born December 29, 1941, Newark; died, spring 1912. Self-taught; on local scene with Charles Earland, Jimmy McGriff, Leo Johnson, Nat Phipps, Irene Reid (1950s–70s); played overseas (1979–97), often with Rhoda Scott; performed in bands led by Art Farmer, John Lewis, Benny Golson, Vanessa Rubin, Jimmy Scott; spent seven years in Lebanon with Three Wheel Drive Trio and Fairuz, a Middle Eastern singer; member, Newark Jazz Elders.

PHIPPS, BILLY   Saxophonist/flutist/music educator. Born December 25, 1931, Newark; died December 3, 2011. From family of pre-eminent musicians that includes twin brother Nat, older cousins Ernie and Gene Phipps Sr., nephew Gene Jr.; originally played clarinet with Nat Phipps Orchestra, scaled-down version of group that featured Wayne Shorter; toured major

East Coast clubs (1960–67) with Megatones; in bands led by Buddy John-son, Dizzy Gillespie, Jack McDuff, Irene Reid, Lloyd Price; led own groups; retired (1992) after teaching (many years) in Newark schools; member, Newark Jazz Elders and NewArkestra.

PHIPPS, ERNIE　Pianist/bandleader. Born February 14, 1923, Newark; de-ceased. Formed Marlarks of Rhythm as teenager; played Dreamland Acad-emy (1941), Savoy Plaza (1943–44); toured Washington, D.C., Virginia, West Virginia (1943); joined Gene Phipps Orchestra upon return from military duty (1946); appeared with vibes band, Caravan Club (1949); played Boba-loo Club, Howard Bar in Newark, Diamond Bar in Orange.

PHIPPS, GENE, JR.　Saxophonist/flutist. Son of Gene Phipps Sr.; on New-ark-New York jazz scene with Max Roach, Abbey Lincoln, Jack McDuff, Jimmy McGriff, Carter Jefferson, Woody Shaw, Tito Puente, Ray Barretto; toured Europe; longtime gig at Priory (early career); co-led Tuesday night jam sessions at DLV Lounge, Montclair, with Bruce Tyler (2011–12).

PHIPPS, GENE, SR.　Saxophonist. Born December 17, 1927, Newark; died November 17, 2013. Active on Jersey jazz scene (1940s–80s); toured as teen-ager with Billie Holiday, then with Oran "Hot Lips" Page, Max Roach, Ike Quebec, Jimmy McGriff, Jack McDuff and Amiri Baraka; played Washing-ton Bar with Gus Young; led own groups.

PHIPPS, LARANAH　Singer/arts administrator. Daughter of Gene Phipps Sr.; former cultural arts director, Convention Hall, Paramount Theater, As-bury Park.

PHIPPS, NAT　Pianist/vibraphonist/bandleader/music educator. Born De-cember 26, 1931, Newark. Leader, Nat Phipps Orchestra, Barringer High School; led smaller groups that included Wayne Shorter; led Megatones; fixture on Newark bebop scene (late 1940s on); active musically, Schenec-tady, New York.

PORTER, BOBBY　Singer. Born December 29, 1929, Orange, New Jersey. Lead vocalist, Brady Hodge Orchestra (1955–62), Newark-based group that included Woody Shaw, Charli Persip; with Nat Phipps Orchestra, smaller group led by Phipps; on two Leo Johnson CDs; member, Newark Jazz Elders.

PURDIE, BERNARD (PRETTY)　Drummer. Born June 11, 1939, Elkton, Maryland. Influenced by Jo Jones, Buddy Rich, Gene Krupa, Art Blakey; prolific recording artist; backed James Brown on *Ain't That a Groove* (1965), *Kansas City* (1967); Aretha Franklin's music director (1970–75); associated with Gil Scott-Heron, King Curtis, Rolling Stones, Isaac Hayes, Steely Dan; accompanied blues singer Carrie Smith (1980s).

PURVIS, PAM   Singer. Born in Bogalusa, Louisiana. Performs with husband Bob Ackerman at clubs throughout New Jersey, out of state; credits include Trumpets, Maize, Priory, Cecil's, Headquarters Hotel.

RASHEEMA   Singer. Born Gloria Smith in Hackensack, New Jersey. Played Las Vegas lounges (early career); favorite at Newark-area clubs including Trumpets (1980s); performed annually in Sweden (1980s); cast member, Amiri Baraka's tribute to Willie "The Lion" Smith, NJPAC (1997); described by *Star-Ledger* jazz critic George Kanzler as "best jazz singer in New Jersey" (1980s).

RAYE, MONA   Singer. Mother of actress Tisha Campbell Martin; talent manager; sang at Mr. Wes's (early career).

REID, IRENE   Singer. Deceased. Former Count Basie vocalist; Key Club favorite (1960s–70)s; appeared frequently at Cleo's in Secaucus, Showman in New York.

ROACH, FREDDIE   Organist. Born May 11, 1931, the Bronx, New York; died in California, 1981; also played pipe organ and piano. Influenced by Jimmy Smith; style considered more subtle than better-known hard-driving contemporaries; began playing professionally with Grachan Moncur's Strollers (late 1940s); record debut on Blue Note with Ike Quebec (1960); best known for Blue Note LP *Mo' Greens Please* (1963); moved to France (late 1960s); ran African-centered theater in Newark (1970s); *Soul Pieces*, his best-known theatrical work.

SAGERMAN, NOEL   Drummer. Born December 23, 1967, Plainfield, New Jersey. Spent a year playing in Japan (1992); started on Newark-area jazz scene, Peppermint Lounge jam sessions; influenced by Don Williams; appeared with Pharoah Sanders, Irene Reid, Big John Patton, David "Fathead" Newman, Oliver Lake; played New York venues including Blue Note, Iridium, Lenox Lounge; taught at Newark Community School of Arts, NJPAC's Jazz for Teens program; travels with gospel singer Joshua Nelson.

SCHWARTZ, RADAM   Organist/pianist/composer/arranger/educator. Born July 10, 1952, New York City. Studied composing at Rutgers University, New Brunswick; associations include Arthur and Red Prysock, Eddie "Lockjaw" Davis, Al Hibbler, David "Fathead" Newman; first Newark gig, Midas Gold with Jimmy Ford (1977); hosted weekly jam sessions, Peppermint Lounge (early career), Crossroads (fifteen years), Skipper's (five years); appears with Gene Goldston at Ideal Bar; music teacher; longtime music director,

Jazz Institute of New Jersey; M.A. degree, jazz history/research, Rutgers-Newark (2012).

SCOTT, JIMMY (LITTLE JIMMY)   Born July 17, 1925, Cleveland Ohio. Toured with dancer Estelle "Caldonia" Young (early career); Lionel Hampton's vocalist (late 1940s–early 1950s); favorite at Newark nightclubs (post-Swing Era); rediscovered at age sixty-eight; longtime favorite of Newark singer Frankie Valli; idolized by Madonna, Liza Minelli.

SCOTT, RHODA   Organist. Born July 3, 1938, Dorothy, New Jersey. Began playing in church at age seven; plays barefooted; known as "Barefoot Contessa"; Key Club and Playbill Lounge favorite (1970s–80s); master's degree, Manhattan School of Music; moved to France (early 1960s); travels Europe, records on Barclay label; often returns to Newark for organ jams; master's degree, research and jazz history, Rutgers-Newark (2014).

SEARVANCE, GREG   Drummer/teacher/composer/bandleader. Born in New Jersey. Self-taught musician; worked with Babatunde Olantunji, Charlie Byrd, Gloria Lynne, Aaron Bell; taught in schools, privately; appears at major venues and clubs, United States, abroad.

SHAW, WOODY, JR.   Legendary trumpeter. Born December 24, 1944, Laurinberg, North Carolina; died May 11, 1988, New York City. Most innovative trumpet player and composer of his era; attended Arts High School; started playing professionally with Eric Dolphy; won acclaim on European circuit as teenager; standout sideman, leader on Blue Note (1960–70s); joined Horace Silver (early 1960s); member, Art Blakey's Jazz Messengers (1970s); later led own groups; Grammy Award winner.

SHORTER, WAYNE   World-renowned tenor saxophonist/composer/band leader. Born August 25, 1933, Newark. Arts High School graduate; led Jazz Informers as teenager; gained experience playing bebop with Newark-based Jackie Bland Band; after serving in Army joined Nat Phipps Orchestra; brief stints with Horace Silver, Maynard Ferguson (1958–59); musical director, Art Blakey and Jazz Messengers (1959–63); with Miles Davis (1964–70); co-founder, Weather Report (1970–86); toured with Herbie Hancock (1998); recipient, National Endowment for Arts Jazz Masters Award; toured with own groups; recipient, nine Grammys, thirteen Grammy nominations; led five-city United States tour marking eightieth birthday (2013).

SIMS, HORACE   Guitarist. Deceased. Husband of singer Lu Elliott; played at the Key Club, Jazz Vespers at West Memorial Presbyerian Church (1970s);

performed at Miss Rhapsody's eightieth birthday tribute, Essex County College (1982).

SLADE, CHARLIE   Drummer/leader. Deceased. Played with Jazz Creations and other groups at area clubs including Priory.

SMITH, CARRIE   Singer. Born, Ft. Gaines, Georgia; died, May 20, 2012, Englewood, New Jersey. Moved to Newark as child; soloist, Abyssinian Baptist Church; gained attention with Greater Harvest Baptist Church Back Home Choir at Newport Jazz Festival (1957); traveled with Big Tiny Little, Al Hirt (early 1970s); stole show at Nice International Jazz Festival (1984); toured Europe (twenty-plus years); starred in Broadway musical *Black and Blue* (1989–91).

SOREY, TYSHAWN   Drummer/pianist/arranger/composer. Born 1980, Newark. Arts High School graduate; won $40,000 *Star-Ledger* scholarship to study music at William Paterson University; travels world with his and other groups; plays frequently at New York clubs; studying for doctorate in music composition, Columbia University.

STEIN BROTHERS   Alex, tenor saxophonist. Born March 7, 1980, New York City. Asher, alto saxophonist. Born March 2, 1983, New York City. Began playing at jams at Peppermint Lounge (1994), when Alex was thirteen; Asher, ten; made the scene at jazz clinic run by Jimmy Owens, Ed Ford at Newark Jazz Festival (1994); longtime students of pianist Barry Harris; popular at Priory (late 1990s–2000s); appearances include Dizzy's Club Coca Cola at Lincoln Center, Smalls in Harlem, Greenwich Village clubs; members, Bud Powell Tribute Band; Alex, doctoral candidate in ethnomusicology, Brown University; Asher, completing medical school.

STEWART, JAMES   Saxophonist. Mainstay with Danny Mixon's Trio; member, Radam Schwartz's Conspiracy for Positivity, Amiri Baraka's NewArkestra, Duke Ellington Tuesday night band at Birdland. Began touring with Sun Ra Arkestra (2011).

TANDY, MADAME PAT   Singer. Born in Newark. Began singing in gospel groups and church choirs; studied jazz with Duke Ellington bassist Aaron Bell, Essex County College; ECC associate degree, music education; singing professionally since 1970s; appears with groups led by Radam Schwartz, Tommy Grice, David Aaron and with Nu Taste Ensemble; performed off-Broadway in *Billie* and *Good Time Blues*.

TAYLOR, JASON (MALLETMAN)   Vibraphonist. Born in Brooklyn, New York. Five-time Grammy award nominee; Lionel Hampton protege; traveled with Hampton's eighteen-piece band throughout United States, Europe, highlighted by appearance at President Ronald Reagan's Inaugural Ball (1985); operated Mallet's Place, downtown Newark (2001–03); president, Mallet Records; hosted *Mallet's Place*, public access TV program.

TERRY, EDLIN (BUDDY) Alto/tenor saxophonist/composer/arranger. Born January 30, 1941, Newark. Played with Dizzy Gillespie, Ray Charles, Lionel Hampton, Horace Silver, Art Blakey, Gil Evans, Charles Mingus, Jimmy McGriff, Joe Morello, Sy Oliver, Thad Jones, Mel Lewis; member, Duke Ellington Alumni Band, Broadway pit band for *Sophisticated Ladies*; original member, TV's *Saturday Night Live* band; Prestige, Mainstream recording artist; member, Newark Jazz Elders.

THOMAS, JOE Saxophonist. Born May 31, 1933, Newark. Fronted own group (many years); toured with Specks Williams, Rhoda Scott; with Scott, fixture at Key Club (1960s–70s); played Sparky J's, Front Room, Lyric Bar, Playbill Lounge, Four Leaf Deli; member, Newark Jazz Elders.

VAN PELT, HAROLD Saxophonist/arranger. Born April 5, 1930, Newark. Began playing (1940s) at Arts High; 753rd Army-Air Force Band; spent two years on Detroit jazz circuit; toured with R&B bands led by Annie Laurie, Sticks McGhee, Joe Morris; regular at Key Club, Lloyd's Manor; founded Jazz Vanguards (1990s); member, Newark Jazz Elders.

VAUGHAN, SARAH Legendary jazz singer. Born March 27, 1924, Newark; died April 3, 1990. Discovered in teens by Billy Eckstine after winning Apollo Theater Amateur Night Contest; signed soon after by bandleader Earl Hines; prolific recording artist; sang in choir, old First Mt. Zion Baptist Church, Newark; attended East Side, Arts high schools; Grammy-award winner; recipient, National Endowment for the Arts Jazz Masters Award.

WALKER, RUDY Drummer/bandleader. Born November 2, 1947, Orange, New Jersey. Influenced by Billy Brooks, Art Blakey, Eddie Gladden, Lionel Hampton, Philly Joe Jones; embraced African drumming after hearing Mongo Santamaria, Willie Bono, Babatunde Olatunji; with Sir Roland Hanna (three years); toured with Sonny Fortune; played for singers Andy Bey, Little Jimmy Scott; leads own group at Priory, Trumpets, other spots.

WASHINGTON, TYRONE Tenor saxophonist. Born June 4, 1944, Newark. Musically inclined since age four; graduate, Arts High School (1964); with pal Woody Shaw considered rising jazz musician as teenager; at Shaw's invitation, joined Horace Silver (1966); recorded *Natural Essence* as leader

(1967); made two subsequent albums; dropped off scene (1968) to devote life to Islam.

WEST, DWIGHT   Singer. Born March 4, 1953, Newark. Sang at Weequahic High with the Decades, R&B group that opened for Barbra Streisand in New York (c1970), Dizzy Gillespie in Branch Brook Park; sang with Armed and Dangerous gospel group; member, Amiri Baraka's BluArk ensemble; with Big John Patton (late 1990s); appearances include Highest Peak, Kimako's Blues People, Priory, New York clubs.

WHITE, CHRIS   Bassist. Born July 6, 1936, New York City. Played with Nat Phipps Orchestra (early on); member, Cecil Taylor's band (1950s); on Taylor's *Love for Sale* album (1959); backed Nina Simone (1960–61); with Dizzy Gillespie (1960s) when Simone, Ramsey Lewis, James Moody, Quincy Jones were part of group; founded Jazz Survivors; played with Prism; executive director, Jazzmobile Inc. (1967–68); director, Institute of Jazz Studies, Rutgers-Newark (1973–76); member, creative arts and technology faculty, Bloomfield College (1966 until retirement).

WILLIAMS, CHERYL (LADY CICI)   Singer. Born March 21, 1947, Newark. Former teacher in East Orange, Newark; sang with Billy Ford's Orchestra; co-leader with husband Don Williams of Jazz Just-Us (thirty-plus years); favorite at Midas Gold, Priory, Skipper's.

WILLIAMS, DON   Drummer. Born December 12, 1945, Newark. Worked with Arthur Prysock, Jimmy McGriff, "Groove" Holmes; forty-year career highlighted by national/international excursions; co-founded Jazz Just-Us combo with wife Lady CiCi (thirty-plus years ago); led Peppermint Lounge house band (several years); co-leads Tuesday night jam sessions at Crossroads with Radam Schwartz.

WING, CHINK (HAROLD WILLIAMS)   Drummer/pianist. Born in Newark; deceased. Began composing, age nine; studied under Herman Bradley, Charlie "Brother" Kelly; worked locally in bands led by Billy Ford, Leon Eason, Larry Ringold, Gene Phipps Sr., Bill Harris; frequently performed with Erroll Garner; recorded on Savoy, Decca, Blue Note, Mercury; backed Ella Fitzgerald on *I Wondered What King of Guy You'd Be*; longtime associate of James Moody; former director, Newark Department of Recreation and Parks.

YOSKO   Singer. Performs at North Jersey clubs including Priory, Skipper's, Crossroads.

YOUNG, LARRY, JR.   Bebop/fusion organist. Born October 7, 1940, Newark; died March 30, 1978. Considered John Coltrane of organ; father owned

Newark clubs and also played organ; Arts High School graduate; sang as teenager with the Challengers; active on European scene (1960s); recorded extensively on Prestige, Blue Note with Jimmy Forrest, Woody Shaw, Elvin Jones, Grant Green, Sam Rivers, Bobby Hutcherson; toured Europe (1962); on Miles Davis's *Bitches Brew*, (Columbia); made bootleg record with Jimi Hendrix (1969); part of fusion trio Lifetime with Tony Williams, John McLaughlin; won *DownBeat* award, Talent Deserving Greater Recognition on Organ (1966).

BIBLIOGRAPHY

Books

Baraka, Amiri (LeRoi Jones). *Blues People*. William Morrow, 1963.

———. *Black Music*. William Morrow, 1968.

———. *Autobiography: LeRoi Jones/Amiri Baraka*. Freundlich Books, 1984.

———. *Digging: The Afro-American Soul of American Classical Music*. University of California Press, 2009.

Bauer, William R. *Open The Door: The Life and Music of Betty Carter*. Jazz Perspectives, 2003.

Carr, Roy; Case, Brian; and Dellar, Fred. *The Hip: Hipsters, Jazz and the Beat Generation*. Faber and Faber, 1986.

Charters, Samuel B., and Kunstadt, Leonard. *Jazz: A History of the New York Scene*. Da Capo Press, 1962.

DeVeaux, Scott. *The Birth of Bebop: A Social and Musical History*. The University of California Press, 1997.

Ellington, Duke. *Music Is My Mistress*. Da Capo Press, 1973.

Gitler, Ira. *Swing to Bop: An Oral History of the Transition in Jazz in the 1940s*. Oxford University Press, 1985.

Gonzalez, Babs. *I Paid My Dues*. Expubidence Publishing Corp., 1967.

Gordon, Lorraine, as told to Singer, Barry. *Alive at the Village Vanguard: My Life In and Out of Jazz Time*. Hal Leonard, 2006.

Gordon, Max. *Live at the Village Vanguard*. Da Capo Press, 1982.

Gourse, Leslie. *Sassy: The Life of Sarah Vaughan*. Scribner, 1994.

Jardim, Gary (editor). *Blue: Newark Culture*. Gary Jardim, 1990.

———. *Blue: Life, Art & Style in Newark*. De Sousa Press, 1993.

Kruth, John. *Bright Moments: The Life and Legacy of Rahsaan Roland Kirk*. Welcome Rain, 2000.

Kukla, Barbara J. *Swing City: Newark Nightlife, 1925–50*. Temple University Press, 1991.

Mercer, Michelle. *The Life and Work of Wayne Shorter*. Penguin Group: Jeremy P. Tarcher, 2005.

Ritz, David. *Faith in Time: The Life of Jimmy Scott*. Da Capo Press, 2002.

Roth, Philip. *American Pastoral*. Doubleday Publishing Company, 1998.

Shipton, Alyn. *Hi-de-Ho: The Life of Cab Calloway*. Oxford University Press, 2010.

Smothers, Ronald. *The Salt Mine: A Cultural History*. AuthorHouse, 2010.

Ullman, Michael. *Jazz Lives: Portraits in Words and Pictures*. New Republic Books, 1980.

Articles

About Moody. James Moody.com.

Alvarez, Peraza. *Chico Mendoza: New Jersey's Favorite 'Latin Sun.'* Latin Beat Magazine, February 1, 2007.

Amiri Baraka. Newark Review, December 1999.

Author unknown. *Allah Means Everything: Thus Spake*. No citation.

Barber, Patricia. *Tickler's Town Spirit of Jazz Returns to Newark, New Jersey*. Jazz-Corner, July 20, 2010.

Berg, Chuck. *Woody Shaw: Trumpet in Bloom*. DownBeat, August 10, 1978.

Berger, Ed. *Overdue Ovation: Grachan Moncur*. Jazz Times, September 2003.

Bernotas, Bob. *James Moody*. Internet, April 19, 2004.

Blumenthal, Bob. *In Conversation With Wayne Shorter*. Internet. No date.

Bright, George. *Getting Into It: Grachan Moncur III*. DownBeat, 1965.

Burns, Jim. *James Moody: The Early Years*. No citation.

Chicago's First Couple of Jazz: Geraldine and Eddie de Haas. Chicago Jazz Magazine, November 15, 2012.

Coleman, Gloria. *Women in Jazz*. Internet. No date.

Davis, Walter, Jr. *Encyclopedia of Jazz Musicians*. Internet. No date.

de Haas, Darius. *Extended Beys*. Internet. No date.

Dope Addiction and the Jazz Musician: A Playboy Panel Discussion. Playboy, November 1960.

Elfman, Donald. *Lest We Forget: Walter Davis Jr*. New York City Jazz Record, July 2013.

Erlewine, Stephen Thomas. *Freddie Roach*. Internet. No date.

Goodman, Amy, and Gonzalez, Juan. *Max Roach 1924–2007: Thousands Pay Tribute to the Legendary Drummer, Educator and Artist*. Democracy News, August 27, 2007.

Guran, Scott. *Revitalizing Newark Through Jazz*. New Jersey Public Radio, October 19, 2012.

Harris. Thom. *Crowd Grooves in time to Jimmy McGriff Quintet*. Hartford Courant, April 5, 1993.

Harvard, Maxine. *Keeping a Great Jazz Tradition Alive and Well in Newark*. Metro Newark, April, 1980.

Hooper, Joseph. *The Ballad of Jimmy Scott*. New York Times Magazine, August 27, 2000.

Hopkins, Marc. *Dennis Irwin: Gone Too Soon*. JazzTimes, January/February, 2009.

Hum, Peter. *Woody & Dex (The Woody Shaw III Interview)*. JAZZBLOG.ca., December 15, 2011.

Jazz Monthly Feature Interview: Mel Davis. Jazz Monthly, March 2007.

Jeske, Lee. *James Moody's Move: Vegas No More*. DownBeat, No date.

Jiminez, Natalie. *A Benefit to Revive Once-Grand Venue*. The Star-Ledger, November 8, 2007.

Kahn, Leslie. *Andy Bey: A Vocal Master Returns*. National Public Radio, January 10, 2008.

Kanzler, George. *Music Crowds Praise Sparky J's, Key Club Tribute*. The Star-Ledger, January 28, 1977.

————. *Jazz Great Recalls Past and Gives Arts High Students a Taste of the Future*. The Star-Ledger, October 11, 1982.

————. *Paying Tribute to a Jazz Innovator: Roy Hargrove Tribute to Woody Shaw*. The Star-Ledger, November 14, 1997.

————. *Paying Tribute to Sassy*. The Star-Ledger, March 29, 1999

————. *Cape May Jazz Festival: Tribute to Jimmy Scott*. JazzTimes, April 25, 2006.

————. *Charli Persip*. All About Jazz, February 12, 2009.

————. *Rhoda's Working Vacation Is a Treat for Jerseyans*. The Star-Ledger, c1972.

Kirk, Dorthaan. *WBGO Announces Tribute to Wayne Shorter; Jazz Great.* WBGO/Jazz 88 Public Radio. No date.

Kukla, Barbara. *From Ballads to Jazz: Ronnell Bey's Magical Voice Packs 'Em In*. The Star-Ledger, January 22, 1998.

————. *Friends Mourn Passing of Two Fine Musicians*, The Star-Ledger, January 3, 1983.

————. *Old Jazzman Reopens Alcazar with Memories of a Golden Era*. The Star-Ledger, January 1, 1980.

————. *Bethany Baptist Church Jazzes Up Vespers*. The Star-Ledger, January 11, 2001.

Lee, Consuela. *Sarah Vaughan: A Voice of Silk & Silver*. Internet. No date.

Leitch, Sylvia Levine. *Dorthaan Kirk: A Life in Jazz*. JazzTimes, June 21, 2012.

Lucas, Caryl. *A Street Named Vaughan Jazzes Newark*. The Star-Ledger, March 26, 1999.

Lustig, Jay. *An Emotional Tribute to the late James Moody*. The Star-Ledger, October 20, 2012.

McCall, Tris. *James Moody Democracy of Jazz Festival Takes Over Newark Next Week*. The Star-Ledger, October 12, 2012.

McGlone, Peggy. *Outside NJPAC: A Walk on State's Creative Side*. The Star-Ledger, May 18, 2006.

————. *Cephas Bowles: WBGO's Leader Who Guided the Station to Nationwide Prominence*. The Star-Ledger, December 26, 2010.

Milkowski, Bill. *James Moody: Playing With the Changes.* JazzTimes, March 2004.

Minunni, Deborah. *Fashions of The Times.* New York Times, Fall 2009.

Morgan, Joyce. *Exploration: Grachan Moncur III.* Internet. No date.

Myers, Marc. *Interview with Rhoda Scott.* JazzWax, October 14, 2011.

Newark Museum Launches Jazz in the Garden Festival. All About Jazz, May 8, 2005.

New Jersey's Jammin': The Garden State Is Fertile Ground for a Growing Jazz Scene. New Jersey Monthly. No date.

Panetta, Gary. *Harlem Blues and Jazz Band to Carry on Tradition with Concert at JCC.* The Journal Star, January 16, 2011.

Potnash, Andrew. *Jazz in 1967 Newark.* The Newark Metro. No date.

Ratliff, Ben. *John G. Gensel, 80, the Pastor to New York's Jazz Community.* The New York Times, February 8, 1998.

Reich, Ronni. *Newark's Yearlong Jazz Party.* The Star-Ledger, April 3, 2013.

Sachs, Lloyd. *Shorter to pour out renewed spirit here.* Chicago Sun Times, November 19, 1985.

Sarah Vaughan. spclarke.com. No date.

Selman, Carol. *Saxophonist, Newark Educator Bradford Hayes Talks, Plays Outdoor Summer Music Throughout City.* Newark Patch, July 2, 2011.

Silvert, Conrad. *Wayne Shorter: Imagination Unlimited.* DownBeat. No date.

Singer, Sean. *The Soul of Trombone: Grachan Moncur III.* Cerise Press: A Journal of Literature, Art & Culture, October 19, 2011.

Smith, Cliff. *Organist Will Open His Own Club.* Rochester Times-Union, October 31, 1970.

Sterling, Guy. *Jazztown USA.* The Star-Ledger, September 26, 2003.

———. *Holiday in Newark: An anniversary remembrance of the jazz legend.* The Star-Ledger, April 15, 2007.

Stewart, Zan. *Jazz Drummer Rudy Walker in Montclair.* The Star-Ledger, November 5, 2009.

———. *At 75, Jazzman Wayne Shorter Looks Forward, Not Back.* The Star-Ledger, November 29, 2008.

———. *A Life's Composition: Examining Newark Native Wayne Shorter's Philosophical Mind and Abstract Jazz.* The Star-Ledger, January 23, 2005.

———. *Eddie Gladden: Drummer Worked with Jazz Greats.* The Star-Ledger, October, 2003.

———. *Dwight West.* The Star-Ledger. No date.

Sutro, Dirk. *Crawford, McGriff Jazz Up Their Careers as Soul Mates.* Los Angeles Times, November 16, 1989.

Teichroew, Jacob. *Jazz and Pop Music: A Response to Wilt Layman.* About.com Jazz. No date.

The Devil's Music: 1920s Jazz. CultureShock. No date.

Venutolo, Anthony. *Celebrating a Jazz Legend.* The Star-Ledger, December 1, 2007.

———. *Keyboardist Braham Adept at Both Playng and Teaching.* The Star-Ledger, March 6, 2008.

Wayne Shorter. New York University Department of Music and Performing Arts Professions. Internet. No date.

Weber, Bruce. *Carrie Smith, Singer in "Black and Blue" on Broadway.* The New York Times, May 26, 2012.

Wells, Jean Nash. *Worshiping the Lord to the Sounds of Jazz.* Positive Community, January 2012.

Wilkins, Tim. *New Fest Celebrates Newark's Jazz Roots.* The Star-Ledger, March 29, 2012.

———. *Master Musician Rhoda Scott Is Back in Jersey, and Back in School.* The Star-Ledger, December 2, 2011.

Wilson, John. *Cabaret: Lu Elliott at Cookery.* The New York Times, March 22, 1981.

Wolff, Carlo. *Hank Mobley Quintet: Newark 1953.* JazzTimes, October 2, 2012.

Woody Shaw: My Approach to Jazz. Jazz Professional, 1977.

Woody Shaw—A Forgotten Trumpet Legend. All About Jazz (from All Music Guide). No date.

Woody Shaw, 44; Jazz Trumpeter. Los Angeles Times, May 12, 1989.

Wyatt, Hugh W. *Jazz Spreads the Gospel at Bethany Baptist Church.* The Spiritual Herald, March 2011.

Other Material

Baraka, Amiri. *Woody III.* Blue Note. Liner notes, 1979.

Baraka, Amiri, and Banks, Robert. Newark Music Project. YouTube, 1997.

Cuscuna, Michael. *Woody Shaw—The Complete Columbia Albums Collection.* Mosaic Records. Liner notes, 2011.

Schwartz, Radam. *Organ Jazz.* Dissertation, Graduate School-Newark, Rutgers University, 2012.

Terry, Buddy. *Natural Soul.* Prestige. Liner notes, 1968.

Thomas, Philip S. *Jazz Marathon* at Newark Symphony Hall. Program, November 15, 2007.

Thomas, Philip S. *Rhoda Scott: Organ Jam With All-Star Jazz Lineup at Newark Symphony Hall.* Program, December 3, 2011.

Washington, Tyrone. *Natural Essence.* Blue Note. Jacket notes, 1967.

Selected Discography (LPs/CDs)

Ackerman, Bob. *The World of Robert Ackerman.* MSR Classics. (3 CD set).

Benson, George. *Breezin'.* Warner Brothers Records, 1976. (LP).

Bey, Andy. *American Song.* Savoy Jazz, 2004. (CD).

Bey, Andy, and the Bey Sisters. *Andy Bey and the Bey Sisters.* Prestige, 2000. (CD).

Bey, Ronnell. *To the Max,* 1991. (CD).

Braham, Dave. *To Be Free.* (CD).

Davis, Mel (with Leo Johnson). *It's About Time.* (CD).

Davis, Walter, Jr. *Davis Cup.* Blue Note, 1959. (LP).

Edwards, Ernie. *Lovely Day.* (CD).

Gibbs, James, III. *Relaxin'.* (CD).

Gladden, Eddie. *Mother Ship.* Blue Note, 1969. (LP).

Gordon, Honi. *Honi Gordon: The Gordons.* Debut, 1953. (LP).

Gordon, Honi. *Honi Gordon Sings.* Prestige, 1962. (LP).

Hayes, Bradford. *The Jazz Life.* (CD).

Holiday, Cynthia. *All the Way, Featuring the Cedar Walton Trio.* Mile High Records. (CD).

Jackson, Carrie. *If I Had My Way.* C-Jay Records. (CD); *A Tribute to Sarah Vaughan, Newark's Own.* C-Jay Records, 2013. (CD).

Johnson, Leo. *It's About Time.* (CD).

Jones, Jackie. *Part of Me.* (CD).

Kettrell, Daille. *The Rite Time, The Right Moment.* Recorded live at the Priory, 2008. (CD).

Kirk, Rahsaan Roland. *Triple Threat.* King, 1956. (LP).

Lady CiCi. *On the Up.* DonCi Records, 2006. (CD); *Lady CiCi Sings Songs from the Heart.* DonCi Records, 2007. (CD).

Lester, Connie. *Man With a Happy Sound,* 1962. (LP).

Logan, Michael. *Night Out.* Muse, 1990. (LP).

McCloud, Andy. *Blues for Bighead.* Mapleshade Records, 2000. (LP).

McCrae, Richie. *Get Here.* 2006. (CD).

McGhee, Cornell. (With Bradford Hayes). *The Jazz Life.* (CD).

McGriff, Jimmy. *Jimmy McGriff at the Organ.* Sue, 1965 (LP); *Skywalk.* Milestone, 1984 (LP).

Mendoza, Chico. *Ocho.* US Latino, 1972 (LP); *Ocho II.* US Latino, 1973 (LP).

Miss Rhapsody (Viola Wells). *Ladies Sing the Blues.* Arista, 1979. (LP).

Mobley, Hank. *Live at the Picadilly,* 1953 (LP); *The Complete Hank Mobley Fifties Sessions.* Mosaic, 1955–58 (LP).

Moncur, Grachan, III. *Homecoming: This One's for Jackie.* Gramon Publishing, 2012 (LP); *Echoes of Prayer,* 1975 (LP).

Montague, Antoinette. *Pretty Blue.* Blues Straight Ahead. (CD).

Moody, James. *Last Train from Overbrook.* Argo, 1958. (LP).

Morgan, Herb. *Mother Ship.* Blue Note, 1948. (LP); reissue, Blue Note Classic, 1969 (LP).

Patterson, Al. *Phipps and Friends.* Pipeline Music, 2009. (CD); *Wheels* (with Oliver Lake Big Band). Passing Through Productions, 2013. (CD).

Persip, Charli. *Charli Persip and Superband.* Stash, 1980s. (LP).

Person, Houston. *To Etta With Love.* High Note, 2004. (LP).

Phillips, Steve (with Rhoda Scott). *The Hammond Organ of Christmas* (CD).

Phipps, Gene, Sr. *After Hours Bounce.* Manor. (78 RPM).

Porter, Bobby (with Leo Johnson). *It's About Time.* (CD).

Purdie, Bernard. *Purdie Good.* Prestige, 1971. (LP).

Purvis, Pam. *Pam Purvis Featuring Bob Ackerman.* MSR Records, 1999. (CD); *Winter Warm.* MSR Records, 1999. (CD).

Reid, Irene. *Million Dollar Secret*. Savant, 1997 (LP); *Queen of the Party*. Savant, 2012 (LP).

Schwartz, Radam. *Songs for the Soul*. AR Jazz, 2000. (CD).

Scott, Jimmy. *Falling in Love Is Wonderful*. Tangerine, 1963 (LP); *All the Way*. Sire, 1992 (LP).

Scott, Rhoda. *The Rhoda Scott Trio: Live! At the Key Club*, 1963 (LP); *Live at the Olympia*, 2002 (LP).

Shaw, Woody. *The Moontrane*. Muse, 1974 (LP); *Rosewood*. Columbia, 1977 (LP).

Shorter, Wayne. *Introducing Wayne Shorter*. Vee-Jay, 1959 (LP); *Schizophrenia*. Blue Note, 1967 (LP).

Smith, Carrie. *Confessin' the Blues*. Evidence Records, 1976 (LP); *Do Your Duty*. Black & Blue, 1976 (LP).

Sorey, Tyshawn. *That/Not*. Firehouse, 2008. (CD).

Spirit of Life Ensemble. *Inspirations*. ZaZou, 1992. (LP).

Stein, Alex and Asher. *Quixotic*. Jazz Media, 2008. (CD).

Tandy, Pat. *Madame Pat Tandy Remembers Irene Reid*. BlueArk. (CD).

Taylor, Jason (Malletman). *Love Attack*. (CD).

Terry, Buddy. *Electric Soul*. Prestige, 1967 (LP); *Natural Soul*. Prestige, 1968 (LP).

Thomas, Joe (with Rhoda Scott). *Live at the Olympia*. Barclay, 2001 (LP).

Vaughan, Sarah. *The Divine Sarah Sings*. Mercury, 1954 (LP); *The Divine One*. Roulette, 1961 (LP).

Walker, Rudy. *Comet Ride*. Miles High. (CD).

Washington, Tyrone. *Natural Essence*. Blue Note, 1967. (LP).

Williams, Don. *Smokin'*. DonCi Records. (CD).

Young, Larry, Jr. *Groove Street*. Prestige, 1962 (LP); *Unity*. Blue Note, 1965 (LP); *Lawrence of Newark*. Perception, 1973 (LP).

INDEX OF NAMES AND PLACES

References to photographs appear in **bold type**.

CPSIA information can be obtained at www.ICGtesting.com
Printed in the USA
BVOW01*2105140114

341583BV00002B/4/P

9 780976 813033